EMPOWERING RURAL CONSUMERS
Opportunities, Challenges and Strategies

About the Editors

Suresh Misra is Chair Professor (Consumer Affairs) and Coordinator, Centre for Consumer Studies at IIPA, New Delhi. He holds his Masters in Political Science from Jawaharlal Nehru University, New Delhi, Masters in Human Resource Management from Pondicherry University and D.Phil. from Allahabad University. He had his advance training in Corporate Management at AOTS, Japan, TQM at U.K. Civil Service College and in Training Techniques and Methodology from the Thames Valley University, UK. Dr. Misra has authored/edited 16 books and contributed several papers to journals of repute. His major areas of interest include Consumer Welfare, Administrative Reforms, Development Administration and Local Governance. He is a member of the Central Consumer Protection Council. He is also the Project Director of National Consumer Helpline & SCHKRM Portal Projects of the Department of Consumer Affairs.

Mamta Pathania holds her Masters, M.Phil. and Ph.D. in Public Administration from Himachal Pradesh University, Shimla. Currently, she is working as Assistant Professor, Consumer Studies at IIPA. Before joining IIPA, she worked with the Department of Public Administration, H.P.U., Shimla and later on with the Department of Public Administration, Regional Centre (H.P.U.), Dharamshala, (H.P.) as a Lecturer in Public Administration. She has authored/edited 8 books and contributed several papers in journers and books of repute. Her major areas of interent include Consumer Studies, Good Governance, Public Sector Reforms and Local Governance. She is a member of the Script Committee of the Department of Consumer Affairs and a Member of the National COPOLCO Mirror Committee of Bureau of Indian Standards (BIS).

EMPOWERING RURAL CONSUMERS

Opportunities, Challenges and Strategies

Editors
Suresh Misra
Mamta Pathania

CONCEPT PUBLISHING COMPANY PVT. LTD.
NEW DELHI-110059

ISBN-13: 978-93-86682-27-7

First Published 2018

Published and Printed by:

Concept Since 1974

Concept Publishing Company Pvt. Ltd.
A/15-16, Commercial Block, Mohan Garden,
New Delhi-110059 (INDIA)
T : 25351460, 25351794
E : publishing@conceptpub.com *W* : www.conceptpub.com

Cataloging in Publication Data--Courtesy: D.K. Agencies (P) Ltd. <docinfo@dkagencies.com>

Empowering rural consumers : opportunities, challenges and strategies / editors, Suresh Misra, Mamta Pathania.
pages cm
Papers presented at a National Seminar on "Globalisation, Markets and Rural Consumers", organised by Centre for Consumer Studies, Indian Institute of Public Administration, New Delhi.
ISBN 9789386682277

1. Consumer education—India—Congresses. 2. Consumer protection—India—Congresses. 3. Panchayat—India—Congresses. 4. Mass media and business—India Congresses. 5. India—Rural conditions—Congresses. I. Misra, Suresh, editor. II. Pathania, Mamta, 1978- editor. III. Indian Institute of Public Administration. Centre for Consumer Studies, organizer.

LCC TX337.I4E47 2018 DDC 381.330954 23

Preface

The Indian rural consumer accounts for over 70 per cent of the population and living in around 6,40,867 villages across the country. While the rural consumer is generally seen as the less affluent, as compared to his urban cousins, things are changing in rural India over the last decade. Like any market that has seen a demand and awareness boom, rural India has also been witnessing considerable rise in purchasing power. A change in consumption pattern and access to communication media have made rural market a vital cog in the sales-growth wheel, especially with demand for many categories of products and services plateauing in the urban markets. In spite of increasing number of rural consumers, provisions for consumer protection and welfare are often based on the general standard and circumstances of those living in big cities and towns.

Rural consumers remain disadvantaged as their right to information, choice, redress, and consumer education are not sufficiently fulfilled. Consequently, such consumers need support in maintaining their rights, so that, they can bargain equally with the producers or the service providers. With the growth in rural markets and due to poor knowledge about their rights and lack of skills to take a rational decision based on information about the product or services, the rural consumers are being exploited in many ways. They are made to endure sub-standard products and services, adulterated foods, short weights and measures, spurious and hazardous drugs, exorbitant prices, endemic shortages leading to black marketing and profiteering, unfulfilled manufacturing guarantees and host of other ills. The rural consumers who generally depend on weekly markets to purchase essential things are often cheated due to lack of choice. Rural markets are full of sub-standard goods and duplicity of branded goods is another major problem in rural areas. As there is no check on production and sale of such products in the rural markets, many consumers of these goods and products also sustain injuries. The expansion of service sector has added to the problem. Services like insurance, banking, electricity and medical have expanded in the rural areas without any checks and balances and the rural consumers continue to be exploited by the service providers. Deficiency in services is a major area of concern. Spurious drugs are causing major health hazards. The vulnerable sections are generally women, children and farmers. It is common to find that farmers are supplied defective seeds, adulterated pesticides and other commodities. The rural consumers are looked upon as a homogeneous entity but the farmers, women, children and elderly consumers have different needs and the resulting exploitation is also different.

Research findings suggest that due to ignorance and lack of awareness about their rights the rural consumers are exploited. Little progress has been made in providing specific safeguards to rural consumers even though their problems are different. There is a need to protect the rural consumers by reorienting the policies and programmes particularly those relating to education and awareness. Unless the rural consumers are taken care of, the consumer movement will remain weak. There is a need to involve the Panchayati Raj Institutions and build the capacity of the local level officials/VCOs (Voluntary Consumer Organisations) and other stakeholders. The media also needs to be involved in enhancing the awareness through various educative programmes.

In order to understand the problems of the rural consumers in the context of globalisation the Centre for Consumer Studies, Indian Institute of Public Administration, New Delhi organised a National Seminar on "Globalisation, Markets and the Rural Consumers". The present book is an outcome of the papers presented in the seminar and contains twenty two papers written by eminent experts working in the area of consumer protection and welfare. They analyse the problems faced by rural consumers, the complex market mechanism and lack of organisations to educate them. They also focus on how the rural consumers can be empowered. Strategies and policy interventions have been suggested by the authors to address the problems faced by the rural consumers.

We are thankful to the Department of Consumer Affairs, Government of India for sponsoring the seminar. We would like to thank all the paper contributors for sending their revised papers in time. We are grateful to Dr. T. Chatterjee, Director, Indian Institute of Public Administration for his help and support. We would also like to thank all the members of the

Centre for Consumer Studies for their support. Thanks are due to Ms. Deepa Rawat for providing excellent secretariai assistance. We hope that the readers will find this book useful in understanding the problems of rural consumer and the ways and means to empower them.

Suresh Misra
Mamta Pathania
Editors

Contents

SECTION II
Strengthening Consumer Movement: Role of NGOs and VCOs

SECTION III
Grassroots Democracy and Consumer Empowerment

SECTION IV
Media, Technology and Rural Consumers

List of Abbreviations

BEE	Bureau of Energy Efficiency
C&AG	Comptroller & Auditor General
CAGR	Compound Annual Growth Rate
CPA	Consumer Protection Act
FICCI	Federation of Indian Chamber of Commerce and Industry
FMCG	Fast Moving Consumer Goods
ICT	Information and Communication Technology
IIPA	Indian Institute of Public Administration
LPG	Liberalisation, Privatisation and Globalisation
LPG	Liquid Petroleum Gas
MART	Marketing and Research Team
MNC	Multinational Companies
MRP	Maximum Retail Price
NCAER	National Council of Applied Economic Research
NCDRC	National Consumer Disputes Redressal Commission
NGO	Non-Governmental Organisation
NSSO	National Sample Survey Organisation
ORG	Operations Research Group
PESA	Provision of the Panchayat (Extension to Scheduled Areas) Act, 1996
PRI	Panchayati Raj Institution
SHG	Self-Help Groups
TNC	Trans-National Companies
ULB	Urban Local Bodies
UN	United Nations
VCO	Voluntary Consumer Organisation

List of Contributors

Benjamin, Dr. Joseph, Associate Professor & Head, St. Francis De Sals' College, Seminary Hillas, Nagpur-440006, Maharashtra. Email: *joseph.sfscollege@gmail.com*

Chadah, Dr. Sapna, Assistant Professor, Centre for Consumer Studies, Indian Institute of Public Administration, New Delhi-110002. Email: *sapnachadah@yahoo.co.in*

Dalal, Dr. Rajbir Singh, Associate Professor, Department of Public Administration, Ch. Devi Lal University, Sirsa, Haryana. Email: *rajbirsinghdalal@gmail.com*

Gopalakrishna, B.V., President, Consumer Forum (Regd.), Zilla Panchayats Office Premiser, Kuvemupu Road, Shimoga-577201, Karnataka. Email: *gopalabalagatte@gmail.com*

Gupta, Dr. Pallavi, Associate Professor (Law), Vivekananda Institute of Professional Studies, AU Block, Outer Ring Road, Pitampura, New Delhi. Email: *pallavigupta2000@yahoo.co.in*

Kapoor, Dr. Sheetal, Associate Professor, Kamla Nehru College, Khel Gaon Marg, University of Delhi, New Delhi. Email: *sheetal_kpr@hotmail.com*

Khan, Mohmmad Azvar, Research Scholar, Department of Law, Aligarh Muslim University, Aligarh-202002, Uttar Pradesh. Email: *khan.azwar@gmail.com*

Kumar, Anju, Adjunct Faculty, Symbiosis Centre for Management Studies, Noida, Sector 62, Block A, Plot Nos. 47 & 48, Noida-201301. Email: *kumaranju16@gmail.com*

Kumar, Arvind, Research Scholar (SRF), IVS-MTA, H.P. University, Summer Hill, C/o. Institute of Vocational Studies (Master of Tourism Administration), Himachal Pradesh University, Summer Hill, Shimla, Himachal Pradesh. Email: *palsara.akumar84@gmail.com*

Mishra, Dr. Pratip Kumar, Reader in Political Science, PRANANATH Autonomous College, NAAC accredited "A", Potential as a Centre of Excellence, Khurda, Odisha.
Email: *pratipmishra@yahoo.com*

Mishra, Prof. Alok, Professor of Law, Amity Law School, Amity University Campus, Sector 125, Noida (NCR).
Website: *www.dralokmishra.com*, Email: *dr.alokmishra@yahoo.co.in, amishra3@amity.edu*

Mishra, Prof. Anil Dutta, Deputy Director, National Gandhi Museum, New Delhi.
Email: *anilduttamishra@gmail.com*

Mishra, Virendra Nath, Research Officer, Centre for Consumer Studies, Indian Institute of Public Administration, New Delhi-110002.
Email: *vn.misra@gmail.com*

Misra, Prof. Suresh, Chair Professor & Coordinator, Centre for Consumer Studies, Indian Institute of Public Administration, New Delhi-110002.
Email: *drsureshmisra@gmail.com*

Murthy, Prof. P.V.V.S., Hon. Professor in Business Management, Montessori Mahila College, Opp. All India Radio, M.G. Road, Vijayawada-520 010, Andhra Pradesh.
Email: *pvvs_murty@yahoo.com*

Padhy, Dr. Mahendra Kumar, Assistant Professor, Department of Mass Communication & Journalism, Babasaheb Bhimrao Ambedkar Central University, Raebareli Road, Lucknow-226025, Uttar Pradesh.
Email: *m.padhy2008@gmail.com*

Pathania, Dr. Mamta, Assistant Professor, Centre for Consumer Studies, Indian Institute of Public Administration, New Delhi-110002.
Email: *mamtapathania@gmail.com*

Poornananda, Prof. D.S., Professor, Department of Journalism and Mass Communication, Kuvempu University, Shankaraghatta, Shimoga-577451, Karnataka.
Email: *poornananda.ds@gmail.com*

Ramesh, C.L., Director, Consumer Forum (Regd), Zilla Panchayath Office Premises, Kuvempu Road, Shimoga-577201, Karnataka.
Email: *clramesh07@gmail.com*

Rao, K. Venugopala, President, Foundation for Rural and Social Development (FRSD), Plot No. 25, Venkatram Nagar Colony, Near Karkhana, Secunderabad-500009, Andhra Pradesh.
Email: *venufrsd@gmail.com*

Roy, Dr. Subhash Chandra, Associate Professor, Chanakya National Law University, Nyaya Nagar, Mithapur, Patna-800001, Bihar.
Email: *scroy2010@gmail.com*

Siddiq, Dr. Abbokar, Associate Professor, Department of Commerce and Management, University College, Hampankatta, Mangalore-575001, D.K. Karnataka, Email: *absiddi@yahoo.com*

Singh, Amit Kumar, Research Officer, Centre for Consumer Studies, Indian Institute of Public Administration, New Delhi-110002.
Email: *amitsinghh@gmail.com*

Singh, Pankaj Kumar, Research Officer, Centre for Consumer Studies, Indian Institute of Public Administration, New Delhi-110002,
Email: *pankaj.bhu@gmail.com*

Soundararajan, Dr. K., Associate Professor, Management Wing, DDE, Annamalai University, Annamalai Nagar-608002, Tamil Nadu.
Email: *spknrajan@gmail.com*

Srivastava, Dr. Abhishek, Assistant Professor, Symbiosis Centre for Management Studies, Noida, Sector 62, Block A, Plot Nos. 47 & 48, Noida-201301.
Email: *abhisheksri05@yahoo.co.in*

Sumathy, Dr. M., Associate Professor, School of Commerce, Bharathiar University, Coimbatore-46.
Email: *sumathivenky2005@gmail.com*

Vijayalakshmi, Dr. N., Ph.D. Research Scholar, School of Commerce, Bharathiar University, Coimbatore-46.
Email: *sahanaviji2007@gmail.com*

Vir, Dr. Vijay, Ph.D. Scholar, Department of Public Administration, Ch. Devi Lal University, Sirsa, Haryana.

Introduction

Globalisation, liberalisation and privatisation have lead to the entry of several private traders, including large multinationals, who have transformed the Indian economy into a vibrant, rapidly growing consumer market. The markets are now flooded with different kinds of goods and services, substantially effecting and changing the purchasing pattern of the consumers. The rural markets, which were earlier ignored by most of the big international market players, are now being seen as a land of great business opportunity. Rural areas currently are home to nearly 70 per cent of India's population and have historically accounted for more than half of Indian consumption. Even with increasing urbanisation and migration, it is estimated that 63 per cent of India's population will continue to live in rural areas by 2025. In terms of economic output, rural India accounts for almost half (48%) of the country's economy, and the rural markets have the potential to reach $500 billion by 2020.

The impact of Globalisation is being felt in rural India as much as in urban. But, it is slow. However, in the long run it will have its impact on target groups like farmers, youth and women. In some states the affluent farmers, today "keep in touch" with the latest information and maximise both ends. Animal feed producers no longer look at Andhra Pradesh or Karnataka. They keep their cell phones constantly connected to global markets. Surely, price movements and products' availability in the international market seem to drive their local business strategies.

The estimated annual business from rural markets is around 1,23,000 crore, comprising 65,000 crore of FMCG, Rs. 5,000 crore of durables, Rs. 45,000 crore of agricultural inputs including tractors and Rs. 8,000 crore of two wheelers and four wheelers. Similarly, India's retail market is expected to touch a whopping Rs. 47 trillion (US$ 782.23 billion) by 2016-17, expanding at a Compounded Annual Growth Rate (CAGR) of 15 per cent, according to a study by a leading industrial body. According to the 68th round of the NSSO (National Sample Survey Organisations) survey the latest data on households' consumer expenditure in 2011-12 reveales that the average rural monthly per capital expenditure went up by 35.7 per cent in the two year period between 2009-10 and 2011-12. Of the total expenditure, rural households spent less than half on food items, suggesting rise in wages.The average monthly per capita expenditure during 2011-12 stood at around 1,430 for rural India, a 35.7 per cent increase compared to the 2009-10 survey and 2,630 for urban India, a 32 per cent jump. The average urban monthly per capita expenditure was 84 per cent higher than rural areas. The share of expenditure on food declined substantially from 53.6 per cent to 48.6 per cent in rural areas and from 40.7 per cent to 38.5 per cent in the urban areas. The faster rise in share of non-food expenditure in rural areas suggests a rise in wages. The rural wages went up from 231.59 a day in 2009-10 to 299 a day in 2011-12, a 29 per cent increase.

For the average rural Indian, food accounted for 52.9 per cent of the value of consumption during 2011-12. This included 10.8 per cent for cereals and cereal substitutes, 8 per cent for milk and milk products, 7.9 per cent on beverages, refreshments and processed food, and 6.6 per cent on vegetables. Within food, the share of protein-based items went up in the consumption basket. The share of milk and milk products went up from 8.6 per cent in 2009-10 to 9.1 per cent. Among non-food items, the share of durable goods in the consumption basket of rural areas went up from 4.8 per cent to 6.1 per cent. Among non-food item categories, fuel and light for household purposes (excluding transportation) accounted for 8 per cent, clothing and footwear 7 per cent, medical expenses 6.7 per cent, education 3.5 per cent, conveyance 4.2 per cent, other consumer services (excluding conveyance) 4 per cent, and consumer durables 4.5 per cent.

Rural consumers are now opting for life improving products and services of real quality or durables that enhance productivity and increase earnings. As the disposable income of the masses is growing, more and more corporate houses are entering into the rural markets with new goods and products. Due to this marketing for rural consumers is becoming more complex. According to experts, the four factors which influence demand in rural India are: access, attitude, awareness and affluence. Some companies have successfully used these to influence the rural market for their products.

In a country like India, where a substantial number of the rural people are living below the poverty line, having high level of unemployment and poor literacy level; consumer awareness continues to remain low.

Several studies have shown that rural consumers are generally ignorant and they are also unorganised. Under these circumstances, the sellers or the manufacturers, exploit the consumers. Though, the consumers in India have been provided with various safety measures against their exploitation, still the sellers and producers are hoarding and black-marketing the essential goods, involving economic corruption and frequently cheating the consumers. Rural markets are full of sub-standard goods and duplicity of branded goods is another major problem in rural areas. As there is no check on production and sale of such products in the rural markets, many consumers of these goods and products also sustain injuries. The expansion of service sector has added to the problem. Services like insurance, banking, telecom, electricity and medical have expanded in the rural areas without any checks and balances and the rural consumers continue to be exploited by the service providers. Deficiency in services is a major area of concern. Spurious drugs are causing major health hazards. The vulnerable sections of the society are generally women, children and farmers. It is common to find that farmers are supplied defective seeds, adulterated pesticides and other commodities. The expansion of mass media has further given impetus to consumerism in the rural areas. Spurious goods are very common in these markets.

Therefore, it has widely been realised that the fate of the consumers cannot be left to the market forces. In view of this the Government of India has taken a number of legal measures to protect the consumers by enlarging the scope of consumer protection. In present situation, consumer protection, though as old as consumer exploitation, has assumed greater importance and relevance. Now, there exist laws and policies which focus on consumer protection and welfare. Special emphasis is being given to consumer education so that people become aware about their rights and responsibilities as consumer and know how to redress their grievances. In India various Acts intended to protect the consumers directly or indirectly against different forms of exploitation were enacted from time to time. However, except for the Monopolies and Restrictive Trade Practices (MRTP) Act, 1969, all the other Acts were mainly punitive and preventive in nature. In spite of these Acts the consumers did not have any effective mechanism or institutional arrangements for the speedy redressal of their grievances and also the lack of effective popular movement isolated the consumer and his plight only increased. Seeing the pressure mounting from various consumer protection groups and the consumers themselves the Parliament enacted the Consumer Protection Act in 1986. Of the various legal remedies, the Consumer Protection

Act, 1986 enacted on 24th December, 1986 is the principal legal remedy available to the consumers. This is an important Act which seeks to provide better protection of the interests of the consumers.

Consumer Awareness in India

The Consumer Protection Act enacted on 24th December, 1986 is a benevolent, unique and highly progressive piece of social welfare legislation providing for simple, speedy and less expensive remedy for the redressal of consumer grievances in relation to defective goods and deficient services. Consumer Protection Act is a weapon in the hands of consumers to fight against exploitation by traders, manufacturers and sellers on one hand and providers of services on the other. The Act provides effective, people oriented, broad based and efficient remedy to consumers against unfair dealings and exploitation. It was enacted with an objective to provide better protection of the interests of the consumers and to make provision for the establishment of Consumer Councils and other authorities for the settlement of consumer disputes. Unlike other laws, which are basically punitive or preventive in nature the provisions of the Act are compensatory. It is a matter of great satisfaction that we can legitimately boast that we now have in our country a statute, which provides more effective protection to the consumers than any corresponding legislation in force in countries, which are considered to be much more advanced and industrialised.

The Act contemplates establishment of adjudicatory and advisory structures in the form of consumer forums and council structure respectively for the protection of consumers' rights. It extends to whole of India except the State of Jammu & Kashmir which has its own Consumer Protection Act. The Act applies to all goods and services unless any good or service is expressly excluded by the Central Government by notification. The Act extends to all sectors—public, private or cooperative. The Consumer Protection Act is an alternative and additional remedy to the remedies already available to the aggrieved persons/consumers by way of civil suit.

To provide cheap, speedy and simple redressal to consumer disputes, a three tier quasi-judicial machinery is set-up at each District, State and National levels called District Forums, State Consumer Disputes Redressal Commission and National Consumer Disputes Redressal Commission respectively. At present, there are 662 District Forums, 35 State Commissions with apex body as a National Consumer Disputes Redressal

Commission (NCDRC). These quasi-judicial bodies are required to follow summary procedure and Principles of Natural Justice to provide quick and speedy justice to the consumers.

After the enactment of the Consumer Protection Act, 1986, the first independent evaluation study of the implementation of this Act was done through a study conducted by IIPA in 1994. It was found that large majority of the consumers belonging to various categories and income groups were completely ignorant of the existence of the CPA and the redressal agencies created under it. Eleven years later, according to a survey commissioned through ORG Centre for Social Research by the C&AG, the position had improved only marginally. The survey was conducted in July-August, 2005 in 25 States/UT's covering 48,732 consumers, 6,237 complaints, 249 manufacturers/service providers, 39 NGOs and 34 laboratories. The report of ORG-MARG revealed that:[1]

- Sixty-six per cent of the consumers interviewed were not aware of consumer rights and 82 per cent were even unaware of the Act.
- Nearly 49 per cent of the aware consumers had come to know about the Act only in the last 4 years though the Act had been in existence for the past 18 years.
- Overall, only 13 per cent of the consumers reported to have been aware of the existence of any redressal agency.
- A majority of the complainants came to know about the redressal agencies through electronic media (48%), print media (61%) and friends/relatives (68%), NGOs were not a popular source of awareness as only 4.9 per cent of the complainants attributed their awareness to the work of NGOs.
- The consumers were not aware of the features of the simple and inexpensive system of lodging complaint in the absence of any focused awareness Programme launched by the Ministry or the States in this regard. The beneficiary survey carried out by ORG-MARG revealed that 78 per cent of the respondents were carrying a negative opinion of the efforts made by the government or had no idea about the same and were not aware that they could directly represent themselves in the Consumer Forums. It is pertinent to note that lack of awareness in this regard had deprived the consumers of the benefit of the adjudication mechanism as out of the total expenditure of Rs. 3,387 incurred by the consumers on each case in the Consumer Forum on an

average, as much as Rs. 2,787 (82%) was the expenditure on advocates.

Therefore, one of the major hindrances on the consumer movement in the country is the lack of awareness among the consumers. The consumers apart from being unorganised do not have the mechanism to understand their rights and responsibilities. These studies reveal not only lack of awareness but lack of consumer education as well. The problem is more acute in the rural areas. A lot more needs to be done on this front. The right to consumer education has been recognised under the Consumer Protection Act, 1986. However, unless awareness increases realising the rights to the consumers, consumer education remains a distant dream. In fact, an educated and aware person is an empowered consumer. Education equips a person with the skill to make discerning choices, to sort out problems effectively and to seek further information and help appropriately.

Rural Consumers

Profile of Rural Consumers

The rural population in India comprises the core of Indian society and represents the real India. According to the 2001 Census, there are 5,80,779 villages in India and about 74 per cent of Indian population lives in these villages. The number of people living in each of these villages also varies considerably. It is found that most of the Indian villages have a population of less than 10,000 while there are only a few villages where more than 10,000 people live (Table 1.1). The country opened up its economy in 1992 and since then due to globalisation and liberalisation the market is flooded with new products and services. Technological revolution and information explosion have also given tremendous boost to consumer culture. The consumers have been sucked into the market economy and today the market determines the needs and preferences of the consumers. This consumer culture and the changing consumption pattern is now not only confined to the urban areas, but is going deep down to the rural markets. The rural markets are the new hunting grounds for the business.

India Brand Equity Foundation (Trust established by Ministry of Commerce with the Confederation of Indian Industry) reports[2] that the Fast Moving Consumer Goods (FMCG) industry is the fourth largest sector in the Indian Economy and creates employment to three million

Table: 1.1: Location and Concentration of Rural Population

Population Range (No. of Persons)	*Number of Villages*	*Proportion to total Villages*	*Proportion to total Rural Population*
Less than 200	82151	13.7	1.0
200 to 499	114732	19.2	4.8
500 to 999	141800	23.7	12.4
1000 to 1999	139164	23.3	23.7
2000 to 4999	96428	16.1	34.6
5000 to 9999	18652	3.1	14.9
10000 and above	4681	0.8	8.7
Total	**597608**	**100**	**100**

Source: Census of India, 2001

people in downstream activities. The current Indian market at present is estimated to be in size of 13.1 billion dollar, which is expected to rise to 33.4 billion dollar by 2015. Also, FMCG and retail giants are making good use of technology to reach out to rural India. From low-cost handsets to tablet PCs, the Indian FMCG and retail sector is latching on to technology and applications to reach out to rural India.

According to NCAER, in 2009, of the 222 million households in India, the absolutely poor households (annual incomes below Rs. 45,000) accounted for only 15.6 per cent of them or about 35 million (about 200 million Indians). Another 80 million households are in income levels of Rs. 45,000-90,000 per year. CIA World Factbook indicates 72 per cent of Indians belong to rural India. Hence, a good enough proportion is distributed mostly in rural area, which offers excellent opportunity for FMCG industries and retailers. The consumer durable market in rural India will witness a 40 per cent growth in the next fiscal year, as against the current growth rate of 30 per cent. The sudden enhancement is due to the change in life style and higher disposable income of the rural populace. India has fascinated the consumer durable market according to a study, "Rise of Consumer Durables in Rural India" undertaken by the Associated Chambers of Commerce and Industry of India.[3] These statistics along with increase in disposable income of rural population proportionately accompanied by their desire to improve existing life style has created the necessary excitement within the producers.

The arenas of untapped rural mass has provided scope away from the saturated market scenario and develop new market with existing products and check for a little while from the cut-throat world of competition. The Bottom of the Pyramid (BoP) is made up of the mass and needs to be addressed to ensure sustainable growth in India. The consumers in BoP are fairly ambitious in their attitude. Even these consumers are focused on improving their lives, use education as a tool to improve life and dream big for their children. The following data by FICCI-Nielsen is a witness to this Figure 1.1.

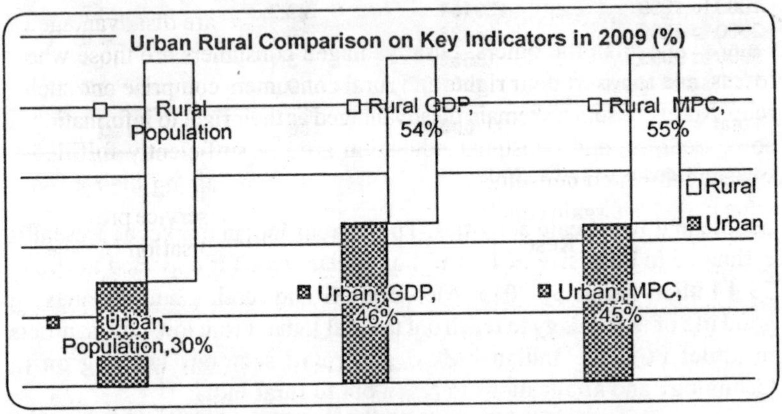

Fig. 1.1: Urban-rural Comparison on Key indicators in 2009
Source: Report: Challenges Before an Integrated India: Bridging the Urban-Rural Divide, 2009.

The reports of National Commission for Applied Economic Research clearly reveals that the rural growth rates have already outpaced urban ones and will continue to do so through the next decade. Rural India accounts for more than 50 per cent of the GDP. Out of 62.97 million households of India those are getting more than 5 lakhs per annum, nearly 28.68 million households (46%) live in Rural India. The rural market in India is projected to be bigger than the urban market for fast moving consumer goods; rural consumption expenditure is accounted for around 60 per cent of the country's total consumption expenditure. The rural consumers need to be educated about their rights and adequate steps be taken to ensure that they get the value for their money as consumers.

The Indian rural consumers live in around 6,00,000 villages across the country and they account for over 70 per cent of the population of the country. While the rural consumer is generally seen as the less affluent, as compared to his urban cousin, things are changing in rural India over the last ten years. Like any market that has seen a demand and awareness boom, rural India has been witnessing considerable rise in purchasing power. A change in consumption patterns and access to communication media have made rural market a vital cog in the sales-growth wheel, especially with demand for many categories of products and services plateauing in the urban markets. In spite of increasing number of rural consumers, provisions for consumer protection and welfare are often based on the general standard and circumstances of those living in big cities and towns. Although consumers as a whole are in an equal bargaining position, there are certain recognizable groups which are disadvantaged in more ways than the others. Disadvantaged consumers are those who are less able to assert their rights and rural consumers comprise one such group. Rural consumers remain disadvantaged as their right to information, choice, redress, and consumer education are not sufficiently fulfilled. Consequently such consumers need support in maintaining their rights so that they can bargain equally with the producers or the service providers.

Marketing and Research Team (MART), an organisation involved for decades in rural marketing research, has over the years built up a veritable trove of research on rural consumers and their consumption patterns. Some of the findings were presented by the President, MART at the Rural Marketing and Communication Conference organised by the Federation of Indian Chamber of Commerce and Industry (FICCI) at Delhi held in 2003. The following are the findings of MART:

1. The rural consumer may not be very educated, but he is certainly astute, with a lot of common sense and practical experience of handling the vagaries and uncertainties of life. He displays great ingenuity and adaptability as evidenced by his learning to repair his tractor, hand pump and motorbike, and finding a host of local solutions in everyday life.
2. Though low on economic resources, he does not go in for only 'cheap' products but looks for value for money. Perception of a premium product is not yet relevant in rural markets, with consumers more concerned with functionality than unnecessary 'frills' with a consumer durable. Too many features with a product tend to confuse the rural consumer.
3. Rural consumers are generally mistrustful and wary of urbanites and turned off by their patronising attitudes. It is not easy for a rank outsider to get the rural consumer to spend money.
4. Brand adherence is high among village consumers. This may not necessarily be on account of loyalties. Limited access to alternatives and lack of information about possible choices do make them 'stick' to tried and tested brands.

5. Brand recognition is often on the basis of logos, symbols, colours rather than the exact brand name. This tendency is partly responsible for the widespread menace of spurious products in rural markets, as it is easy to deceive the rural consumer with look-alikes.
6. A very high degree of involvement characterises purchase of expensive products like consumer durables. A lot of checking and counterchecking is done to seek reassurance on the soundness of the buying decision. Marketers must embody reassurance and provide opportunity to "see and touch" the product in their marketing communication processes.
7. Routine is important to a rural consumer's life as a lot of time consuming activities characterise his everyday life. The routine is governed by nature and seasons, not by the calendar or the clock. Sunday is not typically a holiday. In buying processes, the consumer is not in a hurry and cannot be pushed into a hasty purchase for these segments.
8. Rural incomes show a great seasonality for the segment of large farmers. The segment of petty farmers, farm labour, non-farm workers and the salaried class show a greater regularity of income patterns so the consumption cycles are also more regular and predictable.
9. On account of far higher degree of inter personal communication characterising village life and relatively low penetration of mass media, word of mouth is a very effective medium of influence generation. Existing users, dealers, village influential, youth studying or working in urban locations are all consulted before making purchases.
10. Among the households with TV ownership, TV viewing is the highest among women and children who in contrast to the traditional, household head dominated decision scenario are fast emerging as demand generators for the household goods. Decisions on durables like radio, TV and two wheelers are still male dominated decisions, taken in consultation with other people in the community.
11. The rural youth are increasingly becoming more exposed to urban life styles on account of their frequent visits to urban locations either for higher education or for work. Their media exposure to television is also much higher. This makes urban life styles

an inspirational model for them and their preference for national brands is on the rise.

12. While culture and social norms have a greater hold on rural consumer than urban ones, perceptions, traditions and values vary from state-to-state, sometimes from region to region. It is, therefore, difficult to work with a pan-rural Indian communication package. Two step flow of communication, using opinion leaders and mass media both, seems to work better in rural settings. These observations made on the basis of a host of research-based inputs make it very clear that rural marketing effort cannot be visualised as a simple extension of the urban marketing process. It is a different market and presents a different set of premises on the basis of which suitable marketing.

Rising Rural Prosperity and Changing Consumption Pattern

According to the 66th round of NSSO (National Sample Survey Organisation) survey, the real spending by each person in rural India rose by 6.3 per cent in the five year period from 2004-05 to 2009-10. The year after 2004 saw the government waive unpaid farm loans, announce pay hikes for government employees through the Sixth Pay Commission and put in place its flagship rural employment guarantee programme. The survey also shows that the share of the food basket in total consumption expenditure is coming down in rural India. The share of food in consumer expenditure was 57 per cent for rural India. In rural India people are spending less and less on cereals, edible oils and fruits. They are spending more on pulses, milk, non-vegetarian items and beverages. Consumption of non-food items, which include consumer durables, education and recreation among others has gone up as a result of decline in expenditure on food items. Between 1999 and 2009 expenditure on food increased by about 70 per cent among rural families, but the spending on education jumped up as much as 378 per cent in rural areas. Even after correcting for inflation, the expenditure on education increased by a phenomenal 162 per cent in rural areas during the decade. Compare this to the overall household expenditure on all items, which increased by a mere 8 per cent in rural areas.

Moreover, it is not the same people who are spending more on their children's education. In 2004-05 when the previous survey was carried out, 40 per cent of rural families said that they were spending on education. The latest survey records a big jump in these numbers being 63 per cent for the rural. Expenditure on health too has shown a considerable increase though not as much as education. At current prices, spending on medical care in hospitals increased by 152 per cent in rural areas while spending on non-institutional medical care-medicines, tests, fees etc. jumped by 60 per cent. The NSSO data suggests that there has been an improvement in the living standards of the rural population. The monthly expenditure in rural India was Rs. 953.05 in 2009-10, an increase of 64.6 per cent from 2004-05. Thus, the rural households are spending more on consumer goods like durables, beverages and services. The break-up of the expenditure, or how households spent their money, suggests a break away from mere subsistence for the vast majority. In rural households cereals accounted for only 15.6 per cent of expenditure in 2009-10 down from 22.2 per cent in 1999-2000. During the same period, share of their spending on consumer durables almost doubled to 4.8 per cent from 2.6 per cent. The rise in spending on durables indicates on the overall increasing affluence of the rural population. Infact when the global recession hit the urban demand it was the strong rural demand that rescued the economy. All kinds of consumer product companies—from toothpaste marketers and mobile hand-set-makers to car-makers and television companies have been expanding their rural reach in recent years.

A number of studies have revealed that the rural consumers have acquired importance as India is now seeing a dramatic shift towards prosperity in rural households. Rural India with its traditional perceptions has grown over the years, not only in terms of income, but also in terms of thinking. The purchasing power in rural India is on steady rise and it has resulted in the growth of the rural markets. The market has been growing at 3-4 per cent per annum adding more than one million consumers every year. According to a study by the National Council for Applied Economic Research (NCAER), there are as many middle incomes and above households in the rural areas as are in the urban areas. Moreover, there are almost twice as many lower middle income households in the rural areas as in the urban areas. At the highest income level there are 2.3 million urban households against 1.6 million households in rural areas. As per the NCAER projections, the number of middle income and high income households in rural India was expected to grow from 80 million to 111 million by 2007. In urban India, the same is expected to grow from 46 million to 59 million. Thus, the absolute size of rural India is expected to be double that of urban India.

Rural India Scenario

A survey by NCAER, shows the increase in purchase of durables and expendables by rural consumers in comparison to urban buyers (Table 1.2)[4]:

Table 1.2: Consumer Duables *vs.* Consumer Expendables

	Urban		*Rural*	
	2001-2002	*2009-2010*	*2001-2002*	*2009-2010*
Consumer Durables				
Motorcycle	134.3	320.7	109.0	250.9
T V	942.8	1258.9	616.3	561.3
Car	31.4	52.2	1.6	3.5
Consumer Expendables				
Edible Oil	1000.0	1000.0	1000.0	1000.0
Shampoos	827.8	1000.0	354.5	458.4
Washing Powder	904.7	1000.0	775.4	946.9

Note: Urban Rural Usage Pattern (Per '000 households)

Table 1.2 displays the figures and selling capacity of the sales force and also brings forth the fact that there is a steady rise in the purchasing power of the farmers. The percentage of Below Poverty Line (BPL) families has come to 26 per cent from 42 per cent. At present 42 million rural households avail banking service. A look at the percentage distribution of rural population, a little care for development by creating awareness on the rural front takes greater care on the whole of country. Scope provided by the rural market is wide but entry into it brings forth challenges as poor infrastructure, dispersed settlements, lack of education and a virtually non-existent medium for communication.

In India, out of 6,00,000+ villages, only 10,000 villages have access to organise retailing. This also has a positive indication that these villages have fair connection with the media. The rest, without any guidance or proper awareness are consuming spurious products. In such interior places the conventional mass media techniques turns out to be helpless mainly due to two reasons: First, due to lack of network coverage and secondly, even if there is coverage, conviction of people residing in such interior areas is not easy to be won over. But, at the same time the emergence of the lucrative rural market can also be not forsaken as NCAER reports that rural India is home to 720 million consumers.

Exploitation of Rural Consumers

With the growth in rural markets and due to poor knowledge about their rights and lack of skills to take a rational decision based on information about the product or services, the rural consumers in India are being exploited in many ways. The rural consumer has been made to endure sub-standard products and services, adulterated foods, short weights and measures, spurious and hazardous drugs, exorbitant prices, endemic shortages leading to black marketing and profiteering, unfulfilled manufacturing guarantees and host of other ills. The rural consumers who generally depend on weekly markets to purchase essential things are often cheated due to lack of choice.

The rural consumers in India are generally ignorant and they are also unorganised. Thus, they are exploited by the manufacturers, traders and the service providers in different ways. The rural consumers are not only scattered, but, also diverse and heterogeneous. As a result of globalisation and liberalisation the rural market in India is the largest potential market in the world. Thus, there are vast opportunities for rural marketing. The manufactures and traders take advantage of the condition of the rural consumers. It has been observed that the condition of the rural consumers is deplorable because they are largely exploited in the rural markets on account of lack of competition among the sellers. The rural consumers face various problems like adulteration, short weighing and measuring, lack of safety and quality control in appliances and equipments, electrical and mechanical, unfair warranties and guarantees, imitation, sales gimmicks and unreasonable pricing.

Fake Brands and Spurious Products

One of the major problems being faced by the rural consumers is that of fake brands and spurious products. The brand image of the successful FMCG majors has been imitated by some of the small regional companies. These fake brands have been sold mostly in rural areas. Fake products are of two types – one, counterfeit products and two, pass-off products. Counterfeit products are fake products that bear identical name of a product/packaging/graphics/colour scheme and even same name and address as the genuine manufacturer. Someone produces these to look exactly like real products other than the legal owner of the real product, trademarks and product packaging. Sometimes, it becomes difficult to tell which the real product is. A rural consumer is brand loyal and understands symbols better and this also becomes a problem as it is easy to misguide the rural consumer. The FMCG industry alone has been facing losses of over Rs. 5,000 crore per year, due to counterfeit products, of the Rs. 1,13,000 crore FMCG market in India. Counterfeit products result in an annual loss of approximately Rs. 30,000 crore to the industry and Rs. 15,000 crore to the Government exchequer.[5]

Pass-off products use similar sounding or is similar in spelling. They use similar type of packaging or colour or design. These are look alike products that resemble the original products, mainly through misspelling of the trademark. For example, Sunslik instead of Sunsilk, Clemic Plus or Climic Plus or Cosmic Plus instead of Clinic Plus, Collegiate for Colgate, Vips Rub or Vives Rub as a pass-off for Vicks Vaporub. They come out with the motive to mislead and cheating ordinary consumers who are uneducated or in a hurry in purchasing products.

A study conducted by A.C. Nelson, a leading research agency reveals that FMCG industry loses around Rs. 2500 crore annually to counterfeits and pass-off products. It is also estimated that top brands in India are estimated to lose up to 30 per cent of their business to fake products. Besides the loss of revenue, the trading companies also face the loss of damage to brand image and brand loyalty to consumers. Apart from the loss of revenue and brand image fake products cause immense damage to consumer's health. Ten per cent of all major soft drinks sold are spurious, while 10-30 per cent of cosmetics, toiletries and packaged food are counterfeits. Fake gold and precious metals are worth Rs. 60 billion in India.

Another interesting point is that FMCG counterfeit products only come in smallest size of packing. In the rural segment where fake products thrive, the consumer's low purchasing power makes sachets and smaller packs popular. It is in the case of these small packs that consumers are duped more easily as the quantity is not large enough for the buyer to discern its quality. This is especially so in sachets of shampoo, hair oils, and detergents and so on.

Misleading Advertisements and Role of Media

The media has a greater responsibility towards the vulnerable sections of the society. The rural consumers are one such. Rural consumers today have access to diverse media with the advent of modern technology. Advertising is the major or even the main sources of information about many new products or newly introduced products. The changes in advertising are in part a response to the rapid growth in markets due to globalisation. Due to the entry of a large number of players in the rural market and also due to stiff competition there are large numbers of misleading advertisements in the print and electronic media resulting into exploitation of the consumers.

The advertising firms are studying consumer behaviours to design effective communication strategies without caring for the welfare of the consumer. In most parts of the rural areas in the country there is considerable awareness on various latest products that are available in the market. This has been possible due to the penetration of cable and satellite channels that have brought down the world at the finger tips of the common man. The media has influenced the mindset of the rural consumers to such an extent that people who have money start purchasing the products unmindful of the costs, just to satisfy their needs as well as their ego.

The problem is that there are no effective sanctions against misleading advertisements. What needs to be emphasised is that the poor, uneducated consumers in the rural areas are most likely to be harmed. More generally, as a recent World Development Report rightly emphasised, "information problems are often at the core of the difficulties that poor people in developing countries encounter in their daily struggle to survive and to improve their lives."

Rural Consumers: Need for Education and Empowerment

In the emerging scenario it is necessary to protect the rural consumers by educating them about their rights and empowering them to make decisions based on information about the goods and services. Awareness has to be created among the rural consumers. So far the consumer movement has largely been confined to the urban centres, and with the expanding rural markets now the focus has to shift to protect the rural consumer.

Consumer organisations and similar civil society groups have an important role to play in consumer education. They have the means to provide consumers with information and help them to make informed choices. Consumer information needs to be available at the right time and in the right place before or when purchasing decisions are made. Several NGOs are very active in the rural areas in advocating for consumer rights, but due to their limited ability to put enough pressure on policy-makers, they lack consumer support. This is the dilemma of NGOs in consumer protection. Regardless of these limitations consumer empowerment programmes through regular training and education are very crucial. It is also time to consider consumer education as part of the school and college curriculum.

There is also a need for the effective implementation of various provisions of the legislations enacted to protect the consumers from fake and adulterated products from entering the markets so that the consumers interests could be safeguarded. Various business houses, NGOs and the governmental agencies have to come together to join hands to combat counterfeiting.

Strengthening Redressal Mechanism

Redress of complaints is a major concern for consumers. Having a right to access the redressal mechanism is of prime importance. For the right to redress to have a practical value, a mechanism must exist to ensure that it can be exercised effectively. If consumer confidence is to be built up they need assurances that if things go wrong they can seek redress. The District Consumer Disputes Redressal Forums which act as the first point of contact in case of a complaint have to play a proactive role in building consumer confidence. The district forums should be strengthened and initiatives aimed at promoting access to simple, swift, effective and inexpensive legal channels be taken-up. In many states the District Forums are short of members and also lack the required infrastructure. The State Governments should address the problems of district forums as well as the consumers to make the redressal mechanism more effective and also responsive. Moreover, it becomes difficult for a rural consumer to go to the district headquarters to file a complaint and then pursue his complaint. It will be better if the concept of circuit benches for the district forums is also introduced as in the case of National Commission and the State Commissions so that access to justice is ensured for the rural consumers. There is also a need to set-up more than one district forum in a district to clear-up the pendency of complaints, which has increased substantially. Any further delay in disposal of the complaints will only shatter the faith of consumers in the redressal mechanism.

Role of Voluntary Consumer Organisations

VCOs are advocacy groups that seek to protect people from corporate abuse like unsafe products, deficiency in services, misleading and false advertisements and other unfair practices resorted to by the business. Consumer organisations may operate *via* protests, campaigning or lobbying. They may engage in single-issue advocacy or they may set themselves up as more general consumer watchdogs. One common means of providing consumers useful information is the independent comparative survey or test of products or services, involving different manufacturers or companies which is currently being done by NGOs like VOICE, Delhi and CERC Ahmedabad. The aim of consumer organisations may be to establish and to attempt to enforce consumer rights. Consumer organisations may attempt to serve consumer interests by relatively direct actions such as creating and/or disseminating market information, and prohibiting specific acts or practices, or by promoting competitive forces in the markets which directly or indirectly affect consumers (such as transport, electricity, communications etc.).

In India the consumer movement has been supported by a large network of NGOs operating down to the village-level. They have helped strengthen the consumer movement. But, it is equally true that many of the NGO lack capacity to perform and therefore are ineffective. They lack basic skills of management, advocacy and augmentation of resources. Therefore, there is a need to build the capacity of the NGOs working in the area of consumer protection and welfare so that they can play a larger role in strengthening the consumer movement in the country. Karnataka has a good network of NGOs working in the area of consumer protection and a capacity building programme will help them to discharge their responsibilities in a better way.

Role of Panchayati Raj Institutions

To reach the rural consumers, it is imperative to involve the Panchayati Raj Institutions in not only educating consumers, but also ensuring that fake and spurious products are not sold in the rural markets. These institutions can play a meaningful role in consumer protection and consumer welfare and this has been recogonised by the policy-makers. The recommendations contained in the 20th Report of the Standing Committee on Food, Consumer Affairs and Public Distribution (14th Lok Sabha) on the subject "Consumer Movement in the Country" needs to be effectively implemented. It recommended that the Department of Consumer Affairs should take the desired initiatives to involve Panchayati Raj Institutions in various programmes related to consumer awareness. The publication of the Department specifically "UPBHOKTA JAGARAN" should be brought out in regional languages and distributed to the elected representatives of the PRIs.

The Committee further recommended that the best forum to educate the rural masses about their rights as consumers as well as the techniques to redress their grievances is the meetings of the *gram sabha*. It felt that the Department of Consumer Affairs in consultation with the Ministry of Panchayati Raj should take desired initiatives to have mandatory meetings of the Gram Sabha on 24th December (National Consumer Day), where the villagers could properly be educated about their rights as consumers. No doubt some initiatives have been taken in this direction and capacity building and awareness programmes are being organised through the State Institutes of Rural Development. But to reach such a large number of rural consumers, a vigorous campaign with the involvement of the *panchayats* needs to be taken-up. Specific capacity building programmes for the elected members of the PRIs are to be developed with adequate financial sanctions. All stakeholders need to coordinate their activities and ensure that adequate literature is also made available in the local languages. Street plays and folk songs can be meaningful instruments to create awareness in the rural areas. Apart from these there is also a need to formulate appropriate policies and strategies to protect the rural consumers particularly the farmers, women and children.

The book is an outcome of a National Seminar on "Globalisation Markets and the Rural Consumers" organised by the Centre for Consumer Studies, Indian Institute of Public Administration, New Delhi. The seminar was sponsored by the Department of Consumer Affairs, Government of India. The book contains twenty two chapters written by eminent experts working in the area of consumer protection and welfare and is divided into four sections each focusing on a specific theme. They analyse the rural scenario, the status of the rural consumers, the lack of safety mechanisms and the ways and means to empower them. Various strategies and policy interventions have been suggested by the authors to address the problems faced by the rural consumers.

P.V.V.S. Murthy in his chapter on *Rural Consumers: Need for Education and Awareness* highlights that Consumer Protection Act envisages better protection to consumers, whether one is a rural or an urban consumer. The term "rural consumer" includes semi-urban consumer also. Urban consumer is in a better position than rural or semi-urban consumer, in the sense that at least protection mechanism is available to him in his close vicinity. Further consumers in the rural area are of low literacy and low income. Due to low literacy they cannot read and properly understand the information furnished along with the product. Due to low income they try to purchase low cost products which would provide an opportunity to unscrupulous traders to offer spurious goods or substandard/expired medicines to them. Without proper consumer education and awareness rural consumers are always vulnerable to market frauds particularly the rural women and farmers.

According to him Consumer Education among rural consumers is abysmally low because there are no agencies to take-up such responsibilities. Though Government of India is attempting to create awareness through programmes like "Jago Grahak Jago"; these attempts are not adequate. Though Consumer Protection Act provides a right to consumer education it has not specified the agency that provides this education. The common consumer's view is that as the government brought out this legislation it is its responsibility to provide consumer education. But, government alone cannot undertake this responsibility in a vast geographical nation like India. Necessarily government efforts must be supplemented by other institutions.

His chapter discusses various problems of rural consumers, the reasons for the gullibility of rural consumers, the agencies to be identified to impart such consumer education, how to impart the necessary education, for what age group, and the relevant educative material to be selected for inclusion in the process of consumer education and the extent of government support required for the effective protection of consumers in rural areas.

M. Sumathy and N.Vijayalakshmi in their chapter on *Awareness of Consumer Protection Act among Rural Consumers — A Study of Coimbatore* highlight that about 70 per cent of India's population lives in rural areas. There are about 6,38,365 villages in the country as against about 300 cities and 5,161 towns. Of the 121 crore Indians, 83.3 crore live in rural areas, while 37.7 crore stay in urban areas, as per the Census 2011. The National Council of Applied Economic Research (NCAER) survey report says that there are 720 million consumers across the villages in rural India. Hence, the development of the nation largely depends upon the development of the rural population. Majority of the rural population is dependent upon agriculture for their subsistence. Community Development Programmes, Integrated Rural Development Programme, bringing local self-government to the roots of the village through introduction of Panchayati Raj System ushered a new era of rural development. Schemes for providing effective rural healthcare, guaranteeing 100 days of job, promoting literacy and adult education, expansion of rural industries are other development programmes that have received the thrust of the government's development approach.

They are of the view that islands of poverty still exist, but most of the rural India is transformed beyond imagination, as a result of a host of factors which has put unprecedented wealth into the hands of farmers across the country and turned rural India into a huge consumer market. This study reveals the extent of consumer awareness among rural consumers in Coimbatore.

S.C. Roy in his chapter on *Empowering Rural Consumers: Issues and Concerns* highlights that the rural consumers are the producers of grain, but they are bound to purchase processed goods of brand companies without questioning about their quality, quantity and purity. People are not aware of MRP and INCLUSIVE OF ALL TAXES. According to him the rural population lacks adequate market expansion even in twenty first century. Thus, whatever commodity is available in the local market, they have to purchase at the terms and condition of the vendor. The vendors have their own unions, whereas the purchasers (consumers) are disorganised. Vendors most often charge higher price for substandard goods. More due to illiteracy and ignorance rural folks very easily fall prey to the vendors. Even spurious and expired drugs are sold to them without fear.

He opines that food adulterated is a major problem in the rural areas and are sold without fearing the enforcement agencies. They are also victim of low weights and measurement. Even the vegetable sellers cheat them very easily. The supplies of essential commodities are always in scarcity causing black marketing and high price. Fertilisers, packaged seeds and pesticides are of inferior quality and sold at high price. Thus, from food to agricultural commodities, the rural consumers are very easily deceived by the clever dealers.

In this context, his chapter seeks to study the problems of rural consumers. Whether the rural folks know the remedies available? How can they get relief? Should they fight for small purchases of daily commodities and waste their time, money and energy. Who can provide them protection? Whether the state machinery is not responsible to provide adequate safety to the innocent rural consumers? Are the questions that need to be answered? The answer to all such questions requires to be studied under the concept of consumer empowerment.

Pallavi Gupta in her chapter on *Role of Consumer Courts to Protect "Farmer" as a "Consumer": An Analysis* asserts that rural India is dependent on agriculture. Farmers are the backbone of the rural economy. Today a large number of farmers are committing suicide due to loss in their farms because of various reasons including non-germination and poor quality of seeds, adulterated pesticides, spurious fertilisers etc. A farmer purchases seeds for farming purpose but due to defective seed, he does not get his crop/yield as expected, then what is the remedy in such cases? Although the farmer had applied all the farming steps, like undertaking cultivation by adopting the recognised methods of preparing the field and irrigating at the required time interval, using the prescribed fertiliser, but the output was less and the farmer suffers loss due to defective seed sold by Seed Corporation.

According to her, can the farmer get remedy under the Consumer Protection Act, 1986? Does the farmer come within the definition of 'Consumer' as per section 2(1)(d) of the Consumer Protection Act? Will defective seed be considered 'Defective Goods' under the Consumer Protection Act? Whether 'farming' is considered commercial activity or self-employment? Whether consumer redressal agencies have jurisdiction to try such cases of sale of defective seeds to the farmers or not?

Her chapter attempts to answer the above questions and discuss the role of judiciary to widen the ambit of term 'consumer' under section 2(1) (d) and to protect the 'Farmer' as 'Consumer'.

Pratip Kumar Mishra in his chapter on *Emerging Rural Consumerism in Odisha—Protection and Redressal Initiatives* highlights that India is a huge multi-cultural society having a population and region of sub-continental dimension. It is one of the world's backward regions, with majority of the population in the rural areas in abject poverty, where hunger persists amidst plenty. It is true that the pace of urbanisation has been rapid due to the impact of Globalisation. The new consumerist culture has percolated to rural areas in one of the fastest developing states of the Indian Union—Odisha. But, with it there is a large concentration of the disadvantaged and vulnerable people who are not aware of the new civilisation that is creeping into their neighbourhood in the name of modernisation and consumerism.

He is of the view that LPG—Liberalisation, Privatisation, Globalisation has created unprecedented new opportunities in the sphere of economic development. India is definitely shining in its mega-cities with world class shopping malls and this excitement is slowly travelling to the rural sector where 70 per cent of the potential consumers live. The emerging problem of a new consumer is also surfacing. Various schemes have ensured flow of funds to the rural areas thereby increasing the purchasing power of the people. Sustainable livelihood and steady income has upgraded peoples' choices for a decent living. Once called luxury, TV, Mobile phones, beverages, nutritious food habits. Demand for cosmetics and other fashionable products has now become a necessity. However, in this mad rush to avail the best of things the rural consumer is waylaid. Into buying of spurious, adulterated and fake brand products. With the entry of a variety of private players into the service delivery system, deficiency and delinquency of services has become the major source of concern.

According to him rural India has attracted MNC, TNC (Trans National Companies) and our own corporate houses in recent times. They all maintain a monopoly marketing strategy, as competition in certain areas is remote; this increases the agony of the consumer. There is no proper redressal mechanism in rural areas whereas the quantum of consumer grievances is on the rise, more so after the enactment of CPA (Consumer Protection Act) 1986. Yet the people in periphery villages are not aware of their rights as consumer. There is need for generating a social force.

His chapter analyses the growth of consumerism in rural Odisha, the pattern and strategies for sensitising the rural consumer, the role of community organisations, civil society activist and the Gram Sabha as the lowest organ in the Government people interface. To develop the machinery for interventions that can make consumer rights accessible and people centric.

Rajbir Singh Dalal and Vijay Vir in their chapter on *Consumer Protection Measures in India — A Study of District Jind, Haryana* highlights that in the era of consumerism, market is shifting from the sellers to the buyers and the consumer has been designated as the king therein. In the last decade, the purchasing power of consumers in rural India has increased significantly, hence, their consumption level to upgrade their standard of living due to the various steps taken by the Government for rural development and social welfare. That is why the consumer market in rural areas have multiplied many times having wide scope and potentialities. Therefore, it is the focus of attention to all the marketing forces. Despite of adequate provisions regarding the consumer protection in the country, the ground reality is somewhat in sorry state and the situation is rather worse in rural areas where the consumers are by and large illiterate, ignorant, having poor purchasing and bargaining power due to a number of factors. Therefore, the possibility of exploitation by the rogue traders or sellers is on the higher side. The existing consumer protection mechanism is over 2½ decades old in the country, therefore, it becomes essential to look into it and examine and assess its impact in the rural areas. Accordingly, the present study is carried out with the objectives of assessing the nature of rural consumer, their literacy level as well as level of awareness regarding the Consumer Protection Act (CPA), 1986 and mechanism meant for it. Simultaneously, the challenges before the rural consumers have been pointed out and suitable suggestions have been given to make this consumer protection measure more effective and viable in the rural areas.

They are of the view that rural marketing is somewhat different from the urban where the cash purchase and taking of bills or receipts of purchased goods or services is generally ignored and the personal and informal relations pay their role. The consumers lack consumer protection mechanism at their door step and the market is less competitive. They are exploited due to the monopolised market. Not only the spurious goods are thrown there but also the condition of services provided is also poor in quality. Therefore, special attention needs to be paid in this regard.

Anju Kumar and Abhishek Srivastava in their chapter on *Impact of Education and Awareness on Rural Marketing in India* aruge that rural India is fast emerging as the proverbial goldmine. It is estimated that the rural market size is almost of $425 billion presenting a huge opportunity for marketers to explore this segment. Although poorer than their urban counterparts, the rural consumers are driving volumes of consumption due to their increasing aspirations towards a better life style. Improvement in literacy rates and rising disposable incomes are among the other reasons for their increasing consumption expenditure. Also better access to varied communication media channels has brought about a major shift in the consumption patterns of the rural population making the rural market a vital cog in the sales-growth wheel, especially with demand for many product categories plateauing in the urban markets.

According to them despite the huge potential rural India can offer, one still hears about how very few categories and brands have seen substantial product penetration and how very few marketers have actually been able to successfully tap the market for what its worth. There is a general agreement that there are tremendous growth opportunities which require investment in terms of distribution, product realignment, product-variant creation etc. But at the same time the challenges, pretty unique in character, are many. For instance understanding the pulse of the rural consumers, their typical mindset, physical distribution of goods and services in the face of poor rural infrastructure and inhospitable terrain and finally problems related to generating awareness and communicating to a heterogeneous population. Successful rural marketing calls for a review of the rural marketing environment, developing proper understanding of the nature and profile of rural consumers, designing the right products to appeal to them, and adopting suitable media as well as appropriate strategies for communication and distribution.

Their chapter explores the nature and trends of rural marketing in India, factors affecting the awareness of the rural consumers with a focus on understanding the relationship between education and product awareness in the rural Indian market and how better awareness translates into successful rural marketing.

In the chapter Role of *Consumer Organisations in Rural India: Towards Suggesting Action Agenda for Consumer Organisations* by K.Venugopala Rao discusses the role of Consumer Organisations in rural India. While doing so, he covers aspects like what are Consumer Organisations, what roles they play in increasing consumer awareness and education to protect consumers, importance of Consumer Organisations in rural India, what methods they adopt to increase consumer education in rural areas and what should be an action agenda for them in the context of rural Indian society.

According to him consumer organisations are those organisations which are formed and framed by consumers to fight for their rights, to create awareness among fellow consumers about their responsibility, to enhance consumer welfare through proper coordination with the government and institutions. Theoretically, Consumer Organisations have two roles: (1) the organisations deal with individual consumers, handling consumer complaints and at times acting as a facilitator between the consumers and the service providers; and (2) the organisations focus on policy issues like economic, legal, social and environmental issues affected by various consumer policies of the government. The changing face of rural Indian economy in the entrenching rural market with the given consumer oriented Indian economy; the need for active role by Consumer Organisations becomes imminent. The role of Consumer Organisations becomes further more important because rural market is widening.

His chapter highlights nearly eleven categories of methods/practices which are adopted by the Voluntary Consumer Organisations in rural India to increase the awareness and education of rural consumers. It suggests 21 points Action Agenda which is needed for Consumer Organisations to further protect the rural consumers in India.

Amit Kumar Singh and Pankaj Kumar Singh in their chapter on *Menace of Food Adulteration in the Rural Areas—Need to Empower Women* opine that Food is essential for life. Unfortunately, in recent past the prevalence of food adulteration has become common in India, which is posing a serious threat to the human life and leading towards massive health hazards. Whatever food items are available in the market, whether, it is raw vegetables, fruits, meat, milk, edible oil, sweets or spices, and every single item is mixed with cheap and dangerous ingredients for the purpose of making more profit. Even educated consumers do not pay attention to the menace of adulteration. Many such dangerous chemicals and other items are added while food processing and this has adverse effect on human health. Therefore, there is a need to build the capacity of the consumers as well as the community to fight this menace. Educating the consumers about food safety and hygiene, food adulteration and the way to detect food adulteration is the best way to protect them. In spite of efforts both by Central and State Governments and formulated of several laws and policies to restrict and detect the incidence of food adulteration yet we have not been able to solve this problem.

The authors are of the view that women play a major role in decision-making regarding food, hence, they need to be targeted as far as consumer education and awareness is concerned. Even in rural areas on many occasions the home-makers take independent decision in matters relating to buying of food except the financial aspect. If we want this movement to grow, more women will have to come forward into this movement. It is necessary to generate awareness among the housewives (home-makers) about the existing food adulteration practices of the retailers and manufacturers and equip them with simple household test for detecting adulteration.

Their chapter focuses on how knowledge enhancement and skill development helps rural women to minimise adulteration practices in rural areas. It is based on a case study which was carried out in six districts of Tamil Nadu, where rural women especially the members of Self-Help Groups (SHG) have been trained to detect adulteration in food items. The outcome of the training programme was impressive and this chapter discusses in detail the importance of such type of skill development programmes in the rural areas targeting the home makers to enhance their capacity in fighting the menace of food adulteration.

Sapna Chadah in her chapter on *Role of Civil Society Organisations in Promoting Awareness among Rural Consumers: Challenges and Strategies* opines that Globalisation, liberalisation and privatisation have enabled the entry of several private traders, including large multinationals, who have transformed the Indian economy into a vibrant, rapidly growing consumer market. They have flooded the market with different kinds of goods and services, substantially effecting and changing the purchasing pattern of the consumers. The rural markets, which were earlier ignored by most of the big international market players, are now being seen as a land of great business opportunity. A change in consumption pattern and access to communication media have made the rural market a vital cog in the sales-growth wheel, especially with the plateau in demand for many categories of products and services in the urban markets. The people living in the remote and rural areas do often become victims of unlawful trade practices being adopted by wrongdoers due to lack of education and poor knowledge. Rural consumers remain disadvantaged as their right to information, choice, redress, and consumer education are not sufficiently fulfilled. Consequently, such consumers need support in maintaining their rights so that they can bargain equally with the producers or the service providers.

According to her there are various stakeholders in the consumer movement, but the role played by the civil society organisations especially the VCOs in consumer protection is second to none. The VCOs have the reach as they operate in rural areas and use techniques that are beneficial to the rural population. Moreover, they raise local issues and create awareness about various consumer issues with which it is easy for the rural population to identify with. However, at present many of these organisations lack the required organisational structure and the capacity to carry out meaningful awareness programmes. Moreover, these organisations are also riddled with many problems including lack of both functionaries and finances.

Based on an empirical study her chapter analyses the role of civil society in promoting consumer awareness and advocates that there is a need for accreditation and professionalisation of Voluntary Consumer Organisations (VCOs) to raise their credibility. These VCOs should attract and involve professionally qualified people with service orientation, retain them and motivate them to work for community upliftment. Training and skill development of those who are working with VCOs will no doubt make them more effective to take-up the cause of consumers. But the most important aspect is to identify a credible VCOs and build their capacity to take the consumer movement forward. The chapter suggests a few measures if taken can help the VCOs to enhance their performance.

Abbokar Siddiq in his chapter on *The Role of Voluntary Consumer Organisations in Consumer Protection — An Empirical Study in Rural Karnataka* argues that Consumers are the pillars of economic development of any country as the entire economy revolves around them. The developing and underdeveloped countries at present feel a new 'ism' known as 'Consumerism' to protect consumers from exploitation. In spite of various provisions providing protection to the consumers, very little could be achieved in the field of Consumer Protection. For this purpose, the need for Voluntary Consumer Organisations (VCOs) is gaining momentum to play a vital role to help and to render assistance to the ill-fated consumers in protecting their rights and interests.

The study area comprises two coastal districts of Karnataka State in India, viz., Dakshina Kannada and Udupi. The study highlights the duties, tasks, functions and contributions of VCOs in promoting and protecting the rights and interests of the consumers.

Grassroots Democracy and Empowerment — Rural Consumers and Panchayati Raj Institutions is written by Md. Azvar Khan. According to him everybody is using goods or services in day-to-day life which makes him a consumer. However, the ground reality is that the conditions are not very favourable and conducive for the consumer. He is being exploited and cheated day in and day out. Ignorance is one of the prominent factors contributing in the exploitation of the consumers and is most prevalent amongst the rural masses. The 73rd Constitutional Amendment has established Panchayati Raj Institutions (PRIs) in all the villages. It is through this institution that the consumer movement can get a boost and consumer awareness can be spread among rural masses.

He is of the opnion that the rural consumers in India are generally ignorant and they are also unorganised. Thus, they are exploited by the manufacturers, traders and service providers in different ways. The rural consumers are not only scattered, but also diverge and heterogeneous. As a result of globalisation and liberalisation the rural market in India has become the largest potential market in the world. The manufacturers and traders take advantage of the condition of rural consumers. The rural consumers face various problems like adulteration, short weighing and measuring, lack of safety and quality control in appliances and equipments, warranties and guarantees, imitation, sale gimmicks and unreasonable pricing.

He advocates that the task is gigantic and therefore, it is time to involve the PRIs to reach the rural consumer. The meetings of Gram Sabha can be utilised as a forum to educate the consumer about their rights and obligations and enhance their knowledge about fake and spurious products. An integrated approach is needed to empower the rural consumer. As the largest consumer base in the rural areas protecting the rural consumer has to be a priority in any strategy to protect and empower the consumers. The chapter will highlight how the rural consumers can be empowered through PRIs and what this institution is doing to empower the rural consumers.

Joseph Benjamin in his chapter on *Panchayati Raj Institutions—A Mechanism for Consumer Empowerment* argues that India is one of the biggest consumer markets in the world. But, then how the rights of consumers are being protected is the matter of concern. Most of the rural consumers being illiterate, ignorant and not fully aware of their exploitation by the manufacturers, producers and shopkeepers are unable to get justice. All these happen because the consumers are unaware of their rights. The success of consumer movement mainly depends upon the level of consumer awareness generated in the country by educating the consumers about their rights and responsibilities. Then, who should be educating the rural mass about their consumer rights?

According to him *panchayats* have been the backbone of the Indian villages since the very beginning of history. It is an engine of growth, agent of change and development. The contribution of Lord George Fredrick Samuel Ripon (1827-1909) in starting, in the year 1881-84, local self-government is remarkable. Gandhiji's dream of every village being a republic or Panchayats having powers has been translated into reality after Independence. April 24, 1993 is a landmark in the history of Panchayati Raj in India as on this day the Constitution (73rd Amendment) Act, 1992 came into force to provide Constitutional status to the Panchyati Raj Institutions. Since 1993, the Panchayati Raj Institution has been playing a vital role in educating the rural consumers in their rights. The present chapter is an effort to study how the Panchayati Raj Institution will be a catalyst in making rural mass aware about the consumer rights in their respective areas.

B.V. Gopalakrishna and C.L. Ramesh in their chapter on *Rural Consumers and the Panchayats — A Case Study of a Village in Shimoga District, Karnataka* opine that large population in India mainly in the rural areas is ignorant, innocent and poverty stricken. They live in unhygienic conditions and are deprived of basics of life and even two square meals. As consumers they are exploited and their grievances are unheard. They are the ones who are neglected and not influenced by the various government programmes and policies to protect the consumers. The rural markets are flooded with spurious, adulterated and harmful products. Rural consumers do not have knowledge about their rights and hence lack decision-making skills. They lack information about the products they purchase and the services they are supposed to get from the Utilities/Service Providers like Electricity/Telephone/Health/Insurance/Transport etc.

According to them even after 25 years of enactment of Consumer Protection Act in our country, the rights and facilities provided under this Act have not reached even 10 per cent of our rural population. It is really a pity and sorry state of affairs. Serious thinking and action plan need to be formulated to bring these ignorant, innocent rural consumers to the main stream by providing education and awareness at the grassroot-level that is from village-level. At present in Panchayati Raj system there are three-tier system: (1) Village Panchayat, (2) Taluk Pachayat, and (3) Zilla Panchayat. Lot of funds are directly given by the Central Government to these institutions. Necessary rules and regulations are required to be formulated by the Central Government by involving Consumer Activists in the area and also the District Forums to take up this task and to conduct at least one sitting in Taluk H.Q. and at least one consumer awareness meeting at village Panchayat-level etc.

Their chapter focuses on the status, nature and the problems of rural consumers particularly at the grassroots-level, the role Panchayats can play in consumer protection and also what other strategies are needed to protect rural consumers.

Alok Mishra in his chapter on *Role of Panchayati Raj Institutions in Consumer Protection* asserts that the role of the Panchayati Raj Institutions in Consumer Protection is of prime importance in present times. The evolution of law in the field of consumer protection and the Constitutional status accorded to Panchayati Raj Institutions are closely related. Both of them achieve special significance and meaning in the light of the fact that India is a country with extensive rural base and the bulk of the consumers live in rural areas. Rural markets are feeling the impact of globalisation and liberalisation of economy and law. The economic prosperity achieved by the common men in India has brought about an improvement in the economic status there by making Panchayati Raj Institutions and consumer protection more meaningful.

According to Alok Mishra, the thought process of consumers in rural areas has evolved and is getting rationalised resulting into better and more rational preferences. The behaviour of consumers in rural areas has also changed in a positive direction. In this context the innovations in the field of science and technology have played a crucial role. In a resurgent nation the conumer protection law not only protects the welfare of masses, but also can work as a tool for social development in conjunction with Panchayati Raj Institutions.

The author is of the view that there is an urgent requirement to enhance the role of Panchayati Raj Institutions in consumer protection. Problems of consumers in rural areas are to be taken care of with diligence. Empowerment of consumers and strengthening of redressal mechanisms is the need of the hour.

Anil Dutt Mishra in his chapter on *Gandhian Perspective on Problems of Rural Consumers in India—Issues and Challenges*, highlights that rural markets in India constitute a wide and untapped market for many products and services which are being marketed for the urban masses. There is a demand for all services which are available in cities to be provided in rural area across country. Till now it was the government which was trying to reach the villages through various initiates, but still vast rural areas are still untouched. Better quality of goods and services can be delivered by the introduction of modern and suitable technology along with participation from the private players through public private partnership.

Dr. Mishra opines that Protection of Rural Consumer is not as simple as it looks on chapter. Capabilities have to be built-up, suitable structures have to be valued, and changes have to be brought about in the administrative, technical and political arena. To strengthen the rural consumer movement there needs to be a political and administrative will to decentralise decision-making powers to the lower levels on Gandhian lines with a clear policy enunciation, full political support, and adequate administrative infrastructure. It is expected that the goals of real *swaraj* will be achieved by fulfilling the dream of the Father of the Nation. It is high time for both our policy-makers and the people, to turn the torch within so that they may be inspired to adopt the Gandhian way, if not for any other consideration, but for its pragmatic strength to solve our present day maladies of rural India. There is need to reiterate Gandhian values, and instead of merely garlanding the portraits of Gandhiji, India must translate his ideals into real life and make rural India free from hunger, poverty and exploitation.

The author argues that the village should be the centre of all activity as advocated by Gandhiji. The rural consumer's dependence on external marketers has resulted in his exploitation. The solution to protect the rural consumers lies in the Gandhian model of development.

Suresh Misra, Mamta Pathania and Virendra Nath Mishra in their chapter on *Role of Traditional Media in Consumer Empowerment : Communicating with the Rural Audience* feel that in a country like India, given the scenario of economic disparity and level of education and ignorance, educating the consumers remains a gigantic task. The process of development along with the expanding globalisation and liberalisation has increased the number of consumer related issues. Consumer protection has earned an important place in the political, economic and social agendas of many nations. In India, the Government has taken many steps including legislative enactment, to protect consumers, but still lot needs to be done.

The authors argue that consumer education is a potent tool for empowering consumers. Empowered consumers are knowledgeable, confident and assertive. In present scenario consumer education has an important role to play in supporting those with less developed consumer knowledge and skills. A variety of strategies are needed to communicate with the rural consumers, who lack education and awareness and hence easy to exploit. Perhaps the best way to communicate with the rural audience is through the traditional media like folk art, street plays etc. This form is easy to understand and has been used for centuries to educate the masses. Among these, the Oral tradition and the Performing arts appear to be the main media of communication. Story-tellers, singers, minstrels and other kinds of folk entertainers have acted for centuries as sources for the transmission and dissemination of news and information through face-to-face live communication.

They assert that a good use of traditional folk media for campaigns like consumer awareness and education, particularly in the rural areas can be very effective. Being ancient forms of art, the traditional folk media is very close to the heart of the people. Its appeal is universal and its understanding is direct and at personal level. So, the folk media can effectively be used as mass communication tool among rural people.

Based on a survey, their chapter examines the impact and effectiveness of traditional media on consumers and highlights as to how this media has been successfully used in three districts of West Bengal, i.e. South 24-Parganas, Murshidabad and Hooghly to empower the consumers. A cross-section of the population consisting of 546 persons from the villages of the three districts forms the sample size of the study.

Rural Consumers and the Media written by D.S. Poornananda opines that the consumer market in rural India is expanding like never before. Increasing purchasing power of rural consumers has led to major shifts in their purchasing pattern. The rural share of popular consumer goods and durables ranges from 30 per cent to 60 per cent. Rural markets are growing at double the pace of urban markets and for many product categories, rural markets account for well over 60 per cent of the national demand. While more and more rural consumers are purchasing branded products the awareness about the rights of the consumers, unfair trade practices and grievance redressal mechanisms is lacking.

In the absence of strong consumer movement in the rural area there is no institutional mechanism to help rural consumers enhance their awareness about the ways in which they can protect themselves against unethical and unfair trade practices. In such a situation communication media can play a vital role in educating rural consumers about violation of their rights and available ways of getting their grievances redressed. Just like the business enterprises in the country are making inroads into the rural market to sell their goods and services, the media, too should follow suit. The rural press has shown significant growth in the last two decades, not only because of the increase in the purchasing power of the people, but also because of the increase in the rural literacy rate which has direct relation to circulation figures of the press, readership and its impact.

He is of the view that besides the accessibility of print and electronic media many forms of alternative media have also merged in the rural areas. To what extent does the content in these media caters to the interest of the rural consumers? Do they provide specific information about consumer rights and protection? How can the potential of the alternative media be used to enable rural consumers to make conscious and informed choices? His chapter examines these questions through a content analysis. It also examines cases of district and community newschapters that have provided fora for the consumer to discuss issues related to defective goods and services and practices of unfair trade.

Arvind Kumar in his chapter on *Role of Media in Tourism Marketing and Influencing Consumers in Rural Areas of Himachal Pradesh* examines the role of media in marketing of tourism products (goods and services) and influencing consumers in rural areas of Himachal Pradesh. We know that more than 70 per cent of the population of the country resides in villages. Hence, rural area comprises a large market for various products including tourism products. With better infrastructure, literacy and rise in standard of living, rural tourism has emerged as a potential to market tourism products. With better communication facilities, various forms of media have made inroads in rural areas of the state. Now newspapers, magazines, radio, TV, CDs, DVDs, banners, posters etc. are playing an important role in marketing of tourism products and influencing consumers in rural areas of Himachal Pradesh.

He is of the opinion that different kinds of media have generated awareness and interest among rural people regarding tourism activities and tourism products like garments, fancy articles, souvenirs, brochures etc. and services like transportation, accommodation, site-seeing and ancillary services etc. Various tour operators and travel agents are also approaching consumers directly and influencing them to utilize different tourism products through their exciting offers. Rural consumers are not only utilizing domestic tour packages but also tour packages to foreign countries. Hence, media has played important role in tourism marketing and influencing consumers in rural areas of Himachal Pradesh.

Mahendra Kumar Padhy in his chapter on *Role of Communication Media in Rural Marketing* examines the impact of marketing communication strategies in rural India and shift of multinational corporations focus towards the Indian rural/retail marketing. Marketing consists of the strategies and tactics used to identify, create and maintain satisfying relationships with customers that results in value for both the customer and the marketer. Marketing is the key functional area of creating revenue for any business organisation. Rural marketing is the promotion of a product or service by using promotional strategies to facilitate the flow of goods and services from rural producers to urban consumers and consumer goods from urban to rural. It involves the transmission of manufactured or processed inputs to rural producers or consumers. It is the process of marketing communication to inform, aware, persuade, remind, influence and motivate the consumers in support of the available products and services. Rural marketing communication process includes all aspects of market structures both institutional and functional and covers technical as well as economic aspects. It starts with a decision to produce a saleable commodity and includes all the operations like assembling, grading, transportation, distribution etc.

According to him the rural markets of India are both lucrative and challenging. It offers large scope on account of its sheer size and potential. Even a gradual growth pushes up the sales of a product substantially. The factors chosen by the rural consumers which they consider accountable for deciding the optimal promotion mix confirm the level of awareness among the rural respondents about the elements of promotion mix. Each of the elements of promotion mix has its own impact on the rural masses. The market pioneers are getting rewarded by capturing the rural markets.

His chapter also talks about the changing behaviour of rural consumers due to advertising. It is often said that markets are made, not found. This is especially true of the rural market of India. It is a market meant for the truly creative marketers. The main purpose of the chapter is to identify the various communication media used by the marketers for promoting their goods and services in the rural market.

K. Soundararajan in his chapter on *Information and Communication Technology (ICT): Availability, Awareness, Use and Information Seeking Behaviour of Rural Farmers in Southern India* argues that the use of

Information and Communication Technologies (ICTs) can provide rural farmers with access to information and knowledge and thereby enhance their quality of life and accelerate the pace of rural development. In spite of ICT interventions including projects initiated by the government, non-governmental and other private players like ICT Village Information Centres (VICs) in Tamil Nadu, its acceptability and utilisation of ICT has been very low in the rural areas.

His cross sectional epidemiological study attempts to investigate the utilisation of ICT in agriculture from the perspective of the farmers. The study sample consists of 100 rural farmers' selected randomly in and around village Chunampet of Cheyyur Taluk, Kancheepuram District. Structured questionnaire and interview was used to collect data on socio-demographic pattern, availability, awareness, use and information seeking among rural farmers. Quantitative data was analysed using SPSS software and thematic analysis was used to analyse qualitative data.

Evidence from questionnaire, focus group discussions and personal observations suggests that the ICT has limited impact in terms of meeting some crucial agricultural information needs. Awareness level on ICT among farmers is very low and they mostly relied on middlemen, local and official sources for agricultural information. Although mobile phones are widely available to the farmers, its use is mainly for sale enquiry rather than production efficiency. There is a significant relationship between awareness and information usage and demographic characteristics in addition to the sources of information utilisation. Further, it does not affect the reciprocal relationship between the buyer (middlemen) and seller (farmer).

Sheetal Kapoor in her chapter on *Role of Information and Communication Technology (ICT) in Empowering Rural Consumers* highlights that today, the ultra bright shine of Colgate or some international brand holds more appeal than the traditional methods of cleaning teeth (like tooth powder or '*Dant Manjan*') in rural areas. Consumerism and Globalisation is invading parts of rural India and the villages which were once inconsequential dots on maps are now connected with telephone and internet getting the attention of global marketing and media planners.

According to her information is the key to democracy. With the advent of Information Technology (IT), it has become possible for common man to access global information. Information in a broader sense includes oral communication, voice in telephony, text in fax and newspapers, images in video and television broadcasting, and data in computers. All information can be digitised, transported, stored, retrieved, modified and then distributed. Emerging digital techniques, new network alternatives including intelligent networks, high bandwidth communication technology and state-of-the-art software for network functions and services, are the new technology trends evident in the development of electronic communication systems. The swift emergence of a global "information society is changing the way people live, learn, work and relate." Rural marketers have to successfully communicate with a much larger, but scattered audience characterised by variations in language, culture and life styles. The requirement, therefore, is to develop region specific and right communication strategies to induce target audience to buy the product.

Her chapter discusses the need to focus on Indian rural consumers to empower them to access information, knowledge by deploying the Information and Communication Technologies (ICTs) and to explore the available media at different locations. Analyse the factors preventing rural communities from reaping the benefits of ICTs, government initiatives to overcome the factors, and to identify the bottlenecks and solutions, and lessons learned.

Notes

1. CAG (2006), *Performance Audit of the Implementation of the Consumer Protection Act and Rules—Report of the Comptroller & Auditor General of India for the year ended March 2005*, Union Government (Civil), Performance Audit, p. 9.
2. The Great Indian Bazaar, India Brand Equity Foundation http://www.ibef.co.in/download/indianbazaar_jan19.pdf
3. Rural consumer durable market to grow at 40 per cent in 2011-12 http://news.infibeam.com/blog/news/2011/01/01/rural_consumer_ durable _market_to_grow_at_40_percent_in_2011_12.html
4. NCAER, The Great Indian Market, http://www.ncaer.org/downloads/PPT/thegreatindianmarket.pdf
5. February 2, 2010, India PRwire.

References

Ambi, M.G. Parameswaran (2008). "The Great Indian Rural Consumer", *Business Standard*, Feburary 15, New Delhi.

D.K. Bose (2007). "Marketing in Rural India", *Horizon07*. October 7, IIM Kozhikode.

K.V. Kannan, "Strategies for Chocolate Companies to Kill Fake Products in Indian Rural Market", www.indianmba.com/Faculty

Kaptan, S.S. (2004). *Rural Consumer and Consumer Protection*, Sarup & Sons Publication, (pp. 19, 83), New Delhi.

Preeti Mehra (2001). "Crusade against Counterfeit", *Business Line*, Monday, July 02, 2001.

Pushma Girimaji (2008). *Misleading Advertisements and Consumer*, IIPA, New Delhi.

S. John, Mano Raj and P. Selvaraj (2007). "Social Changes and the Growth of Indian Rural Markets: An Invitation to FMCG", International Marketing Conference on Marketing and Society, April 8-10, IIM, Kozhikode.

Sarangapani, A. (2009). *A Textbook on Rural Consumer Behaviour in India—A Study on FMCGs*, Oxford University Press, New Delhi.

Venkatesh Tamlurkar, "Assessing the Marketing for Rural India", www.indianmba.com/Faculty

who are out of school. The scientific methods of teaching are well-known to the teachers and hence they become the best of the lot to impart consumer education. Further, consumer clubs are already established in many schools and colleges which can render wonderful service in spreading consumer education. Members of consumer clubs can even discuss the issues they have learnt through consumer club with their family members.

SECTION I
Consumer Education and Awareness

and needs to be addressed to ensure sustainable growth in India. The consumers in BoP are fairly ambitious in their attitude. Even these consumers are focused on improving their lives, use education as a tool to improve life and dream big for their children. The following data by FICCI-Nielsen is a witness to this figure 1.1.

Fig. 1.1: Urban-rural Comparison on Key indicators in 2009

Source: Report: Challenges Before an Integrated India: Bridging the Urban Rural Divide, 2009.

The reports of National Commission for Applied Economic Research clearly reveals that the rural growth rates have already outpaced urban ones and will continue to do so through the next decade. Rural India accounts for more than 50 per cent of the GDP. Out of 62.97 million households of India those are getting more than 5 lakhs per annum, nearly 28.68 million households (46%) live in Rural India. The rural market in India is projected to be bigger than the urban market for fast moving consumer goods, rural consumption expenditures are largely more around 60 per cent of the country's total consumption expenditures. The rural consumers need to be educated about their rights and adequate steps be taken to ensure that they get the value for their money as consumers.

The Indian rural consumers live in around 6,00,000 villages across the country and they account for over 70 per cent of the population of the country. While the rural consumer is generally seen as the less affluent, as compared to his urban cousin, [illegible] looking to rural India over the last ten years, like any market that has seen a demand and awareness boom, rural India has been witnessing considerable rise in purchasing power. A change in consumption pattern, and access to communication

1
Empowering Rural Consumers: Need for Education and Awareness

P.V.V.S. Murthy

Introduction

"India lives in villages and continues to live in villages." There are no two opinions on this statement. More than 70 per cent of our population is still living in villages, away from the fruits of progress the urban India is making. Rural-Urban divide is a cause for concern to the economists as well as policy-makers. Urban Indian consumers are confined to approximately 3,200 towns/cities whereas the rural consumers are living in more than 6,40,867 lakh villages, occupying vast areas compared to consumers living in urban areas. The literacy rate is low and the income levels too are very low when compared to their urban counterparts. A large part of the rural consumer's income is spent on basic necessities leaving a negligible amount for other consumer goods. They have very low purchasing power. In a vast country like India consumer protection is difficult particularly with regard to the consumers living in rural areas. Villagers are gullible consumers and more vulnerable to the deceitful market practices. Hence, it becomes necessary to empower the consumers with necessary education to enable them to protect themselves.

Before any attempt is made to discuss the modalities on imparting consumer education to the rural consumers we need to understand the term 'consumerism' and also consider various aspects that cause problems to them. Ralph Nader, the father of the consumer movement in the world, suggested that consumerism is not a fight against anybody, but an effort to improve the quality of life of consumers. If we look at consumerism from this point of view, the quality of life of rural consumers is low when compared to the quality of life of people living in the urban areas. There are three important parameters usually considered to measure the quality of life, namely education, health and income. In villages the health care delivery is absolutely unsatisfactory. No medical professional lives in villages and in case of emergencies the villagers have to run to nearby towns for medical care. Similarly, educational facilities are inadequate and many of the villages do not have higher school education facilities. Income is considered in this context just to assess the purchasing power of the rural consumer, though it is not a matter that no government can ensure. But the term 'income' is of importance to know the 'consumer surplus' which provides purchasing power to consumer. Income depends on the opportunities and the hard work of the income earner. A study of these three parameters would reveal the plight of rural consumers and the quality of their lives.

In a rural set-up, we find two sections of people representing the consumer groups predominantly. Firstly, the people who are engaged in agricultural operations and secondly, those who are engaged in house management. In other words, the farmers and housewives are the prominent consumers in villages. These two sections of consumers account for majority spending in villages; farmers spend large amount of money for the purpose of agricultural operations, whereas housewives spend considerable amount of money for the domestic needs. If we look at the village markets and the quality of goods sold, we can understand that they are prone to many unfair and unethical business practices. While spending their hard earned money they are exposed to many malpractices prevailing in the rural markets which they are not aware of. If these two sections of consumers are educated and made aware, there will be tremendous improvement in the lives of these consumers. Hence, imparting consumer education and creating awareness on such malpractices is the better way to protect these gullible consumers.

Consumer education is a herculean task and associated with many problems. Though Consumer Protection Act provides a right to consumer education, it is not very clear whose responsibility is to provide consumer education. Primarily, it is the responsibility of the respective governments to impart consumer education. But, in a vast country like India imparting consumer education and creating consumer awareness is not possible by a single agency. It has to be taken-up simultaneously by many agencies like educational institutions, consumer clubs, manufacturers, women organisations, consumer organisations, farmers' organisations, cooperative societies etc. As these agencies are controlled by different departments and associations it requires coordinated effort by all these agencies to impart consumer education. The Ministry of Consumer Affairs should take up this issue with various departments and agencies and coordinate with them for successful implementation of consumer awareness programmes. It is only the educational institutions that can successfully take-up this responsibility and spread the consumer education to several generations effectively. Hence, the educational officers have the onerous responsibility to implement the consumer educations scheme. The most important aspect in this exercise is to develop consúmer education syllabus afresh. Consumer Education can be taught as a separate subject or can be included in various existing subjects like economics, social studies, mathematics, natural science etc. By no stretch of imagination one can think of providing consumer education outside schools or colleges because it is a continuing education.

While preparing the syllabus for consumer education one has to keep in mind various problems encountered by rural consumers and accordingly teach them on how to face these problems and overcome the difficulties. We need to consider the problems faced by the farmers as well as women while discussing the rural consumer problems. Farmers are purchasing several items for their agricultural operations spending huge sums of money. For instance purchase of fertilisers, pesticides, farm equipment involve in heavy expenditure. It is in the knowledge of everyone that farmers are not getting required quantities of fertilisers thus, forcing them to-go-to unscrupulous traders for the supply. These unscrupulous traders supply them substandard quality of fertiliser resulting in low yield of crop. There are no facilities to find out whether the fertiliser supplied to them is genuine or adulterated. Same is the case with pesticides. Due to these malpractices farmers are incurring heavy losses and ultimately ending their lives.

Departments of Agriculture are unable to supply the required agricultural seeds at the appropriate time forcing the farmers to approach other sources. Now-a-days, we find mushroom growth of seed manufacturers, making all false claims about the yield luring the farmers to purchase their seeds. The seeds thus, purchased do not sprout, even suppose if they sprout they may not flower, even if they flower there is no guarantee that they would yield as expected/promised. This is all due to the substandard quality of seeds sold by the dealers/manufacturers. In this modern bio-technological world, the farmers are facing a new problem and uncertainty with genetically modified seeds. In order to safeguard the farmers, governments enacted Seeds Act and appointed Seeds

Inspectors to safeguard the interests of the farmers against spurious seeds. But, the farmers are not aware of the existence of such a mechanism and where these seeds inspector are to be contracted. They do not even know to demand a bill from the seller; even if the bill is issued they do not preserve the bill. It becomes difficult for them to fight against these unscrupulous traders in the Consumer Forum, in absence of the bill.

Farmers purchase tractors and other farm equipments for the purpose of agricultural operations. In case of failure of these equipments during busy agricultural season their agricultural operations come to a standstill resulting in heavy loss. The guarantees or warranties offered by the manufacturer would not really help them because the service centres are located far away from their villages. In case of such problems there would be nobody in the village to properly guide them. Hence, imparting necessary education on warranties and guarantees *vis-à-vis* consumer rights would be of great assistance to them to assert their rights. If farmers do not receive necessary consumer education and assistance they are bound to lose heavily and ultimately fall into the debt trap. It is a well known fact that farmers are committing suicides because farming has become un-remunerative. Agriculture has become un-remunerative because of substandard fertilisers, pesticides and farm equipments. In addition to providing consumer education it is also equally necessary to provide effective mechanism to check the quality of agricultural inputs supplied to farmers and at the same time violators of quality norms must be punished severely.

Though farmers are consumers of many agricultural inputs they are at the same time producers. Farmers are the food providers to the nation. Hence, the farmers must be trained on healthy and scientific methods of cultivation to protect the health of millions of consumers in general and the health of the soil. Use of fertilizers and pesticides in agricultural operations has become a great threat and health hazard to the consumers as well as to the soil. Due to indiscriminate use of chemical fertilizers and pesticides, the food that is made available to consumers becomes health hazard. Further, the excessive use of fertilizers and pesticides is polluting the underground water. Pesticides sprayed on vegetables are causing concern to the health of consumers, as the pesticidal residue is found not only on the vegetables sold, but also in curries. The unscientific methods used in the preparation of jaggery may cause damage to the health of consumers. In the manufacture of jaggery, it is found that farmers are using industrial chemicals to gain attractive colour to the jaggery. Farmers must be made to understand that mixing industrial chemicals in the manufacturing process of jaggery is a health hazard. Presently many agricultural lands are converted into fish ponds for better income. Even in this aqua-culture farmers are using unhealthy farming practices causing health problems to fish eaters. Indiscriminate use of antibiotics is a cause for concern in aqua-culture. As these practices are fatal to the health of consumers, the farmers are also to be educated on all these aspects.

Farmers, depend much on electricity without which it becomes expensive for them to supply water to the growing crop. With the meagre supply of electricity, farmers are finding it difficult to manage water supply to the fields. With the limited availability of electricity these farmers need to be trained on power management systems. Farmers must understand the provisions of Conservation of Energy Act, 2001. While using electricity the farmers are expected to follow the guidelines given by the electricity supply companies. Due to lack of proper knowledge on the selection of economical and trouble free motor and pump sets, they are put to inconvenience and financial loss. Bureau of electricity efficiency is labelling energy efficient equipments and hence, the farmers must look for BEE label before purchasing electrical equipment. In some federal states like Andhra Pradesh electricity is supplied to farmers free of charge and in other states the governments are giving subsidy on the power tariff. When electricity is supplied free of cost the human tendency would be to use the facility to its maximum. In this process there is every possibility that the underground water is pumped out more than their requirement. Farmers need to be educated on the importance of underground water and its conservation. If underground water depletes to dangerous levels the farmers may not even get water for their drinking purposes.

In many recent studies it has come to light that the rural consumers are evincing interest to invest in mutual funds, chit funds and other non-banking financial companies. As the nationalised or other scheduled banks could not set-up their branches in many villages, these villagers have no option except to deposit their savings in some private financial institutions. Many a time these financial institutions are defrauding them. For instance Sahara India has collected around Rs. 26,000 crore from the rural areas and failed to pay them back their deposits. In such cases, the rural consumers become helpless and await help from others. Traditionally, villagers are reluctant to go to a court of law to seek remedy. Taking advantage of the situation some people promising them to get back their money would try to collect money to fight out the case. Voluntary Consumer Organisations are not available in the rural areas, to represent the aggrieved consumers' cases in consumer courts.

Villagers are also purchasing health care policies, without having any knowledge, whatsoever, on the terms and conditions of such insurance policies. They believe whatever the insurance agent says is right and they sign the agreement. But, they realise after making the claim and face the repudiation of the insurance claim that the policy is not suitable to them. Similarly, insurance companies are reluctantly issuing crop insurance policies which do not benefit the farmers. United Nations Organisation in its guidelines for protection of consumers, laid down clearly that the economic interests of consumers need to be protected. In consonance with the spirit of U.N. Guidelines it is necessary to provide education to the rural consumers on investment opportunities and the precautions to be taken while making such investments. Farmers are facing many problems with micro-finance companies while repaying their debt and these companies are even threatening with dire consequences, if the payments are not made as demanded by them. Taking such threats seriously, farmers are even putting an end to their lives. In fact, voluntary consumer organisations or farmers co-operative societies can help the farmers in a better way, by creating awareness, to come out of the clutches of these micro-finance companies.

The plight of the rural women consumers is totally different from that of their counterparts in urban areas. When compared to rural women urban women are more informed and make informed choices. But rural women are on a different footing. They need to purchase whatever is made available to them. There is no choice for them. Villages are becoming haven for unscrupulous traders and they are able to sell all sub-standard items to villagers because these villagers do not know the quality parameters. Spurious goods, adulterated food products, expired medicines are put to sale in the village markets because there is no government machinery to check the rot. On the face of it the prices appear to be cheap, but in reality they do not worth even that price when compared to the quality of material supplied. Usually, there will be only one provision store in each village and whatever the store-keeper sells, the villagers must accept them as there is no choice or another supplier. As these villages do not have cloth shops they depend on those hawkers who come on bicycles to sell the dress material, now and then. No guarantees are given to any product sold in villages. Even if guarantees are given villagers do not know how to claim the guarantees.

Falsification of weights and measures is a bigger problem in villages because the department of legal metrology is a non-existent in the villages. Every year it is estimated that the Indian consumers are cheated to a tune of Rs. 2000 crore cumulatively. They are not aware where to make a complaint, in case of falsification of weights and measures. If proper information is given to them about false weights and measures, at least they will take necessary precautions to avoid deceptive practices. It should be made mandatory to the department of legal metrology to conduct awareness camps in villages to educate the consumers. For example government has enforced a law whereby the edible oil should not be sold loose and it should be sold only in packets. But, how many villagers are aware of this rule? The poorer section of consumers need 50 ml or 100 ml of edible oil and no merchant is prepared to sell the edible oil in such small packets. Ultimately, villagers get edible oil loose and no one complains about it.

Use of LPG cylinder and electricity is associated with risk to life and property of consumers. In order to protect consumers' interests government insisted that all LPG dealers must necessarily obtain multi-peril insurance policy from the insurance companies to cover the risks associated with the supply and use of gas cylinders and to protect the economic interests of consumers from the possible hazards and loss to life and property. Similarly, Electricity Supply Act has provisions to protect the user of electricity from the risks associated with the use of electricity. It is needless to mention that the rural consumers are not aware of these provisions. Hence, it is necessary to educate them on the provisions of these legislations and to encourage them to proceed against the suppliers in case of loss or damage to the lives and property. Many incidents took place in which major fire accidents took place due to LPG cylinder blast or short-circuit of electricity, claiming many lives in addition to destruction of property.

In villages majority of the people seek their livelihood through agricultural operations. Villagers are from low income group (LIG) and hence must receive the benefits of Public Distribution System (PDS). They have been issued ration cards to enable them to draw supplies of essential commodities from the fair price shops/ration shops. Some of the villagers are pledging these cards with the ration shop dealers being unable to pay money for the commodities purchased from them. The dealers in turn are using the quota of such ration card-holders and making extra money by selling them in black market. Thus, the rural consumers are deprived of the use of their ration cards. Further, these ration dealers are not keeping the shops open at the scheduled timings making consumers to visit the shop number of times. They are also not providing essentials under the pretest that they have not received supplies yet. The general complaint against these dealers is that they are resorting to deceitful weighment practices and short delivering the commodities. Consumers should be motivated to form into a vigilance committee to have a check on their shoddy deals and to fight against the malpractices.

Gold has become part of the Indian Culture and this metal is treated as God that brings luck and prosperity. Whether one is a rural consumer or an urban consumer the desire to acquire gold is strong. At the time of marriages the yellow metal plays an important role. It is no exaggeration to say that no marriage is performed without gold. In villages there are no gold shops and hence villagers go to nearby town for gold purchases. Fully aware of their innocence and ignorance, the jewellers try to cheat them in terms of quality and weight. In a survey conducted by Government of India in the four metros a few years ago, it had come to light that consumers are getting low quality gold. On an average, consumers are delivered 19 carrot gold as against 22 carrot. Villagers do not even know that there is an electronic devise that can measure the quality of gold. Goldsmiths are available even in villages to make ornaments. Consumers are taken for a ride by these jewel-makers both by weight and quality. At present the craze is for KDM gold as the seller assures that there would be no loss of gold at the time of remaking the jewellery. India is consuming 1,000 tonnes of gold per year and Indian consumers are losing thousands of crore of rupees due to low quality and low weight. For each carrot of gold consumers lose around Rs. 182 with the present rate, if the gold quality falls short of required carrots. As the gold rate is souring day-by-day rural consumers must know how they are cheated in gold transactions. They should also be trained to verify Hallmark before they purchase gold ornaments. Consumers must be advised to obtain bill whenever they purchase something, particularly gold.

Water is the elixir of life without which human race cannot survive. Unfortunately, the villagers are not getting potable drinking water. Some villages do not have access to drinking water. They fatch even drinking water from the irrigation canals and rivers, use without filtering or purifying the water. As the use of pesticides is prevalent and the water in irrigation canals are polluted by the poisonous substances, hence is not fit for drinking. Added to this, there are many waterborne diseases that cause health problems to villagers. If there is no facility of protected water in the village they should be advised to take boiled cool water. Hepatitis-B, diarrhoea and other waterborne diseases are dangerous and even kill the infants. Public defecation is another problem in the villages, that is spreading various contagious diseases. Considering all these issues, it is also necessary to impart health education to these villagers.

Villages do not have adequate health care facilities. Though Public Health Centres are set-up, doctors who are appointed in such hospitals do not live in villages and come from a town or city for their duties. Their services are not available to the villagers in an emergency. Taking advantage of this situation quacks are entering into villages posing themselves as qualified doctors, playing with the lives of villagers. There are no maternity facilities in villages allowing the unfortunate women who conceived, to deliver the child in a crude manner. There is no prenatal care. As a result many women die at the time of delivery and the infants' lives are also at risk. As medical practitioner is not available in the village, rural consumers are approaching a nearby pharmacist for their ailments, and using medicines according to their prescription. There is an urgent need to correct this situation by providing the required education to them.

Villagers are absolutely not aware of Consumer Protection Act and the establishment of Consumer Fora. Consumer education should also include information about the legislative protection and how they can have access to this three-tier judiciary. Particularly, rural consumers must have the knowledge about the rights of consumers as envisaged in the Consumer Protection Act, 1986. While advocating consumer rights they should also be taught about the responsibilities of consumers. Without having knowledge on Consumer Protection Act and its advantages no consumer would try to assert their rights.

Imparting consumer education to rural consumers is not an easy task in view of low rate of literacy. Illiterates receive consumer education only through oral communication. They cannot make use of printed matter. Though, radio and television are the best modes to impart consumer education to the illiterates. They are not used intensely, because of prohibitive costs. Particularly, the adults will not show interest to learn consumer related topics. With great difficulty government and voluntary agencies are imparting adult education. The same problems might surface in adult consumer education also. Hence, the best way is to impart consumer education at a tender age. The best principle for consumer education is "Catch the Consumers Young". In countries like France, Italy, Japan, Sweden, Dutch and United States Consumer education is successfully implemented and India has to take some lessons from their success.

Before identifying the agencies that can be entrusted with this onerous responsibility, we have to first decide what syllabus can be adopted for consumer education. Even after 25 years of the enactment of Consumer Protection Act, 1986, no significant efforts have been made either by

Central Government or the State Governments to impart consumer education at all levels. Unless the Indian consumer is educated on a national priority basis, his protection will be a far cry. Consumer education should try to develop skills in consumers to make informed choices and become knowledgeable about the law, their rights in order to participate actively in the market economy to fuel the economic progress and at the same time to protect himself.

Without developing a consumer culture we cannot think of a civilised and uniform behaviour of consumers. Informed consumers are the asset to the nation. Hence, it is necessary to develop critical eye for consumers. The consumer culture or consumer eye can be developed by making the consumers to question themselves on some important aspects before they go for purchase, such as,

1. Do I need this product at this moment?
2. Am I encouraging bad trends in the market?
3. Is this product and its packing environment-friendly?
4. Am I infringing the rights of fellow consumers?
5. Is it beneficial to purchase this product or take it on hire?
6. Do I have the purchasing capacity?
7. Does my action cause damage to the country's economy?

As consumer is a catalyst for the progress of Economy Consumer Culture stimulates him and empowers him to distinguish between bad and good consumption. Consumer education must provide basic knowledge and life skills that are necessary to improve the quality of their lives.

Imparting consumer education is not as easy as developing the course content. The problem in including it in school or college curriculum is the resistance from the teachers. They are of the opinion that the students are already overburdened with many subjects and consumer education becomes an additional burden. Hence, teaching it as a separate subject may attract further resistance from teaching community. It is necessary to first convince the teaching community before any attempt is made to include consumer education as a special subject. Alternatively, this can be included in various subjects like, economics, social studies, mathematics, natural science etc., wherever appropriate. In Germany consumer education is taught at all four levels of secondary education. In Sweden kids are given consumer education in preparatory school at the age of six. India can emulate one of these models and go ahead with the preparation of consumer education. At present we do not have any uniform policy. This falls short of the guidelines adopted by United Nations Organisation for consumer protection. When once the course content is finalised we need to search for the agencies that can effectively impart consumer education.

As regards the implementation agencies for consumer education, it is needless to emphasise the importance of educational institutions. We can rely on the educational institutions for imparting proper consumer education. The second agency that can take up this responsibility is Voluntary Consumer Organisation who can create awareness to consumers from their experience. Unlike the educational institutions they may not have classrooms to deliver this service. However, by organising awareness meets they can provide good consumer education. Thirdly, farmers' co-operative societies can impress upon the farmers the need for consumer education and accordingly motivate them to learn the essentials of consumer life. Fourthly, women organisations can impart best education to women who can in turn educate the entire family. Fifthly, consumer co-operatives have more access to these consumers and hence can take up consumer education.

When we contemplate to do something in rural areas, immediately it comes to our mind that the local bodies can render better service. Even some subject experts advised to involve panchayats to promote consumer education. Panchayats may not be able to deliver these services properly because they do not have adequate means to even manage their statutory duties. It is likely that these panchayats may consider this responsibility as an additional burden. Further, the local bodies do not have any powers to make any decision on funding the scheme or otherwise. For the purpose of imparting consumer education they may require additional funds. It may be difficult for them to mobilise required funds unless the government grants financial assistance to carry out this job. Further, panchayats do not have adequate number of employees even to execute their assigned duties and as such carrying out this additional responsibility may not be within their means.

Schools are better place to impart consumer education because they have experienced teachers to handle different subjects of consumer education like economics, social studies, mathematics, natural science etc. Further, in school laboratories they can conduct tests to detect food adulteration with a bit of training. These teachers can impart consumer education for generations together and the motivated teacher can take time to impart consumer education even outside the school for adults who are out of school. The scientific methods of teaching are well-known to the teachers and hence, they become the best of the lot to impart consumer education. Further, consumer clubs are already established in many schools and colleges which can render wonderful service in spreading consumer education. Members of consumer clubs can even discuss the issues they have learnt through consumer club with their family members.

2

Awareness of Consumer Protection Act among Rural Consumers

A Case Study of Coimbatore

M. Sumathy and *N. Vijayalakshmi*

Introduction

India is one of the biggest rural consumer markets in the world. Even now, 70 per cent of India's population lives in rural areas. There are about 6,40,867 villages in the country as against about 300 cities and 5,161 towns. Of the 121 crore Indians, 83.3 crore live in rural areas while 37.7 crore stay in urban areas, as per the Census 2011. The National Council of Applied Economic Research (NCAER) survey report says that there are 720 million consumers across the villages in rural India. Hence, the development of the nation largely depends upon the development of the rural population. Majority of the rural population is dependant upon agriculture for their subsistence. The rural consumer is likely to exhibit different purchase behaviour as compared to his urban counterpart. This is basically due to the unique characteristics of rural markets. The composition of Indian rural market is probably the much more complex than the whole market in Europe in terms of cultural, linguistic and other diversities. The social and religious customs, climatic considerations, dual ownership due to prevalence of joint family system, mould the buying habits of rural consumers. The rural consumers tend to be more subject to local religious, cultural and social pressures and there are regional variations in tastes and habits.

Changing Face of Rural India

Over the past few years rural India has witnessed an increase in the purchasing power of consumers, accompanied by their desire to upgrade their standard of living. The steps taken by the Government of India to address the poverty have improved the condition of rural masses. As a result, rural consumers have upgraded their life styles through making changes in their consumption patterns by adding more nutritious food and are purchasing life style products such as cosmetics, beverages, mobile phones etc., which have become necessities for them. A number of schemes and programmes of the government have changed the rules of the marketing game in rural India. The flagship schemes of Government of India especially Mahatma Gandhi National Rural Employment Guarantee Act (MGNREGA) scheme, which has a budget of more than 40,000 crore have given the rural population an opportunity to meet their daily needs. With the initiation of various rural development programmes there have been an upsurge of employment opportunities for the rural poor. NREGS guarantees 100 days employment to a rural household and provides much needed bargaining power to battle the exploitation in the farming sector as a labourer. Also the increased demand for labour in the urban projects such as Jawaharlal Nehru National Urban Renewal Mission (JNNURM) has resulted in more money being sent back home by the immigrant worker. Bharat Nirman, an Indian plan for creating basic rural infrastructure, is having a budget of Rs. 58,000 crore for 2011-12. It is a step towards bridging the gap between rural and urban areas and improving the quality of lives of rural masses. It comprises projects on irrigation, roads (Pradhan Mantri Gram Sadak Yojana), housing (Indira Awaas Yojana), water supply, electrification and telecommunication connectivity.

Consumer Law

Consumer rights are the rights given to a "consumer" to protect him/her from being cheated by salesman/manufacturer. Consumer protection laws are designed to ensure fair trade competition and the free flow of truthful information in the marketplace. The laws are designed to prevent businesses that engage in fraud or specified unfair practices from gaining an advantage over competitors and may provide additional protection for the weak and those unable to take care of themselves. Consumer Protection Laws are a form of government regulation which aims to protect the rights of the consumers.

Consumer Awareness

Consumer awareness is about making the consumer aware of his/her rights. Consumer awareness is a marketing term. It means that consumers note or are aware of products or services, its characteristics and the other marketing P's (place to buy, price, and promotion). With the growth of private sector there is a greater need for discipline and regulation of the market. Consumers must be aware of not only the sale and purchase of goods, but also the health and security aspects. Ensuring the safety of food items sold in the market is essential these days. Legal measures for consumer safety and consumer awareness must be uniform, and transparent in terms of prices, quality of goods, and stocks. Consumers must have the tools to combat malpractices and protect their rights.

Consumer Protection and Role of Local Bodies

Like in many other countries consumer movement in India as a social force originated with the necessity of protecting and promoting the interest of consumers' against fraudulent, unethical and unfair trade practices. The movement initially reflected a common perception, which characterised traders and manufacturers as people who were out to maximise profits by means of fair or foul with scant regard for consumers' well-being. Selective shopping could be the only form of consumer resistance at the early stages, the basic tenet governing the legal position of consumers being "buyers beware". The movement gained a momentum after enactment of CoPRA in 1986. Over time, the movement found expression in efforts to bring pressure on business firms as well as government to correct business conduct that may be unfair and against the interest of consumers at large. The movement, which has been confined to the middle class citizens in urban centres by large, is now having a presence in the rural areas as well. But it needs to be spread and strengthened further among the masses in rural and semi-urban areas.

Objectives of the Study

1. To evaluate the awareness level among the rural consumers.
2. To identify the sources of information that creates consumer awareness.
3. To understand impact of the socio-economic factors on consumer awareness.

Methodology

This study attempts to know the awareness level among the rural consumers of Coimbatore district in Tamil Nadu by collecting primary data. For that purpose the researcher has adopted convenient sampling technique. One hundred twenty five sample respondents were approached for the study to collect the information through structured schedules and personal interview. The Secondary data was collected relating to consumer awareness level from bulletins, journals, magazine, newspaper, previous research record and e-sources. Primary data was collected through structured schedule. This was used to collect information from the rural respondents regarding their awareness level of consumer rights. The primary and secondary data so collected were analysed. The independent variables identified were socio-economic factors such as, income, education, age, and gender. The collected data were analysed using appropriate statistical tools.

Statistical Tools Used

Reliability: After collecting the primary data it has been subjected to reliability test. The Alpha and Guttman's reliability test found to be 0.63 and 0.72 since the value is more than 0.50, the reliability is established. The tools used to analyse the data were measures of central tendency, chi-square and ANOVA.

Analysis and Interpretation of Data

Respondents Level of Consumer Awareness

Consumer protection is a key concept of consumerism. Every consumer has the rights to ask the manufacturers towards their purchased products. In this study intent was to evaluate the consumer awareness towards the certain consumer issues. The respondents were asked questions to rate their awareness level. Their views are displayed in Table 2.1.

The researcher developed eight statements relating to the consumer protection awareness with Five-point Likert Scale. Their opinions were grouped and calculated the mean and standard deviation. From the mean value it was observed, the respondents are experienced that the advertisement has not educated consumer on their rights and they were also worried about false weights. But the respondents were unfamiliar

Table 2.1: Respondents Views on Consumer Law Awareness

Statement	*Mean*	*Standard Deviation*
Adulteration in Food	2.203	1.481
Short Weight of Measures	2.325	1.220
False Weights	3.526	1.101
Using Stones for Weights	2.254	1.436
Using Hand Made Balances	2.020	1.084
Using Deceiving Advertisement	3.646	1.083
Using Fraudulent Packaging	2.534	1.154
Unfair Warranties and Guarantees	2.528	1.175

Source: Based on Field data.

with their rights regarding adulteration, misuse of weights and measures. Packaging is also a big problem for the rural respondents. Respondents were felt that they are getting deceitful packaging. The respondents were not much aware about protection laws relating to using store for weights, using hand made balance and adulteration of food. It is found that the respondents are some what aware of law on protection of false weights. Advertisements have exaggerated the product quality and quantity also. It is understand that the consumers are less aware of consumer legal law.

Sources of Information Regarding Consumer Protection Awareness

Table 2.2 explains the role of mass media for creating consumer legal law about product standard. The respondents are asked to view their opinion, how they are get the information regarding the product standard.

Table 2.2: Sources of Information that Create Consumer Protection Awareness

Sources of Inter Motion	*Useful in Creating Awareness*	*Frequency*	*Percentage*
Television	Yes	69	55.2
	No	56	44.8
Radio	Yes	72	57.6
	No	53	42.4
Newspaper	Yes	57	45.6
	No	68	54.4
Outdoor Advertisement	Yes	59	47.2
	No	66	52.8

Source: Based on Field Data.

Majority of the respondents got information on consumer issues from radio (57.6%) followed by television (55.2%) than through outdoor advertisement (47.2%). Newspaper is the media least commonly used as source of information by the respondent (45.6%). It is found that most of the rural consumers gained awareness of consumer issues through radio and television. It is a fact that the rural consumers highly favour listening radio programmes. It was found that in every village there is a tea shop, in where, most of the villagers assemble every morning and go through the newspaper and then they pass on the message to others.

Awareness of Standardisation Marks

The consumers need to be aware not only of the commercial aspects of sale and purchase of goods, but also of the health and security aspects. Food safety has become an important element of consumer awareness these days. In case of food products, its quality depends not only on its nutritional value, but also on its safety for human consumption. Consumption of contaminated or adulterated food is a major cause of human illness and suffering. The standardisation and certification of products is an assuance of the quality and safety of the products. Therefore, the respondents were asked question regarding awareness of standardisation marks.

Table 2.3: Awareness of Consumer Law

Standardisation Mark	*Level of Awareness*	*Frequency*	*Percentage*
Agmark	Yes	82	65.6
	No	43	34.4
ISI	Yes	84	67.2
	No	39	32.8
916 KDM	Yes	86	70.4
	No	37	29.6
BIS	Yes	64	51.2
	No	61	48.8
Hallmark	Yes	73	58.4
	No	52	41.6

Source: Based on Field Data.

Level of awareness regarding various standards is observed in Table 2.3. The data showed that 70.4 per cent of the respondents were aware of 916 KDM. 67.2 per cent of the respondents were aware about ISI. 65.6 per cent of the respondents were aware of Agmark. 58.4 per cent were aware of Hallmark and 51.2 per cent of respondents were aware about BIS. It is found that the rural respondents have better awareness of the popular terminology like 916 KDM, ISI, Agmark. It is understood that the rural consumers are having some level of awareness when they purchase gold and food.

Level of Awareness among Various Age Groups

Hypothesis: There is no significant difference in level of awareness on consumer issues on the basis of respondent's age. Table 2.4 indicates the respondent's awareness level on the basis of their age. The data were grouped and mean value was calculated for each of the age group. From the mean value, it is observed that, the awareness of adulteration of food is comparatively high among the young age respondents than others. But, more than 30 years old people are having very low level of awareness towards food adulteration. In the case of awareness level regarding misuse of weights and measures, short weights and measures and giving contents without weighting is very low among the old aged people.

But others are having some awareness on this aspect. With regard to false weights and using stones instead of weights, middle aged respondents are having moderate awareness level.

Table 2.4: Respondent's Views on Consumer Protection Awareness and Age

Statement	*Age*	*Mean*	*S.D.*	*ANOVA (P-value)*
Adulteration in food	Less than 30	4.432	0.656	0.000
	31-40	1.170	0.832	
	41-50	1.620	0.970	
Short weight of measures	Less than 30	3.671	1.682	0.000
	31-40	2.869	1.263	
	41-50	2.164	0.480	
False weights	Less than 30	3.778	1.139	0.121
	31-40	3.937	1.127	
	41-50	3.375	1.070	
Using stones for weights	Less than 30	2.400	1.313	0.001
	31-40	2.740	1.421	
	41-50	1.625	1.070	
Using handmade balances	Less than 30	1.555	0.818	0.002
	31-40	3.248	1.741	
	41-50	2.718	1.197	
Using deceiving advertisement	Less than 30	3.044	1.278	0.017
	31-40	2.437	1.442	
	41-50	2.312	0.692	
Using fraudulent packaging	Less than 30	3.324	1.752	0.000
	31-40	2.604	1.267	
	41-50	1.806	1.613	
Unfair warranties and guarantees	Less than 30	1.281	0.796	0.030
	31-40	2.681	1.367	
	41-50	3.044	0.888	

Source: Based on field data.

In order to test the stated hypothesis one-way ANOVA was applied. While reading P-value, explain that there is a significant difference of opinion towards various consumer issues according to the respondents' age. Since, the hypothesis is rejected.

Relation between Age and Sources of Information for Awareness

Hypothesis: There is no significant association between age of the respondents and sources of information accessed.

CHI- SQUARE

Table 2.5: Relation between Sources of Information and Age

Sources	*Chi-square*	*P-value*
Television	61.446	0.001
Radio	38.097	0.021
Newspaper	15.919	0.000
Outdoor Advertisement	26.139	0.001

Source: Based on field data.

Table 2.5 explains the opinion of respondents of different age groups towards the sources of information for gaining knowledge on different consumer issues. In order to verify the stated hypothesis, chi-square value is applied. The calculated chi-square value and p-value indicates that there is a significant association between age and sources of information used to gain knowledge. Hence, the hypothesis is rejected.

Comparative Statement of Consumer Protection Awareness

Hypothesis: There is no significant difference of level of awareness towards consumer issues on basis of gender. Table 2.6 shows the respondent's level of awareness based on gender of the respondents. From the mean value it is observed that the male respondents were having comparatively higher level of awareness towards consumer affairs. But, females are having comparatively more awareness towards consumer affairs. In order to test the stated hypothesis t-test is employed. The calculated t-value and p-value show that the respondent's views on significantly varied based on gender expecetancy.

Recommendations: Measures to Increase Consumer Awareness

- Promote General Awareness of the rights of the consumer by encouraging consumer education and supplying information.

Table 2.6: Comparative Statement of Consumer Protection Awareness

Statement	*Gender*	*M*	*S.D.*	*t-value*	*P-value*
Adulteration in Food	Male	2.5802	1.7604	3.123	0.010
	Female	1.7865	0.8325		
Short Weight of Measures	Male	3.0875	1.24578	–3.272	0.001
	Female	3.4587	1.13462		
False Weights	Male	3.5926	1.31060	1.432	0.250
	Female	3.5926	1.31060		
Using Stones for Weights	Male	2.9155	1.55606	4.034	0.000
	Female	1.8579	1.32334		
Using Handmade Balances	Male	1.7465	0.98152	1.784	0.040
	Female	2.4259	1.34026		
Using Deceiving Advertisement	Male	3.5352	1.16902	4.034	0.000
	Female	3.3704	1.37767		
Using Fraudulent Packaging	Male	2.4507	1.41208	1.155	0.250
	Female	2.8579	0.99825		
Unfair Warranties and Guarantees	Male	2.21131	1.1104	–5.570	0.000
	Female	2.8704	1.40143		

Source: Based on field data.

- Banners with slogans and appeals should be used in public places and on public buildings. In order to transfer messages to uneducated people, representation of contents in the form of pictures should be thought of for rural consumers.
- Enlighten the business community on its ethical and legal obligations to maintain quality of the products or services and to be transparent in dealing with consumers.
- Encourage consumer activities to strengthen the existing institutional set-up of consumer dispute redressed by acting as a facilitator between consumer and the institution.
- Cable TV which is increasingly available in villages should be made better use of for consumer information.
- Local radio programmes (in the language of the region) should be considered.
- All available media of consumer information should be used, including documentary films, street plays, competitions etc. to spread consumer awareness.

Conclusion

The present research focused evaluation of the awareness level of rural consumer towards consumer issues. It has been conducted among the 125 rural respondents from Coimbatore district on the basis of convenient samples techniques. The collected data are coded and analysed with appropriate statistical tools. The findings gave in to the extent of lack of awareness among consumer of many facts that are of much relevance for their own welfare. Rural respondents are lacking knowledge of their rights and responsibilities. They should be educated and trained towards their own welfare.

References

Bijapurkar, Rama & Rajesh Shukla (2008). *Spotlight on Rural Consumers*, December 3.

Bijapurkar, Rama & Rajesh Shukla (2009). '*The Rural Consumer Myth – II*', March 26.

Chandwani and Sanjay (2009). "Marketing To Rural Consumers", *Vision*, April-June 2009, Vol. 13, Issue 2.

History of Panchayati Raj in India, available *at: http://en.wikipedia.org/wiki/History_of_panchayati_raj_in_India*

Livemint.com

Pradeep S. Mehta (1998). "How to Survive as a Consumer", *CUTS*, CUTS Publication.

The "Bird of Gold" (2007). *The Rise of India's Consumer Market,* May, McKinsey & Company.

Velayudhan, Sanal Kumar, *Rural Marketing: Targeting the Non-Urban Consumers*, Response Books, Sage Publications, Second Edition.

3
Empowering Rural Consumers
Issues and Concerns

S.C. Roy

Introduction

Where there is life there is consumption of goods and services. Life without consumption cannot be imagined. Even the beggars consume the goods and the services without which they have no physical existence of which the Constitution guarantees[1] to all citizens of this country. Consumerism seems to be different in meaning from the ordinary meaning of consumer. It seems that one who spends much on goods and services, i.e. the elite class or high income group spending money on consumption. In other words consumerism is associated with criticism of consumption. But, in positive sense consumerism is social and economic order that encourages the sale and purchase of goods and services in great amounts. The term consumerism also refers to the "Consumerist Movement", "Consumer Protection" or "Consumer Activism" which seems to protect and inform the various consumers by various modes of advertisements, consumer education, consumer awareness and protection through legal provisions and machineries. It is the movement to regulate the products, services, methods and standard of manufacturers, sellers and advertisement in the interest of buyers. It is the public concern over quality of consumer goods and honesty of advertising agencies.

This ideology came into full focus in 1962 after the President John F. Kennedy introduced the Bill "Consumer Bill of Rights" which provided that consumers have right to be safe, to be informed, choose and to be heard. This was shift from theory of caveat emptor[2] to caveat vendator.[3]

This movement brought a shift in American culture from "Producer Oriented Society" to "Consumerists". It was a check on the monopoly for better goods and services to conscious consumer. This movement affected all the countries and entered into the Indian System also. Although, India had various legal provisions to protect interests of the consumers under Indian Penal Code, 1860, the Dangerous Drug Act, 1930, Sales of Goods Act, 1930, Drugs and Cosmetics Act, 1940, Banking Regulation Act, 1949, Industrial Development and Regulation Act, 1951, Prevention of Food Adulteration Act, 1954, the Essential Commodities Act, 1955, Indian Standard Institution (Certification of Marks) Act, 1952, Monopolies and Restrictive Trade Practices Act, 1969, Prevention of Black Marketing and Maintenance of Supplies of Essential Commodities Act, 1980, the Provisions of Maintenance of Internal Security Act, 1971 which has been replaced by National Securities Act, 1980.

The United Nations General Assembly also adopted guidelines for protection of consumers[4] after extensive negotiation and discussion among the governments on the scope and content of guidelines. Since the consumers often face imbalances in economic, educational, and bargaining term, they must be protected from defective goods or deficiency in services, spurious drugs, adulterated food items, deceit in weights and measures, arbitrary price fixation, black marketing, artificial scarcity of essential commodity in the market so that the consumers enjoy their lives with decency, check the drain of money for future consumption in their lives. The UN General Assembly is concerned with Global Peace, Security, and Prosperity along with Socio-economic Justice.

Thus, influenced by the General Assembly Resolution, 1977, a high powered expert committee was constituted under the chairmanship of Justice Rajender Nath Sachar to study the social responsibility of business concern to the community so that the corporate sector should function as being responsible to the society like any other individual. The corporate accountability is not limited to the shareholders alone, but to the best of the community at large. With the recommendation of the report the concept of unfair trade practices was brought in MRTP Act, 1969 in 1984 for the protection of Consumer and Indian Companies Act, 1956 was amended in 1988. But, it was not enough to protect the interest of the consumer so, in 1986, the Government of India enacted Consumer Protection Act, 1986 in order to provide easy remedy to consumer and check on the business and service providers.

The Act[5] defined the term Consumer.[6] Consumer means a person who buys goods or is a user of such goods on price paid or promised but it does not include the person who obtains such goods for resale or any commercial purpose. However, the person who buys such goods exclusively for the purpose of earning livelihood by means of self-employment is put under the heading consumers. Consumers also include the person who hires or avails of any services for consideration and includes beneficiary of such services excluding services for any commercial purpose. But the term consumer does not classify either rural or urban. The definition treats all the consumers equally, therefore, the question arises here—Why should there be specific talk on Rural Consumerism? Since, India is a country of villages and around 70 per cent population resides in rural area, therefore, the concern of rural consumerism is obvious. The corporate sectors have very good market in the rural areas too, though, the per capita income of rural people is less in comparison to urban consumer. Secondly, the urban consumer is mostly educated and aware of their rights whereas the rural consumers are generally naïve persons believing the sellers, service providers etc. without, in real sense, "good faith". The rural consumers do not know the meaning of MRP, service tax, VAT (Value Added Tax) etc. They do not know how to check the spurious drugs. They also do not know about food adulterations, weights and measures, food safety. They also do not know about the quality of seeds and fertilizers. The rural people are easily cheated by grocers and cloth and other merchants. They are not in a bargaining capacity. This is why in spite of consumer reddressal mechanism, the rural folks are far away from the protection from profit mongers, unfair traders, and gullible service providers. Thus, here is the requirement of empowerment of the rural consumers urgently. In this developmental concept, this chapter seeks to study the various ways and means to empower for socio-economic justice in India.

Rural Markeing and Rural Consumers

Rural areas are the areas of the country that are not urbanised. Thus, the consumers residing in rural areas depend on goods of consumption in rural market where industrial as well as local goods are sold. In the rural marketing, the dominant participants are from the rural area that are naïve and lack bargaining capacity. The rural market is different from urban market. The urban people are powerful in word of mouth and bargaining. Rural consumers easily fall prey to the sweet alluring words of the traders who are trained in salesmanship malpractices. Rural consumers are slow to collect any brand commodity because of high price, lack of selection intelligence, and the economic status. Thus, the rural sellers do not keep goods of high brands, but duplicate goods in the same brand name are easily sold. The purchasers do not know about the trademark or brand name. Every consumer has to spend year long, whereas income in rural area is seasonal. Hence, purchasing is high in income season in rural markets whereas surplus goods/rejected goods or goods of very low qualities are sold in rural market at the same price. More so, rural market was completely unorganised even in twenty first century. It is agriculture-based marketing. With the advent of Green Revolution in 1960-1990, the agriculture production increased and purchasing capacity of people boosted up. Since 1990, Indian industrial sector has gained strength and maturity. Not only fertilisers and Seed Company entered the rural market but consumer companies also entered with their brands for the vast rural market.

At the same time, the development in education and employment has poured cash into totally agriculture-based economy improving the purchasing capacity of the people. The communication facilities and transportation also connected the rural people to urban market and the desire to purchase and consume the commodities increased. Thus, the rural market started to cater to the demand of the people, realising the potential of rural consumers. But along with this the expansion-*cum*-development saga starts and there starts exploitation of rural consumers. The reasons are various, i.e. the low rate of literacy, the problem of English language, lack of road and rail connectivity, lack of media (TV and Radio), lack of electricity, lack of adequate and scientific storage facilities, awareness of goods and services, competitive pricing, bargaining technique, redressal mechanism etc. Rural consumer does not know how to examine the quality of goods and services even for medical services; they are ignorant of their rights with doctors and knowledge of purchasing medicine, where they easily purchase even spurious drugs. Rural market is also ignorant of banking and insurance utility. Thus, in all cases, there is waste of income without proper advantages.

Rural Consumer Behaviour and Consumer Rights

Consumer behaviour refers to the buying behaviour of the individual household for personal consumption. Thus, all the individuals and households living in the rural area are rural consumers help in the formation of the rural market. There are more than 6,40,867 villages in India as against 300 cities and 5000 towns. The rural consumers have different taste in comparison to urban consumers in terms of products, colour, and sizes of the commodities. Their purchasing behaviour is guided by their motive and by reason regarding orientation, purchase, use, maintenance, and disposal of goods. The environment and geographical influences affect the purchasing behaviour of the consumers. The influence of the occupation, place of purchase, durable and creative use of product, all influence the rural consumer's behaviour.

The rural consumers do not choose the 'best' option, but the satisfying option.[7] Whereas they have to pay for the best at same time they are unknown about their right if their goods and services are of low quality and deficient. The M.R.P. that is maximum retail price that is inclusive of all taxes, levies, charges, fees, duties etc. But, there is no minimum retail price which can be understood for M.R.P. There is no cost of production written on package, the rural consumer is not aware of these facts. Along with medical and health care are the basic needs like shelter, food and education. The rural consumer under this sector is also cheated from medical shop to doctor's clinic. They become the victim of doctor's negligence. Generally, they avail the services of the doctor on the propaganda of touts. Though the rights are available to the consumers under Consumer Protection Act, 1986 yet what are the rights and how it can be availed are quite absent. No mechanism are available in the market for immediate education, information, suggestion and confidence build up for the purchase of the commodity. Thus, the psychological behaviour of the consumer is also responsible for the deception in the market. Consumer confidence is key to a competitive and flourishing market in European Union.[8] The European Union has evolved 10 basic principles of consumer protection:

1. Buy what you want, where you want.
2. If it does not work, send it back.
3. High safety standards for food and consumer goods.
4. Know what you are eating.
5. Contract should be fair to consumers.
6. Sometimes, consumers can change their mind.
7. Make it easier to compare price.
8. Consumer should not be misled.
9. Protection while you are in holidays.
10. Effective redress for cross-border dispute.[9]

The Consumer Rights under EU seems more comprehensive in comparison to Indian counterpart. The CPA 1986, ensures the right to be protected against the marketing of hazardous goods, against unfair trade practices, to be assured to access to variety of goods at competitive prices, the right to be heard and to be assured that their interests will receive due consideration at appropriate forum and right to consumer education. The Act provides three-tier facilities in order to redress the complaints in District Consumer Forum, State Consumer Redressal Commission and at National Consumer Dispute Redressal Commission. No doubt, the Consumer Protection Act (CPA), 1986 has brought revolution and awareness among the consumers for their rights, yet the maximum rural consumers are far away from the reach of Redressal Mechanism. The reason is obvious, the lack of knowledge of their rights, lack of confidence to fight against the organised business guilds, delay in the redressal from the forum, expenditure of money etc. One of the most important reason is that one does not want to spend money and time in litigation for small purchase whereas every one is every time being cheated for the small purchase of utmost need due to these reasons the empowerment is an urgent need of the rural consumer.

Empowerment Mechanism

Generally, empowerment is understood in terms of rights conferred for the redressal if there is no violation by any one. But the term is not providing the power legally rather mentally and psychologically with confidence. Many of us are being cheated because of naive character without utilising the cognitive faculty of mind. Therefore, in spite of CPA 1986, and different dozens of legislations for different goods and services, the actual benefit is out of the reach of the people. Though the rights conferred under CPA 1986, are nothing but to empower the consumers in general, i.e. either rural or urban, yet the consumers are unable to decide the quality, brand, local made or industry made. Nor there is any agency to guide for their selection according to their means. There is no mechanism or organisation to keep watch on artificial scarcity and over charge in the market. Therefore, market functions entirely on the behaviour of consumer and alluring tactics of the sellers. The rural consumers completely depend upon the fate and luck. Voluntary organisations are not working in this area.

In case of insurance sector, the rural consumers are easily cheated by the insurance agents in misguiding in the selection of the plan, premium amount, and deposit of the same in the insurance office and discharge of the maturity amount. Likewise, banking services are far away from the rural folk. Grameen Banks are not working properly nor available in the rural areas. Therefore, every market requires a "consumer watch" as a governmental institution or NGO to educate the consumer immediately, protect them from gullible traders, and provide immediate local protection. If the matter is related to the durable goods, the dispute can be referred to the consumer forum through the "consumer watch". Therefore, empowerment programmes need to be started from the "Gram Panchayats Level" every week and information related to various consumer friendly legislations. In this movement, the empowerment of the women needs first priority because most of the rural purchases are made by the rural women.

Another requirement for the support of empowerment is expansion of rural market. Population is increasing but market expansion is not keeping pace with such increase. Therefore, the number of business entities is not in adequate number where competition among the sellers may develop and the consumer may be ultimately benefited. Therefore, market expansion and encouragement for entrepreneurship is also required. The seasonal character of market has to be changed. It has to be converted into perennial markets and all the markets are required to be 'watched' by the specific agency as a free aid to consumer awareness. Traders are also required to be motivated for their social responsibility through making the appropriate goods and services available to the "potential consumers" on reasonable price. Thus, the Consumer Protection Act, 1986 can work sufficiently and protect the interest of rural consumers.

Role of Mass Media in Empowerment

Media, i.e. print, audio-visual disseminate information about the various goods and services through advertisement, but they do not explain the quality, quantity, price, durability, safety, comfort etc. However, the goods are purchased on the basis of trademarks and the advertisement which is the silent salesman. More so, the trademarks are only suggestive not descriptive, but its impression is vital. The visual advertisers are concerned with increase in sale by dazzling attraction. The media—audio, visual or print—is not only to provide political, or social events or sports news, rather consumer friendly problems in the nature of Frequently Asked Questions (FAQ) requires to be made available to the consumer. Since, media has a greater reach for twenty four hours, it can be a great help in consumer empowerment. Along with, the voluntary organisation can be a great aid to help fight manipulation. As to certain channels, i.e. AWAZ deals with stock market, financial institutions analysis, likewise media has to establish rural market channels for their empowerment. With the help of the analysis, the stock market consumers are benefited. Likewise, the rural market analysis will help the rural consumers, rural salesman, entrepreneurs, rural management graduates, transporters etc.

Conclusion

With about three-fourth or 70 per cent of the country population living in the villages, and their ever increasing consumption power, their empowerment is a primary concern to avail them goods and services at reasonable price and save them from exploitation. Since in the era of globalisation, many business houses, big companies and even MNCs have placed special emphasis on rural areas to promote their products as well as services. They have designed special communication messages to draw their attention and thereby their purchasing power. But, judging from the consumer point of view, no special care is taken to address the issues arising out of the differentiation between urban consumers and rural consumers. The product usage guidelines, manufacturing date, date of expiry of medicine and foils, MRP, description of the content on the packages, weights and price variation etc., are printed on international standard which is out of the common understanding of the rural consumer. More so, they lack bargaining capacity. The information on any package, carton is not in local language. They are not able to examine the trademarks or trade names and the quality of the goods underneath. Therefore, In spite of various consumer friendly legislations and CPA 1986 some guidelines/ training of marketing is required.

In this context, the role of NGOs and establishment of an institution as "consumer watch" in each market is urgent need to protect the rural consumer's interest. The easy access to "consumer watch" in the existing market is first before working on any major plan to educate them. Therefore, in order to build-up confidence seminars, workshops in rural areas closely linked to the market is essential for practical training on the spot with expert advisers. This will generate employment too. The Indian concept of consumer rights and education requires simplification and expansion in terms of European Union (EU) and China. EU model of consumer protection principles can build up confidence among the rural folk. At the same time, right to information has to be applied towards the private business entities/sellers also as practised in China.

The product liability law[10] of China has stipulated obligation upon the business operators to present true product information, any 'flaw' in the product, i.e. does not possess good quality or standard of services, is punishable. Here under the CPA, 1986, the term 'flaw' requires to be added in order to widen the scope of the Act. More so, the efficiency of the consumer redressal forums also requires to be enhanced by addition of more members and benches to *Panchayats* level for speedy disposal of consumer problems. The network of consumer forums along with the "consumer watch" can reduce the exploitation of the rural consumer. Confidence building is a long term strategy and ongoing process. Consumer's laws and redressal mechanism are the secondary part of the problem. Primary concern for rural empowerment is to make the people aware about the market trends and commodities available in the market, their pricing and quality. China has also amended product quality law[11] to protect the consumers from any deviation from quality.

Thus, in the age of global market the rural market in India is still in the pre-liberalisation stage and the rural consumers are struggler in between the traders and manufacturers for quality goods, fair price, fair services and immediate redressal. The rural consumers who are guided by their psychology and emotions attached to particular trading house, businessmen, requires to be rationalised through another consumer movement, i.e. "empowering rural consumerism". It is possible through the establishment of "consumer watch" in the market, organising the rural consumers under "Consumer Manch" or "Consumer Cooperative Society" to combat the "Business guild". At the same time, various consumer laws require to be unified or consolidated. The empowerment and enlargement of the consumer forum at *panchayat* level is also a need. Through seminars, workshops in rural areas, confidence building and purchasing skill can be developed for the fair access to market, consumption and socio-economic justice.

Notes

1. Article 21 of Constitution of India, right to Life which reads as "No one shall be deprived of his life and personal liberty except for the procedure established by the law."
2. Let the buyer be aware.
3. Let the seller be aware.
4. General Assembly Resolution No. 39/248.
5. The Consumer Protection Act, 1986.
6. 5.2 (1)(d) of the Consumer Protection Act, 1986.

7. G. Radha Krishna, *Consumer Behaviour*, ICFAI Books, ICFAI University Press, Overview III.
8. Saba Nazmi, *Consumer Rights, Your Right As A Consumer*, ICFAI Books, ICFAI University Press, p.162
9. *Ibid.*
10. *Product Liability Law in the Peoples Republic of China*, 2010.
11. Product Quality Law as amended in 2000 (Peoples Republic of China).

4

Role of the Consumer Court to Protect "Farmer" as a "Consumer" with Reference to Farming

An Analysis

Pallavi Gupta

Introduction

Whether farmers or growers can avail remedy under the Consumer Protection Act, 1986 as rural consumer against loss suffered in their farming due to defective seeds supplied by authorised person. This issue is answered after interpretation of The Seeds Act, 1966, The Seeds Rules, 1968, and The Consumer Protection Act, 1986. It is done by Apex Court of the country in the case of *National Seeds Corporation Limited* versus *M. Madhusudan Reddy & Another.*[1]

Facts of this case show that farmers/growers/agriculturist labours were engaged in the agriculture/horticulture activities/seeds production either in their own land or on lease and cultivate the same for livelihood. M/s. National Seeds Corporation Ltd.[2] entered into an agreement with these growers/farmers/agriculturist labours for selling foundation seeds of sunflowers, bitter gourd, tomato, castor and chilli. However, seeds were sowed in the supervision of company's officers. Farmers adopted prescribed modes of preparing the field, irrigation and fertilizer for cultivation.

When the farmers/growers/agriculturist labours noticed that there was no germination and growth of the plants were uneven consequently no yield from the plants, they approached the company's to inspect the field and assess the damages, but the company did not respond. They, then, filed complaint against company in the Consumer Forum that they have suffered loss due to failure of crops/yield, alleging that they did not get the expected yield because the seeds sold by the company (NSCL) were defective. They asked compensation for the cost of seeds, fertilisers etc.

District Consumer Forum appointed the Commissions to inspect the field. Commission after inspection of the field, submitted the report in favour of farmers that foundation seeds supplied by company for farming were defective. District Consumer Forum rely on the report of Commission and direct the company to pay compensation. The State Consumer Forum and the National Consumer Forum approved the decision of District Forum.

Company objected the order of the Consumer Redressal Agencies and filed an appeal in the Supreme Court and raised several objections and argued as follows:

- Initially company argued that the crop of the farmers had failed because after sowing the seeds the farmers/growers/agriculturist labours did not take necessary precaution and they did not get proper steps for cultivation, therefore, they suffer loss.
- Since in the agreement, between farmers and company, arbitration clause is mentioned, farmers/growers/agriculturist labours can, in case of any grievance about the quality of the seeds, seek remedy only under the Seeds Act by way of filing a complaint to the seed inspector or by way of prosecution, in this situation the Consumer Protection Act cannot entertain complaint filed by farmers.
- Farmers/growers/agriculturist labours cannot seek remedy under the Consumer Protection Act, because they are not consumer as per section 2(1)(d) because they have purchased seeds for commercial purpose.
- Finding of the Consumer Forums, that the Seeds sold by the company were defective, is liable to be set aside because the procedure prescribed under Section 13(1) (c) of the Consumer Protection Act was not followed and the State and National Commissions committed grave error by maintaining the complaints of the farmers.

In the view of objections raised by the company, Apex Court of the country framed several issues as follows :

- Whether the Seeds Act, 1966 is special legislation and bars the jurisdiction of the Consumer Forum to entertain complaint filed by the farmers under the Consumer Protection Act, 1986?
- Whether the Seeds Act, 1966, the Seeds Rules 1968 bar jurisdiction of the Consumer Protection Act, 1986 for agricultural products?
- What is object of the seeds Act?
- Whether defective seeds provided by the company will come within scope of defective Goods under the Consumer Protection Act, 1986?
- Whether the farmers/growers of seeds can seek remedy only under the Seeds Act, 1966?
- If remedy is available in the form of arbitration in case of dispute, can this remedy be used as optional remedy or only remedy?
- If only remedy is available in the form of arbitration, can provision of CPA be applied for additional relief in favour of growers/farmers?
- Whether purchasing of seeds by farmers from supplier of foundation seeds does come within the scope of commercial purpose under section 2(1)(d)(i) of CPA?
- Whether the person, who has purchased foundation seeds from seller of foundation seeds, can claim relief under CPA as consumer?
- Whether the District Forum has committed a jurisdiction error by awarding compensation to the farmers without complying with the procedure prescribed under section 13(1)(c) of CPA?
- Whether interpretation of municipal law, in implementation of international law, can be against the interest of consumers?

Analysis of Decision of the Supreme Court

To recognise the rights of farmers as consumer Apex Court of the country examined the Seeds Act, 1966, the Seeds Rules, 1968 and the Consumer Protection Act.

Scope of the Seeds Act with reference to Farmers Right

The examination of the provisions of the Seeds Act, 1966, the Seeds Rules, 1968 shows that object of the Seeds Act is to regulate the quality of certain seeds for the purposes of agriculture including horticulture.[3]

To achieve this object the Seeds Act specifying the minimum limits of germination and purity of notified kind or variety of seeds. This Act provides to affixes mark or label to indicate that such seed conforms to those limits. It restricts the sale of any notified kind or variety of seed unless the same is identifiable with certificate as to its kind or variety and conforms to the minimum limits of germination and purity. It has provisions for grant of certificate and by the certification agency to certain category of person to sale these seeds. The Seed Analysts and the Seed Inspectors will have the power to take sample of any seed of any notified kind or variety from any person selling such seed and send the same for analysis by the State Seed Laboratory or the Central Seed Laboratory in case of any doubt. The Seed Inspector can launch prosecution for violation of any provision of the Seeds Act or any Rule made thereunder. If a person is found guilty then he can be punished with imprisonment or with a penalty of fine or with both. If an offence is committed by a company, then every person who, at the time of commission of offence, was in charge of and was responsible to the company, of the conduct of its business, can be punished.

The Seeds Rules casts a duty on every person selling of any seed of notified kind, to keep complete record of each lot of seeds sold for a period of three years. He is also required to keep sample of the seed, which can be tested for determining the purity.

This Act further says that if farmer has lodged a complaint that the failure of the crop is due to the defective quality of seeds of any notified kind or variety supplied to him, the Seed Inspector shall have power to take possession of the seed containers and a sample of unused seeds from the complaint to investigate the causes of the failure of the crop by sending samples to the Seed Analyst for detailed analysis at Laboratory. In case, report concludes that the failure of the crop is due to the quality of seeds being less than the minimum standards notified by the Central Government, Seed Inspector shall launch proceedings against the supplier for contravention of the provisions of the Act.

And to maintain the complaint of the farmers/growers/agriculturist labour under the Consumer Protection Act, 1986 as consumer, Supreme Court has looked into the object, legislative history[4] and the preamble to the Consumer Protection Act, 1986. It shows that the Consumer Protection Act, (CPA) is enacted to provide for better protection of the interests of consumers and to provide for better redressal also through cheaper, easier, expeditious and effective redressal mechanism for the settlement of consumer disputes after following a prescribed procedure.

Scope of the Consumer Protection Act with reference to Farmers' Right

Regarding scope of the Consumer Protection Act, number of judgements[5] has been considered. In these judgements judiciary noticed the background, reasons, and the purpose for which the Consumer Protection Act was enacted and held in clear and unambiguous terms that the provisions of the Consumer Protection Act shall be in addition to and not in derogation of the provisions of any other law for the time being in force.

Regarding who can be consumer, the definition of 'consumer' under the Consumer Protection Act, takes within its fold any person who buys any goods for a consideration paid, and it also includes any person who uses the goods though such use is with the approval of the buyer, although it excludes a person who obtains the goods for resale or for any commercial purpose. It is also clarified that the expression "commercial purpose" used does not include use by a consumer of goods bought and used by him for the purpose of earning his livelihood by means of self-employment.

Regarding '*Defect*' in the goods the Consumer Protection Act provides that any fault, imperfection or shortcoming in the quality, quantity, potency, purity or standard which is required to be maintained by or under any law for the time being in force or under any contract, express or implied, or as is claimed by the trader in any manner whatsoever in relation to any goods. If complaint is admitted, the Consumer Forum shall follow a prescribed procedure under the CPA.

Analysis of the Decision

Farmers—A Consumer: Yes or No

The Supreme Court, in deciding the issue that Consumer Forum has no jurisdiction to entertain complaint of farmers as consumer, consider the conflict of two Acts, i.e. the Seeds Act and the Consumer Protection Act.

The Supreme Court held that in the context of farmers/growers and other buyer of the seeds, the Seeds Act being a special legislation, ensure that there is no compromise with the quality of seeds sold to the farmers and that those engaged in agriculture and horticulture get quality seeds and if any person violates the provisions of the Act, shall be punished. However, *there is no provision in that Act for compensating the farmers, who may suffer due to loss of crop or get insufficient yield on account of defective seeds supplied by a person authorised to sell the seeds.*

Undoubtedly, the agriculturists and horticulturists are the largest consumers of seeds. They suffer loss of crop due to various reasons, one of which is the use of defective/sub-standard seeds. *If a farmer who suffers loss of crop due to defective seeds can approach the Seed Inspector only and can make a request for prosecution of the person from whom he purchased the seeds, but this cannot redeem the loss suffered by a farmer.*

The Supreme Court further cleared that the Seeds Act and its Rules do not indicate that the provisions of the Consumer Protection Act are not available to the farmers, who are very much covered by the wide definition of "consumer" under Section 2(d) of the CPA. Any attempt to exclude the farmers from the ambit of the CPA by implication will make that Act vulnerable to an attack of unconstitutionality on the ground of discrimination.

The trend of the decisions[6] of Apex Court is that the jurisdiction of the Consumer Forum should not and would not be curtailed unless there is an express provision prohibiting the Consumer Forum to take up the matter which falls within the jurisdiction of civil court or any other forum as established under some enactment. Even if two different fora have jurisdiction to entertain the dispute in regard to the same subject, the jurisdiction of the Consumer Forum would not be barred and the power of the Consumer Forum to adjudicate upon the dispute could not be negated.

Term 'consumer' was interpreted by Supreme Court in several judgements[7] as —"it is in two parts. The first deals with goods and the other with services. The Act thus aims to protect the economic interest of a consumer as understood in commercial sense as a purchaser of goods and user of services. The defect in goods and deficiency in services may have to be removed and compensated differently. The former is, normally, capable of being replaced and repaired whereas the other may be required to be compensated by award of the just equivalent of the value or damages for loss."

The Supreme Court held that since the farmers/growers purchased seeds for livelihood by paying a price to the company, they would certainly fall within the ambit of "Consumer" under the Consumer Protection Act and there is no reason to deny them the remedies which are available to other consumers of goods and services.

Nature of Remedy provided by Arbitration Act or Consumer Protection Act

In the context of next issue that the only remedy available to the farmers/ growers, for loss of crop due to defective seeds, was to apply for arbitration only, means the only remedy available to the farmers and growers was to file complaints with the concerned Seed Inspectors for taking action under the Seeds Act, Supreme Court answered this issue by interpreting its own judgement[8] and held that the grievance of a farmer/grower is not remedied by prosecuting the supplier of the seeds. Even if, such person is found guilty and sentenced to imprisonment, the aggrieved farmer/grower does not get anything. Therefore, the so-called remedy available to an aggrieved farmer/grower to lodge a complaint with the concerned Seed Inspector for prosecution of the seller/supplier of the seed is illusory and they cannot be denied relief under the Consumer Act on the ground of availability of an alternative remedy.

Therefore, it can be said that the remedy of arbitration/prosecution is not the only remedy available to a grower. Rather, it is an optional remedy. He can either seek reference to an arbitrator or file a complaint under the Consumer Act. If the grower opts for the remedy of arbitration, then he cannot, subsequently, file complaint under the CPA. However, if he chooses to file a complaint in the first instance before the competent Consumer Forum, then he cannot be denied relief under the Arbitration and Conciliation Act, 1996, even the existence of an arbitration clause will not be a bar to the entertainment of the complaint by the Redressal Agency, constituted under the Consumer Protection Act, since the remedy provided under the Act is in addition to the provisions of any other law for the time being in force. It does not extinguish the remedies under another statute, but provides an additional or alternative remedy.[9]

Farming—Commercial Purpose: yes or not

Regarding next issue that grower is excluded from the definition of 'consumers' because the foundation seeds produced by him are required to be supplied to the company under an agreement that is for commercial purpose and as such their cases would fall in the exclusion part of the definition of 'consumer', interpretation of the expression "commercial purpose" is necessary. In several cases[10] judiciary observed that the expression "commercial purpose" is also not defined in the Act. In the absence of a definition, we have to go by its ordinary meaning. Term 'Commercial' denotes "pertaining to commerce, it means connected with, or engaged in commerce; mercantile; having profit as the main aim whereas the word 'commerce' means "financial transactions especially buying and selling of merchandise, on a large scale." Therefore, Consumer Forums appear to have been taking a consistent view that where a person purchases goods with a view to using such goods for carrying on any activity on a large scale for the purpose of earning profit; he will not be a 'consumer' within the meaning of section 2(d)(i) of the Act.

Here, the Supreme Court observed that the company had selected a set of farmers/growers in the area for growing seeds on its behalf and by way of entering into agreements with the farmers, the company supplied foundation seeds to them for a price and assured them that within few months they will be able to earn profit. The agreements clearly assumed supply of the foundation seeds by the company with an assurance that the crop will be purchased by it. It is neither pleaded by the company nor any evidence produced before any of the Consumer Forums that the growers had the freedom to sell the seeds in the open market or to any person other than the company. Therefore, the objection of the company cannot be sustained that the growers had purchased the seeds for resale or for any commercial purpose and they are excluded from the definition of the term 'consumer'. As a matter of fact, the evidence shows that the growers had agreed to produce seeds on behalf of the company for the purpose of earning their livelihood by using their skills and labour.

Jurisdictional Error: Committed or Not

Regarding the issue that the consumer forum has committed a jurisdiction error by awarding compensation to the farmers/growers without complying with the procedure prescribed under the Consumer Protection Act, the Supreme Court said that provisions of this Act shows that the District Forum can call upon the complainant to provide a sample of goods, if it is satisfied that the defect in the goods cannot be determined without proper analysis or test. After that the sample, which is obtained, is required to be sent to an appropriate laboratory for analysis or test for the purpose of finding out whether the goods suffer from any defect as alleged in the complaint or from any other defect.

The Supreme Court further observed that the District Forums had appointed agricultural experts as Court Commissioners/Advocate Commissioner with liberty to avail the services of agricultural experts for ascertaining the true status of the crops. The reports of the agricultural experts clearly revealed that the crops had failed because of defective seeds/foundation seeds. After examining the reports the District Forums felt that the seeds were defective and this is the reason why the complainants were not called upon to provide samples of the seeds for getting the same analysed/tested in an appropriate laboratory.

The Supreme Court held that in our view, the procedure adopted by the District Forum was in no way contrary to Section 13(1)(c) of the Consumer Protection Act and the company cannot seek annulment of well-reasoned orders passed by three Consumer Forums on the baseless ground that the procedure prescribed under section 13(1) (c) of the Consumer Protection Act had not been followed.

Logic of Supreme Court in Favour of Illiterate and Rural Consumers

Therefore, decision given by Consumer Forum on the basis of expert opinion of Commission is deemed to be followed the procedure of CPA for analysing the defect the laboratory. Here Supreme Court gave reasoning of its decision *in favour of rural and illiterate consumers* as, majority of the farmers in the country remains illiterate throughout their life because they do not have access to the system of education. They have no idea about the Seeds Act and the Rules framed thereunder and other legislations. They mainly rely on the information supplied by the Agricultural Department and Government agencies, like the National Seeds Corporation Ltd. (NSCL). Ordinarily, nobody would tell a farmer that after purchasing the seeds for sowing, he should retain a sample thereof so that in the event of loss of crop or less yield on account of defect in the seeds, he may claim compensation from the supplier. In the normal course, a farmer would use the entire quantity of seeds purchased by him for the purpose of sowing and by the time he finds that the crop has failed because the seeds purchased by him were defective nothing remains with him which could be tested in a laboratory. In some of the cases, the farmers had categorically stated that they had sown the entire quantity of seeds purchased from the company. Therefore, it is naïve to blame the District Forum for not having called upon the farmers to provide the samples of seeds and send them for analysis or test in the laboratory.

It may also be mentioned that there was abject failure on the company's part to assist the District Forum by providing samples of the varieties of seeds sold to the farmers. Such samples could have been easily made available to the District Forums for being sent to an appropriate laboratory for the purpose of analysis or test. Why the appellant did not adopt that course has not been explained. Not only this, the officers of the company, who inspected the fields of the farmers could have collected the samples and got them tested in a designated laboratory for ascertaining the purity of the seeds and/or the extent of germination etc. Why this was not done has also not been explained by the company.

These omissions lend support to the plea of the farmers that the seeds sold/supplied by the company were defective.

Here Supreme Court held that the Consumer Forums did not commit any error by entertaining the complaint of the farmers and awarding compensation to them.

Conclusion

- Object of the Seeds Act is to ensure the quality of seeds in this context it should read with CPA provisions. And this case focus on shortcoming of the Seeds Act—it has substantive provisions to punish a person only if he found guilty of violating the provisions relating the quality of the seeds, but it is silent on compensating the farmers/growers of seeds who may suffer loss of crop or who may get insufficient yield due to use of defective seeds sold/supplied by the any authorised person. In author's view activities of these authorised selling person should be consider as unfair trade practice for the purpose of Consumer Protection Act.
- The Seeds Act, 1966 and Seeds Rules, 1968 does not bar jurisdiction of CPA for agricultural products, livestock and markets.
- This case expands the definition of 'consumer' by considering farmers, agriculturist and horticulturist as consumer as purchasing of seeds for their farming is for livelihood by using skill and labour and purchasing of seeds do not come under "commercial purpose".
- Defective seeds do come within the definition of defective goods as per provisions of CPA.
- Commission's expert opinion (with agriculture expert) may be treated as the procedure to analyse defect of goods under section 13 of the Consumer Protection Act.
- Municipal law cannot be interpreted against the interest of consumer or against the object of international treaty.

Suggestions

- Since, there is conflict between two Acts, therefore, it is suggested:
  —to make amendment to insert provisions for compensation also to the farmers/growers in case they suffer loss of yield

due to defective seeds in this Act itself as to redeem their loss; and

— to enhance penalty provisions also in the Seeds Act to fix them for unfair trade practice specially when wrong is committed by a company.

- There is a need of consumer education programme to the illiterate or rural consumers specially farmers to get them aware about the provisions of Consumer Protection Act.
- This awareness programme can be done by Media, NGO, Panchayat system, by Choupal in village, by FM radio.

Notes

1. (2012) 2 SCC 506, this case has involved several civil appeals, Civil Appeal No. 622 of 2012 [arising out of SLP(C) No.32750 and 35350 of 2009], in which G.S. Singhvi, granted SLP, are impounded with civil appeal No. 7543 of 2004, 3499 of 2009 and 4519 of 2009.
2. Incorporated with a purpose to arrange quality seeds of different varieties for production, in the farms of registered growers and supply the same to the farmers.
3. The Seeds Act contains definitions of various terms like — '*seed*' means any of the following classes of seeds used for sowing or planting. I. seeds of food crops including edible oil seeds and seeds of fruits and vegetables, II. Cotton seeds. III. Seeds of cattle fodder and includes seedlings, and tubers, bulbs, rhizomes, roots, cuttings, all types of grafts and other vegetatively propagated material, of food crops or cattle fodder; *"Kind"* means one or more related species or sub-species of crop plants each individually or collectively known by one common name such as cabbage, maize, paddy, wheat etc.; *"Notified kind or variety"*, in relation to any seed, means any kind or variety thereof notified under Section 5; *"Variety"* means a sub-division of a kind identifiable by growth, yield, plant, fruit, seed, or other characteristic.
4. This Act was enacted after taking into account the proliferation of international trade and commerce and vast expansion of business and trade and finally to implement guidelines of the UN on consumer protection (Resolution No. 39 of 243); Reference: (2012) 2 SCC 506, para 50.
5. *Secretary, Thirumurugan Cooperative Agricultural Credit Society* vs. *M. Lalitha,* (2004) 1 SCC 305, *Lucknow Development Authority* vs. *M. K. Gupta,* (1994) 1 SCC 243, *Fair Air Engineers Private Limited* vs. *N. K. Modi,* (1996) 6 SCC 385, *Skypay Couriers Limited* vs. *Tata Chemicals Limited,* (2000) 5 SCC 294, *State of Karnataka* vs. *Vishwabharathi House*

Building Cooperative Society, (2003) 2 SCC 412, *CCI Chambers Cooperative Housing Society Limited* vs. *Development Credit Bank Limited,* (2003) 7 SCC 233, *H.N. Shankara Shastry* vs. *Assistant Director of Agriculture, Karnataka,* (2004) 6 SCC 230 and *Trans Mediterranean Airways* vs. *Universal Exports and Another,* (2011) 10 SCC 316.

6. In *Kishore Lal* vs. *Chairman, Employees' State Insurance Corporation,* (2007) 4 SCC 579, p. 593, para 17.
7. *Lucknow Development Authority* vs. *M. K. Gupta,* (1994) 1 SCC 243, pp. 253-54, para 3.
8. *Fair Air Engineers (P) Ltd.* vs. *N.K. Modi,* (1996) 6 SCC 385, p. 393, para 15 & 16.
9. *Skypay Couriers Limited* vs. *Tata Chemicals Limited,* (2000) 5 SCC 294, para 2, *Trans Mediterranean Airways* vs. *Universal Exports* (2011)10 SCC 316 para 41.
10. *Laxmi Engineering Works* vs. *P.S.G. Industrial Institute,* (1995) 3 SCC 583, para 11.

5

Emerging Rural Consumer in Odisha

Protection of Rights and Redressal Initiatives

Pratip Kumar Mishra

Introduction

India is a classic example where Consumer Protection is always high in the government agenda. There is a consumer friendly legislation and with amendments from time to time it has become friendlier. But, in reality consumers find it very difficult to solve their problems in a manufacturer centric globalised market. Further, the helplessness of the consumer is felt both in the urban and rural areas due to cumbersome legal procedure and delay in redressal of their grievances.

With the gradual withdrawal of the interventionist state, where the state is more of a facilitator, it is expected that consumers will be more empowered and better protected. The Consumer Protection Act, 1986, Act gives better protection to consumer interests by setting-up quasi-judicial bodies for quick disposal of complaints and giving six basic rights to consumers. Experience in the past has revealed that consumer complaints have not been dealt with reasonable expediency and complaints are only mounting. The market is booming and the consumer is getting exploited more-and-more. "The demand revolution has penetrated down to middle India and these towns will behave like the metros of tomorrow".[1] The growth has been attributed to factors like increased consumption, rising income level, changes in lifestyle and demographic changes. There is a 33 per cent revenue each year from food (52%) and non-Food (45%).

Changing Face of Rural India

Over the years rural India has witnessed an increase in the purchasing power of consumers, accompanied by their desire to upgrade their standard of living. The government initiatives to address poverty have improved the conditions of rural masses. As such rural consumers have upgraded their life styles at par with their urban and semi-urban counterparts. Consumption patterns, nutritious food, cosmetics, beverages, mobile phones and other necessities have found their place in the rural household.

Mahatma Gandhi National Rural Employment Guarantee Act (MGNREGA) and Jawaharlal Nehru Urban Renewal Mission (JNURM), the two flagship programmes of the government have increased the purchasing power in rural areas. The former guarantees work in the lean agricultural season and the other fulfils the demand for labour in urban projects. Rural Marketing Association of India (RMAI) and MART, New Delhi based research organisations have highlighted that the rural economy has not been impacted by the global economic slowdown. Rural income is on the rise, this is due to a boom in agriculture production for the past four years showing a record harvest which has given a boost to the rural economy.

The rural consumer as a buying class is a post-globalisation phenomena and thus, recent in origin. Commercialisation of agriculture, rapid industrialisation, green revolution and operation flood has greatly contributed in the funds transfer from the urban to the rural. Special initiatives taken by successive governments have also improved rural connectivity and rural markets. Development of cold storage facilities and warehouses has in a big way increased the productive quality and storage capacity. Implementation of various social and economic development schemes by the government, cooperative credit, micro-finance through commercial banks and establishment of self-help groups (SHG), regulated markets and insurance schemes to support has impacted a change in the rural heartland.

Poverty and lack of skill for employability in rural areas has also made people to migrate to distant lands in search of better jobs, economic status and bring about improvement in the quality of life. This interaction between cities, towns and villages has also led to the growth of a new consumer class in rural areas who have the purchasing power. The phenomenal increase in the size of this buying population and their changing profile has resulted in many physical, cultural and economic changes. The concept of sophisticated markets is slowly taking roots in the rural areas. The new class of buyers has developed a complex taste and liking towards the new products that enters the market each day. But this has a negative consequence too. In the rush of changing habits the rural class is still unaware and unfamiliar with the rules of market and also has limited knowledge about new products. There are a lot of expectations of the rural consumers from the government.

1. They feel that it is the responsibility of the government to protect the consumers.
2. Traders should be punished for cheating and malpractices.
3. Initiations of practical measures that can help safeguard the consumer interest.
4. The consumers on their own cannot stop the malpractice in the market place.
5. However, the concept of educating the rural consumer about their rights and duties is still missing.

Problems Faced by the Rural Consumer

Venturing into a new world of consumerism the rural consumer is faced with a variety of problems and this sometimes influences their consumer behaviour and purchasing decisions. Poverty, low purchasing power, ignorance, lack of knowledge of the legal system and its implementation has been some of the major problems faced by the consumers in the backward regions of a state like Odisha. Moreover, there are no special initiatives for mitigation of these problems. In the tribal and backward regions people are illiterate and unaware of their rights and the methods of redressal of complaints. Having no organisational set-up to assist them their voice is unheard. Therefore, consumers fall an easy prey to the manufacturer, retailers and brokers. Several research studies have revealed that there has been an alarming rise in sub-standard and spurious products which have at times proven dangerous and fatal to the consumers. With the entry of many more private players into the service sector has resulted in large scale deficiency in service quality. This is a major area of concern.

Further India is having a high demographic profile and anything produced finds a market. This has attracted the Transnational and Multinational organisations to dump their products in the Indian market and to a less resilient rural market. They not only maintain a monopoly of their products and services, but prevent competition by following various marketing strategies. The fall out is in the form of fake brands, spurious products, misleading advertisements, adulteration, less weights, misleading warranties and gurantees on products, services and unreasonable price tags.

What the Consumer Ought to Know

Being a consumer is not easy; one has to pass the rigorous litmus test in selecting and buying of products. Therefore, one has to go by certain guidelines to avoid being duped by the prevailing market conditions. The enumeration of these rights and their effective enforcement will pave the way for a healthy consumerist society. A consumer has the right to seek redressal for any defects in goods, deficiency in services and loss incurred due to unscrupulous trade practices. Each day the manufacturers are finding new ways of cheating and duping the consumer. As the markets are globalising the direct link between the manufacturer and the user is also receding.

Strategies to Protect the Consumers

There is no doubt that the vulnerable consumer needs protection. Thus, it becomes necessary to promote consumer education and raise awarness among the people on various issues like:

1. The existence of consumer rights and need to protect it.
2. Role of government in protecting and promoting consumer rights.
3. Independent agencies working in the field of consumer protection.
4. Making comparative analysis of consumer protection methods in developing countries and the advanced countries.
5. Evaluating the effectiveness of legislations designed for consumer protection.
6. Legal support and resources available to consumers and the proactive roles possible for marketer to ensure consumer protection.

The next important issue is to what extent the consumer needs protection? An ideal relationship between consumer and producer arises out of a voluntary act between equal partners. However, in practice it is like any other relationship, the party that is more empowered tries to impose its will on the other in an unfair manner. In a consumer and producer (marketer) relationship, it is usually the producer who is more empowered and always better organised side.[2]

Absence of access to redressal mechanism in rural areas has led to quantum rise in consumer grievances. For the benefit of rural consumers the Gram Sabha must be convened to educate them. There is also negligence on the part of consumers, who are responsible for not seeking correct and reliable information.[3] Therefore, to educate the consumers there is a need to include consumer education in school and college syllabus, involve the panchayat, NGOs and the Media and build the capacity of the local officials of the SIRDs. Formulation of specific policies for the consumers, particularly farmers, women and children, strengthening the consumer redressal mechanism at the district-level can be the other measures that can be taken-up.[4]

Odisha Consumer Redressal Machinery

Odisha is largely rural, therefore, the focus of consumer empowerment has to be the rural consumers.The introduction of the Right to Information Act (RTI) has given a boost to non-governmental organisations to work in the area of grievance redressal against those in authority. With the third tier of governance in the form of Panchayati Raj Institution coming in after the 73rd Amendment in rural areas, the role of local bodies has become the focus of attention. It is pertinent that these bodies have to play a very significant role in consumer redressal initiatives. Manpower management and effective utilisation of functionaries are required. Capacity building and training in redressal mechanism has to be a continuous process to handle complaints.The gram panchayat being the base of deliberation there can be a better government-people interface in resolving consumer related issues. Proper infrastructure and the E. gram project has to be implemented. Non-official members and people's representative have to play a positive role in building up a progressive redressal forum. There should be effective utilisation of key persons like the *sarpanch, gram sevaks* and *sevikas* and the VLWs. They should act as change agents in the awareness campaigns among rural consumers specially women and youth.

There are a number of steps that can be taken to strengthen the consumer movement in the State. A few are indicated below:

1. Initiative has to be taken to make the rural consumer aware and sensitise to the use of grievance redressal mechanism.
2. Consumer information system needs to be improved.
3. The civil society has to partner with the officials in education and awareness programmes.
4. Efficiency and accountability in the functioning of consumers forum is to be ensured.

Conclusion

Globalisation is expected to create unprecedented and new opportunities for economic development. Developing economies and states are buoyant with their growth. The feel good factor is perceived in the mega shopping malls that has changed the landscape of cities and towns and with it created a euphoria and excitement among potential consumers like youth, women and children who are more guided by the flashing advertisements than the quality of products. Yet over three quarters of the people of developing scciety like India are under great stress and frustration unable to negotiate the rising tide of the process of integration. There is a contrast seen today in our country, the affluence of mega cities and towns with a sizeable concentration of urban poor and the trend of food insecurity, starvation deaths, under nourishment, malnutrition and unemployment. Modernisation of traditional society is not easy. Urbanisation should not be misconceived with the hyper growth of consumerism nor should industrialisation be a gamble in the game plan of development. Consumerism cannot be wished away in a global world, but its side effects can be reduced with a strong will of consumer grievance redressal mechanism.

Notes

1. Ranjeet Executive Director Nielsen India.
2. M.S. Raju, Dominique Xardel, (2009). *Consumer Behaviour: Concepts, Applications and Cases*, New Delhi: Vikas Publishing House, p. 215.
3. *Workshop on Consumer Protection and Awareness.*
4. Mamta Pathania (2011). "*Globalisation and Consumer Rights*", presentation at IIPA Odisha Regional Branch, SIRD, Bhubaneswar, November.

6
Consumer Protection Measures in India

A Study of District Jind, Haryana

Rajbir Singh Dalal and *Vijay Vir*

Introduction

In the present age of consumerism and competitive trade practices, the market is shifting from the sellers to the buyers. The consumer has been designated as the king of the market who controls and steers the market. However, on one hand the consumer has been decorated with higher profile in the market, on the other attempts are being made to protect his rights and sovereignty as a consumer against the exploitation made by the market forces. Over the past few years rural India has witnessed an increase in the purchasing power of consumers, accompanied by their desire to upgrade their standard of living. The steps taken by the Government of India to address the poverty have improved the condition of rural masses. As a result, rural consumers have upgraded their life styles through making changes in their consumption patterns by adding more nutritious food and are purchasing life style products such as cosmetics, beverages, mobile phones etc., which have become necessities for them.

A number of schemes and programmes of the government have changed the rules of the marketing game in rural India. The flagship schemes of Government of India especially Mahatma Gandhi National Rural Employment Guarantee Act (MGNREGA) scheme, which has a budget of more than Rs. 40,000 crore have given the rural population an opportunity to meet their daily needs. With the initiation of various rural development programmes there have been an upsurge of employment opportunities for the rural poor. NREGS guarantees 100 days employment to a rural household and provides much needed bargaining power to battle the exploitation in the farming sector as a labourer. Also the increased demand for labour in the urban projects such as Jawaharlal Nehru National Urban Renewal Mission (JNNURM) has resulted in more money being sent back home by the immigrant worker.

Bharat Nirman, an Indian plan for creating basic rural infrastructure, is having a budget of Rs. 58,000 crore for 2011-12. It is a step towards bridging the gap between rural and urban areas and improving the quality of lives of rural masses. It comprises projects on irrigation, roads (Pradhan Mantri Gram Sadak Yojana), housing (Indira Awaas Yojana), water supply, electrification and telecommunication connectivity. That is why in spite of adequate provisions regarding the consumer protection in the country, the ground reality is somewhat in sorry state and the situation is rather worse in rural areas where the consumer is by and large illiterate, ignorant, having poor purchasing and bargaining power due to a number of factors. Therefore, the possibility of exploitation by the rogue traders or sellers is on the higher side. As the rural market is rapidly growing and new dimensions of its expansion are opening everyday hence the people at the helm of affairs or attached with consumer protection movement had to pay attention in this regard to take stock of the situation prevailing therein. Further, the existing consumer protection mechanism is over 2½ decades old in the country, therefore, it becomes essential to look into it and examine and assess its impact in the rural areas. Accordingly, the present study is carried out with the objectives of assessing the nature of rural consumer, their literacy level as well as level of awareness regarding the Consumer Protection Act, 1986 (CPA) and mechanism meant for it. Simultaneously, the challenges before the rural consumers have been pointed out and suitable suggestions have been given to make this consumer protection measure more effective and viable in the rural areas.

Historical Perspective

Consumer protection movement has a long history. The people in the world are today enjoying a variety of services, goods and commodities. LPG syndrome has not only strengthened the multinational corporations, but also internationalised the market. Therefore, a number of new products are available in the market before the consumer which is making it difficult to decide the quality of the product and to make a judicious selection. MNCs captured the market and protection of consumer's interest against their hegemony was felt necessary at national and international levels. This movement emerged in U.S.A., Britain and gradually spread to all the countries. The General Assembly of the UNO passed a resolution regarding protection of consumer's interests on 9-4-1985 that directed the Third World countries to make legislation on the subject. Government of India has made a number of laws to protect the consumers from the market forces, yet the consumers in India are not aware of their rights.

The most important is the Consumer Protection Act of 1986. It came into force w.e.f. 15-4-1987 all over the country except Jammu & Kashmir. This Act is considered as a milestone in the historical development of Judicial Institutions in India. It was amended in 1991, 1993 and 2002 for speedy disposal of the cases and making these courts effective in real sense. The consumer courts have been given powers of first class magistrate and creation of new benches and appointment of additional members in State and National Commissions have been made for quick decisions. Moreover, some concrete steps have been taken to fill up the vacancies in Zila Forums and State Commissions without unnecessary delay. In absence of the President of State Commission, the selection committee can be presided over by any judge of High Court. Similarly, the senior most members can work as presiding officer and work accordingly in absence of the President at any level.

The pecuniary limits of hearing complaints have also been raised at all the levels. Now, District Forum can hear cases up to Rs. 20 lakh whereas the State Commission above Rs. 20 lakh up to Rs. 1 crore and the National Commission has power to take up cases more than Rs. 1 crore. The Act makes provisions for two types of institutions: Consumer Protection Councils and Consumer Disputes Redressal Agencies or Forums. The various decisions delivered by the Hon'ble Supreme Court in different cases have widened the scope of the Act and activities concerned which have further geared up the consumer protection movement.

Conceptual Framework

Consumer Disputes Redressal Forum which is popularly known as District Forum is the basic unit of Consumer Disputes Redressal Agencies established by the State Government in each district of the State by notification. Whereas the term consumer stands for any person who buys or hires or avails of any goods or service for a consideration, which has been paid or promised or partly paid and partly promised or under any system of deferred payment and includes any user of such goods or service with the approval of such person other than the person who buys or hires or avails of such goods or service for re-sale or for any commercial purpose. The 'consumer dispute' means a dispute where the person against whom a complaint has been made, denies or disputes the allegations contained in the complaint. However, Consumer Protection means the protection of consumers from their exploitation by the unfair trade practices of the traders or producers who can exploit the consumers in many ways, i.e. by giving derogatory information about the quality of product, adulteration, underweight supplies, supply of low quality of product, poor or negligent services, delay in supply after giving advance; spiralling prices, misleading and deceptive advertisements and offering gifts and prizes etc. In a liberal competitive economy, the consumer is designated as God and he/she enjoys a number of rights which are right to purchase or reject the product displayed for sale, right to safety, right to information, right to education and to be heard besides the right to seek redressal of grievances.

Research Framework

The present chapter is exploratory and analytical in nature-based on primary data collected from 210 respondent consumers of district Jind in Haryana, which is primarily a rural dominated and agrarian district. Stratified simple random sampling technique was adopted to collect the data from respondents with the help of interview-schedule and observation methods. Simple statistical techniques were used for analysing the data collected.

Major Findings

The findings of the present chapter are based on the information received from the respondent consumers of district Jind for which age, education, awareness level and mode of redressal of dispute adopted in case of default or deficiency in goods purchased or service hired were taken as the main variables for assessing the actual status of Consumer Protection Act and mechanism related to it.

Age-wise Classification of Consumers

Age has been considered as a criterion to determine the behaviour of consumers. Accordingly, the respondent consumers have been classified on this basis so that their views can be ascertained. Table 6.1 given below reflects the data in this regard:

Table 6.1: Age Status

Age Status (Years)	*Number*	*Percentage*
Below 18	22	10.47
19-30	61	29.04
31-40	47	22.38
41-50	55	26
51-60	25	11.90
Total	**210**	**100**

On the basis of the data given in above table, it can be concluded that maximum respondent consumers (29.4%) are in the age group of 19-30 years followed by one-fourth in 41-50 years age group. Whereas the number of respondents below 18 years is lowest (10.47%) followed by (11.90%) in the age group of 51-60 years. Thus, majority of the respondent consumers are between 19 to 50 years age who are mature and can have a better understanding of market and consumer behaviour.

Education-wise Classification of Consumers

Education has vital role in human life. If a person is educated, he can have a better understanding of his rights and related provisions. Further, a literate person can make proper utilisation of his rights whereas illiterate person has a comparatively lesser knowledge of consumer protection measures. Therefore, the possibility of unfair trade practical increases. Data given below in Table 6.2 reflects the distribution of consumers on the basis of the literacy-level.

Table 6.2: Education Status

Education Status	*Number*	*Percentage*
Metric	85	40.47
10+2	55	26.10
Graduation	32	15.23
Post Graduation	13	6.19
Others	25	11.90
Total	**210**	**100**

The data from Table 6.2 infers that the largest number (40.47%) of respondent consumers were educated up to metric-level followed by one-fourth who were literate up to 10+2 level. The percentage of respondents, who were graduates and above was insignificant. Thus, two-thirds of the respondent consumers were literate up to 10+2 level and their number with higher qualifications was far lesser.

Knowledge about Consumer Protection Act

The level of knowledge regarding CPA is an effective variable to determine its success. Accordingly, the opinion of the respondents has been given in Table 6.3 given below whether the consumers are aware regarding the provisions of the Act concerning their protection or not.

Table 6.3: Knowledge about Consumer Protection Act

Status	*Number*	*Percentage*
Yes	21	10
No	140	66.66
To some extent	49	23.33
Total	**210**	**100**

The data from above table states that when the consumers are aware regarding their consumer's rights, they can protect these rights easily, but two-third of the respondent consumers reported that they are not aware regarding the Consumer Protection Act. Whereas about one-fourth of the respondents stated that they are aware to some extent regarding this Act. However, only 10 per cent of the respondents admitted that they have knowledge regarding the Consumer Protection Act and related provisions. Thus, it can be concluded that after a fairly long period of 26 years of implementation of the Consumer Protection Act, a greater segment of the rural population is not aware regarding the Act.

Modus Operandi of Making Complaint

The success of CPA can be ascertained on the basis of number of consumers approaching the consumer redressal forum for remedies of their grievances. To find the extent to which the Consumer Protection Act is effective, an attempt has been made in the present table to assess the information of respondents regarding the *modus operandi* adopted by them for redressal of their grievances as a consumer. The data given in Table 6.4 below reflects the mode of complaint made by the consumer in case of any deficiency or defect in the consumer goods purchased or services hired.

Table 6.4: *Modus Operandi* of Making Compliant

Modus Operandi	*Number*	*Percentage*
Sellers	135	64.28
Companies	15	7.14
Consumers Redressal Forum	8	3.80
No Complaint Made	52	24.76
Total	**210**	**100**

From the data given in Table 6.4, it can be observed that about two-thirds of the respondent consumers made the complaint regarding the defective items or deficiency in service to the sellers concerned, whereas about one-fourth of them did not make any complaint in case of any default or deficiency. A small number of them (7.14%) reported regarding making complaint to the company concerned, whereas an insignificant number of respondents (3.80%) approached the Consumer Forum for redressal of their grievances which is a serious matter and reflect the level of ignorance or lack of awareness among the consumers regarding the Consumer Protection Act and related provisions.

Conclusion

No doubt, the CPA 1986 has contributed a lot in providing security to the consumer in the present era of consumerism to a great extent. But, its impact is not so satisfactory in case of the rural consumers. As the rural consumer market in India has multiplied many times in the last two decades and its potentialities are far and wide, hence, it becomes essential that due attention should be paid to the needs and problems of rural consumers so that, they can be saved from the unfair and deceptive trade practices. The present chapter is based on the primary data collected from the consumers of district Jind which is primarily a rural dominated area. The largest segment of the consumers (29.04%) is between 19-30 years age group followed by 41-50 years age group. The percentage of the respondent consumers with age group under 19 years and 51-60 years group is lowest. Thus, more than three-fourth of these respondent consumers are between 19-50 years who are not only mature, but also physically and mentally fit to take appropriate decision regarding the goods or services consumed or purchased. They should be aware of their rights and duties as a consumer. Proper bills or receipts of the goods purchased or services hired should be taken. Moreover, the quality, quantity, brand and price of such goods must be ascertained.

Among the respondent consumers a greater chunk (40%) is literate up to metric followed by one-fourth educated up to 10+2 level. Thus, about two-third of the rural consumers are literate up to 10+2 level and very small number of them are educated up to graduation level and above. Their low level of education certainly effects their consumer behaviour. Generally, lesser educated people are not aware of the branded items and other requirements under the CPA to safeguard their interests. In case of any deficiency in purchased goods or hired services most of the consumer's complaint the seller and insignificant number of them (3.80%) have made complaint to the Consumer Forum in this regard. Thus, either the consumers are not aware of their rights or feel that the consumer grievances redressal mechanism a futile exercise or they prefer to get these remedies through the sellers directly. So far as their response about the knowledge of CPA is concerned, two-third of them stated that they did not know about it, about one-fourth of them pointed that they have knowledge about its set-up and relevant provisions is to the same extent. Only a small number of them admitted that they knew about the CPA.

The findings indicate that majority of the rural consumers are illiterate and ignorant about the consumer protection mechanism. Therefore, need to be made aware regarding the CPA and related grievances redressal mechanism. Amongst the consumers who are aware regarding the CPA, only a few of them have used the available mechanism and that too against the government and semi-governmental agencies. Hardly any of the respondent consumers intimated that the provisions of CPA were used against the market forces. Therefore, it is required that the consumers should be made aware regarding it. The reasons behind not applying the CPA against market forces are lack of invoice/cash receipt/bills which generally are not in practice in rural marketing. Thus, cash purchase and taking of bills or receipts of purchased goods or services should be ascertained in rural marketing.

The consumer protection mechanism is also confined to urban areas and it is also becoming complex and expensive day by day. That is, why the rural consumers cannot get redressal of their grievances due to a number of factors, hence, it is essential that the mechanism meant for protection of rural consumers should be extended up to the level of block and village. Moreover, the awareness campaign regarding CPA among rural consumers is the need of hour and might be an effective tool to combat the unfair and deceptive trade practices prevailing in rural market.

The educational institutes, PRIs, NGOs and government machinery of concerned department can prove instrumental in empowering the rural consumers through awareness campaign or working with them. The existence of competitive market and availability of branded goods therein may be helpful in doling out the rural consumers from exploitation of monopolised market of the day. As the service sector has expanded rapidly in the country in the last two decades, hence due attention must be paid on it to protect the interests of rural consumer. Generally, it has been observed that the services provided in the rural areas are not only poor in quality, but also delayed one which need to be boosted-up. Special precaution needs to be taken while purchasing unbranded items or spurious goods from the rural market or desist from purchasing goods in sale when there is no guarantee or warranty of any defect or deficiency.

References

Consumer Protection Act, 1986.
Government of India, Ministry of Consumers Affairs, New Delhi.
Government of India, Ministry of Rural Development, New Delhi.

7
Impact of Education and Awareness on Rural Marketing in India

Anju Kumar and *Abhishek Srivastava*

Introduction

India is a land of diversity and about 70 per cent of the population lives in villages. These villages contribute in the economic development of the nation through the production of food grains, vegetables, fruits etc. Export of these agricultural commodities result in the generation of capital and earnings of foreign exchange. Indian rural market has a vast size and demand base. The villages are the backbone or the soul of India. With more than two-thirds of the Indian population living in rural areas, rural India reflects the very essence of Indian culture and tradition. A holistic development of India as a nation rests on a sustained and holistic development of rural India.

Rural marketing involves the process of developing, pricing, promoting, distributing rural specific product and a service leading to exchange between rural and urban market which satisfies consumer demand and also achieves organisational objectives. It is a two-way marketing process wherein the transactions can be:

1. *Urban to Rural:* It involves the selling of products and services by urban marketers in rural areas. These include: Pesticides, FMCG Products, Consumer durables etc.
2. *Rural to Urban:* Here, a rural producer (involved in agriculture) sells his produce in urban market. This may not be direct. There generally are middlemen, agencies, government co-operatives etc. who sell fruits, vegetables, grains, pulses and others.

3. *Rural to Rural:* These include selling of agricultural tools, cattle, carts and others to another village in its proximity.

Features of Indian Rural Markets

- *Large, Diverse and Scattered Market*: Rural market in India is large, and scattered into a number of regions. There may be less number of shops available to market products.
- *Major Income of Rural Consumers is from Agriculture*: Rural Prosperity is tied with agriculture prosperity. In the event of a crop failure, the income of the rural masses is directly affected.
- *Standard of Living and Rising Disposable Income of the Rural Customers*: It is known that majority of the rural population lives below poverty line and has low literacy rate, low per capita income, societal backwardness, low savings etc. But, the new tax structure, good monsoon, government regulation on pricing has created disposable incomes. Today the rural customer spends money to get value and is aware of the happening around him.
- *Traditional Outlook:* Villages develop slowly and have a traditional outlook. Change is a continuous process but most rural people accept change gradually. This is gradually changing due to literacy especially in the youth who have begun to change the outlook in the villages.
- *Rising Literacy Levels*: It is documented that approximately 45 per cent of rural Indians are literate. Hence, awareness has increase and the farmers are well-informed about the world around them. They are also educating themselves on the new technology around them and aspiring for a better life style.
- *Diverse Socio-economic Background*: Due to dispersion of geographical areas and uneven land fertility, rural people have disparate socio-economic background, which ultimately affects the rural market.
- *Infrastructure Facilities:* The infrastructure facilities like cemented roads, warehouses, communication system, and financial facilities are inadequate in rural areas. Hence, physical distribution is a challenge to marketers who have found innovative ways to market their products. As part of planned economic development, the government is making continuous efforts towards rural development. In this age of liberalisation, privatisation and globalisation, rural market offers a big attraction to the marketers to explore markets that are untapped.

Roadblocks of Indian Rural Markets

There are several factors that act as roadblocks and hamper the growth of rural markets. Marketers encounter a number of problems like dealing with physical distribution, logistics, proper and effective deployment of sales force and effective marketing communication when they enter rural markets. The major problems are listed below:

1. *Standard of Living*: The number of people below the poverty line is more in rural markets. Thus, the market is also underdeveloped and marketing strategies have to be different from those used in urban marketing.

2. *Low Literacy Levels:* The low literacy levels in rural areas leads to a problem of communication. Print media has less utility compared to the other media of communication.

3. *Low Per Capita Income:* Agriculture is the main source of income and hence spending capacity depends upon the agriculture produce. Demand may not be stable or regular.

4. *Transportation and Warehousing*: Transportation is one of the biggest challenges in rural markets. As far as road transportation is concerned, about 50 per cent of Indian villages are connected by roads. However, the rest of the rural markets do not even have a proper road linkage which makes physical distribution a tough task. Many villages are located in hilly terrains that make it difficult to connect them through roads. Most marketers use tractors or bullock carts in rural areas to distribute their products. Warehousing is another major problem in rural areas, as there is hardly any organised agency to look after the storage issue. The services rendered by Central Warehousing Corporation and State Warehousing Corporations are limited only to urban and suburban areas.

5. *Ineffective Distribution Channels*: The distribution chain is not very well organised and requires a large number of intermediaries, which in turn increases the cost and creates administrative problems. Due to lack of proper infrastructure, manufacturers are reluctant to open outlets in these areas. They are mainly dependent on dealers, who are not easily available for rural areas. This is a challenge to the marketers.

6. *Many Languages and Diversity in Culture:* Factors like cultural congruence, different behaviour and language of the respective areas make it difficult to handle the customers. Traits among the sales force are required to match the various requirements of these specific areas.

7. *Lack of Communication System:* Quick communication is the need

of the hour for smooth conduct of business, but, it continues to be a far cry in rural areas due to lack of communication facilities like telegraph and telecommunication systems etc. The literacy rate in the rural areas is rather low and consumer's behaviour in these areas is traditional, which may be a problem for effective communication.

8. *Spurious Brands:* Cost is an important factor that determines purchasing decision in rural areas. A lot of spurious brands or look-alikes are available, providing a low cost option to the rural customer. Many a time, the rural customer may not be aware of the difference due to illiteracy.

9. *Seasonal Demand:* Demand may be seasonal due to dependency on agricultural income. Harvest season might see an increase in disposable income and hence more purchasing power.

10. *Dispersed Markets:* Rural population is highly dispersed and requires a lot of marketing efforts in terms of distribution and communication. The entire points discussed above offer challenges to the marketer. He tries to uncover newer ways to market his product as he cannot afford to miss this huge opportunity existing in rural markets. He tries to identify solutions to these marketing problems.

Profile of Rural Consumers

Indian Market Research Bureau (IMRB) and National Council for Applied Economic Research (NCAER) have made available a few studies based on which rural consumers profile can be arrived at.

- *Literacy:* Twenty-three per cent of rural Indian population is literate and people are getting added to this list year after year. There are still some villages which are underdeveloped. Maximum education is primary school or in some cases high school. To this group the marketing promotional strategy to be adopted is demonstration of product features and advantages. Print media and posters do not make any impact.
- *Income:* An average rural consumer has a much lower income than his urban counterpart. The disposable income has increased in the recent years to considerable extent. In spite of this, the common traits of rural consumers are low purchasing power, low standard of living, low per capita income and low economic and social positions.
- *Density:* Rural population is scattered across 7 lakh villages. This implies that rural demand is scattered and urban demand is concentrated.

- *Influencers:* There are many reference groups in a village. These include teacher, doctor, *panchayat* members, health workers, bank manager and co-operative board workers. These influencers need to be kept in mind when a marketer decides on rural marketing.
- *Occupation:* The main occupation is agriculture. The size and ownership of land determines the basis for differentiation and consumption patterns.
- *Culture:* Rural consumers are traditional in their outlook. They associate faster with messages that match their cultural behaviour.
- *Language:* English is not a language of rural India. Hence, a marketer should aim for communication in the local language.
- *Media Habits:* Television, radio, video and theatre are some of the traditional media that a rural consumer identifies with.

The above are some of the factors that differentiate the rural consumer from his urban counterpart. A marketer has to decide on all the above parameters while designing a marketing plan.

Changing Profile of Rural Consumers

Rural consumers were generally illiterate and ignorant and lacked awarness about products and services available to them. This was due to their poor paying capacity. However, this scenario is slowly changing with the increase in literacy and disposable income. Multi-national companies are flocking rural markets to establish their brands as rural markets today are critical for every marketer be it for a branded shampoo or a television. With expansion of information and communication technology today a consumer in the rural area is quite literate about myriad products that are on offer in the market place. Media penetration has helped many companies to enter the rural markets and launch new products and services.

The rural youth is playing a far more significant role in influencing purchase decisions. They travel frequently out of the village and are the drivers of purchase decisions regarding FMCG products and durables. They may not be the end customers, but often are the people who influence the purchase of high value products and they decide which brands to choose. Penetration levels of consumer durables in the rural sector have risen dramatically in the last decade or so. Slowly even in rural areas women are becoming the decision makers as far as household goods are concerned.

Influencing the Rural Consumers

The biggest challenge today is to develop a scalable model of influencing the rural consumers' mind over a long period of time and still keep it going. This needs to be achieved in a limited or a reasonable budget and it is here that the marketers, who really understand rural markets and advertising agencies can make a difference and develop a scalable media/ communication model. The mass media has the drawback that the time, gap between the point of exposure and the time of purchase is long. Hence, it is difficult to use it in rural communication. The most important element in rural communications is that the marketer has to integrate three things in communication:

1. Exposure of a message,
2. Trial or demonstration, and
3. Final sale.

There is minimal brand loyalty in rural consumers mainly due to a bigger problem of brand recognition. A number of look alikes are available in the rural market. Through communication strategies, the challenge is to develop communication strategies that would help the rural consumers in recognising brands, logos, visuals, colours etc., so that, he or she actually buys the actual brand and not something else.

Awareness

A large part of rural India is inaccessible to conventional advertising media. Only 41 per cent rural households have access to TV. Enhancing awareness is another challenge in rural marketing. For a rural consumer, outing is confined to local fairs and festivals and TV viewing is confined to the state-owned Doordarshan. Use of branded products is treated as indulgence. Some companies have their own media firms to educate the consumers. Hindustan Lever has its own media company through which they organise promotional events. Godrej Consumer Products, which is trying to push its soap brands into the interior areas, uses radio to reach the local people in their language. Coca Cola uses a combination of TV, cinema and radio to reach the rural households. It has also used banners, posters and tapped all the local forms of entertainment. The media penetration in rural areas is only about 57 per cent. It has been seen that, two out of five Indians are unreached by any media: TV, Press, Radio and Cinema put together making *haats*, *mandis* and *melas* as the biggest opportunity to reach the consumers.

Promotion

Communication with rural consumers is mainly through the organised media. More number of rural consumers (~70%) has access to and listens to radio than any other form of communication. Rural communication can be through conventional media or through a non-conventional media. The most common conventional media include: Print, Cinema and Television. The non-conventional media include: Theatre, Posters, *Haats* and *Melas*. The conventional media has excellent reach, less expensive and create a better impact. But, at the same time, it is not customised to each village and also offers unnecessary coverage at times. Low literacy rates, culture, traditions, rural reach, attitudes and behaviour are the other problems in rural communication. An effective promotion plan should have a proper mix of media. This is very important to create an impact on the rural mind. Hence, talking to the customer in a language known to him, advertising the functional benefits and demonstrating the product go a long way in capturing the rural market.

The Indian rural market today accounts for only about Rs. 8 billion (53%—FMCG sector, 59% durables sale, 100% agricultural products) of the total *ad pie* of Rs. 120 billion, thus, claiming 6.6 per cent of the total share. So, clearly there seems to be a long way ahead. Hindustan Lever is the first company that comes to mind while thinking of rural marketing. Amul is another case in point of aggressive rural marketing. Some of the other corporates that are slowly making headway in this area are Coca Cola India, Colgate, Eveready Batteries, LG Electronics, Philips, BSNL, Life Insurance Corporation, Cavin Kare, Britannia and Hero Honda to name a few.

Conclusion

The future lies with those companies who see the poor as their customers says C.K. Prahalad in his book "*The Fortune at the Bottom of the Pyramid*". He clearly pinpoints on the raw fact that there is vast potential for profits in the rural markets. But a large number of businesses merely scratched the surface of the potential for profitable growth in rural India. And, they have made only a dent in the social infrastructure challenges that keep so much of India's population in the shadows. But, as Accenture's latest research reveals, there is now real momentum on both fronts. Whether it is LG's impressive market-creation activities, Hero Honda's customer outreach during village festivals or Thomson Reuters' mobile content services helping farmers to protect their crops, there are now abundant stories to demonstrate that businesses can and should make rural markets a central plank of their long-term strategy for growth. We believe that there is ample evidence to indicate that the best businesses help lift-up the lives of those less privileged.

In a nation where income disparities and differences in living standards are so stark, it is the obligation of those tapping rural markets to help boost education levels as well as awareness about the products thereby providing plethora of employment opportunities and to also think in terms of their long-term involvement in and contributions to the rural communities in which they work. The high-performance businesses will be those that deliberately learn from their experiences in India and quickly apply those experiences elsewhere, not only in other emerging markets but in highly mature markets as well. These are the companies that also understand that today's multi-polar world of dispersed economic power does not simply refer to the growing economic might of hubs such as Mumbai, Sao Paulo and Dubai. It also means that global investment and growth will come increasingly from rural regions and populations the world over.

References

Aarati Krishnan, "Sachet Revolution – Buy Less, Save More", www.blonnet.com, January 21, 2001.

Advertising in Rural India: Language, Marketing Communication, and Consumerism; Institute for the Study of Languages and Cultures of Asia and Africa, Tokyo University of Foreign Studies; Tokyo Press, Tokyo, Japan. 2000.

Aileen Ionesca-Somers and Ulrich Steger, "*Hindustan Lever – Leaping a Millennium*", IMD Case, 2002.

Ajita Shashidhar; *"Colas' Countryside Crusade"; The Hindu Business Line;* Financial Daily from THE HINDU Group of Publications; Thursday, July 3, 2003.

Anant Kulkarni, "*Another look at Rural marketing*" USP AGE, September 2004.

C.K. Prahalad and Stuart Hart, "*Strategies for the Bottom of the Pyramid*", www.wri.org.

Development Informatics: *Reaching the Rural India; Role of NIC*; D.C. Misra, Senior Technical Director and Head, Rural Development & Panchayati Raj

Divisions; National Informatics Centre; Dr. N. Vijayaditya, Director General, National Informatics Centre.

e m e r g i c. o r g; Rajesh Jain's Web log on Emerging Technologies, Enterprises and Markets.

G. Krishnan; *Challenges in Rural Marketing*; Strategic Marketing Forum.

Harish Bijoor; *A Market in Waiting; The Hindu Business Line*; Business Daily from THE HINDU Group of Publications; Thursday, August 17, 2006.

Hetal Adesara; *Making Inroads into the Hinterlands*; Indiantelevision.com's Perspectives; 23 October, 2004.

Hind Lever to Expand Project Shakti Reach", *Business Standard*, November 18, 2003.

HLL Aims for Rural Market", www.blonnet.com, May 10, 2000.

HLL Plans Rural Campaign to Reposition Lifebuoy – to Pitch on Hygiene Platform", www.blonnet.com, February 13, 2002.

HLL Rewrites Strategy for Greater Penetration of Rural Markets", www.domain-b.com, February 4, 2003.

HLL Takes Pepsodent Rural with a Vengeance", www.blonnet.com, October 12, 2002.

Ishita Ayan Dutt and Sambit Saha, "*Hind Lever in Plans to Raise Rural Spoils*", *Business Standard*, July 20, 2002.

Mohanbir Sawhney, McCormick Tribune, Professor of Technology, Kellogg School of Management, USA; *ITC's E-Choupal Movement* – Initiatives of Rural Development in India by ITC Limited.

Namrata Singh, "*10 per cent of HLL's Rural Sales from Project Shakti*", www.financial express.com, November 24, 2003.

Namrata Singh, "*Project Bharat to Push HLL's Rural Sales to 50 per cent by 2004*", www.expressindia.com, August 9, 1999.

P. Balakrishna; B. Sidharth; *Selling in Rural India*; *The Hindu Business Line*; Financial Daily from THE HINDU Group of Publications; Monday, February 16, 2004.

Preeti Mehra, (2001). "*HLL Doing a Grameen Bank – Leverages Microcredit to Tap Rural Market*", www.thehindubusinessline.com, May 21.

Purvita Chatterjee (2002). "*HLL Plans Rural Thrust for Toothpaste Brands*", *The Hindu Business Line*, February 21.

Ramkishen, Y., *New Perspectives on Rural Marketing*; Jaico Publishing House.

Rashmi Vasudeva (2003). "Empowering Women", *Deccan Herald*, June 15.

Rekha Balu (2001). "Strategic Innovation – Hindustan Lever Ltd.", *Fast Company, Issue 47*, June.

"*Rural Sales Drive Growth*", *Business Standard*, April 12, 2004.

Rustom S. Davar (1998). *Modern Marketing Management,* New Delhi: University Book Stall.

Shanthi Kannan (2002). "Rural Market: A World of Opportunity"; *The Hindu*; Online edition of India's National Newspaper; Thursday, October 11.

Sourav Majumdar and Namrata Singh (2004). "HLL Project Shakti to Cover All Rural India", *The Financial Express,* March 2.

Sushma (2005). "Indian Rural Marketing: Knowing the Potential", *Marketing Mastermind*, July.

Swati Bharadwaj (2004). "HLL Target 1 Cr Rural Consumers by '05", www.economictimes. indiatimes.com, January 30.

V.S. Ramaswamy and S. Nama Kumari (2002). *Marketing Management–Planning, Implementation and Control*, MacMillan India Limited.

Vinay Kamath (2003). "Where HLL's Shakti comes from", *The Hindu Business Line – Catalyst, May 29.*

Vinay Kamath (2004). "HLL's 'Shakti' to Help Partners in Rural India", www.thehindu businessline.com, April 26.

Websites: www.domain-b.com, www.hll.com.

SECTION II
Strengthening Consumer Movement: Role of NGOs and VCOs

8
Role of Consumer Organisations in Rural India

Action Agenda for Consumer Organisations

K. Venugopala Rao

Introduction

The Importance of Voluntary Consumer Organisations (VCOs) to increase consumer awareness and education in rural India is well recognised by the Department of Consumer Affairs, Government of India. In the report of working group on Consumer Protection, Twelfth Five Year Plan (2012-17) Vol. I of Department of Consumer Affairs, Ministry of Consumer Affairs, Food and Public Distribution, VCOs role is realised by mentioning that campaigns of the Ministry of Consumer Education and Awareness can be deepened by inducting VCOs in rural areas.[1] The report mentions that utility of VCOs in the area of consumer protection is second to none by virtue of their operational domain at the grassroots level. They are useful in many ways. They can effectively contribute in promotion and propagation of the programmes and schemes relating to consumer education and awareness especially in grassroots level. They can play the role of catalyst to mobilise the rural communities in organising awareness activities such as Consumer *Melas*, Road Shows, *Nukkad Nataks* etc. VCOs in rural areas are contributing to the overall efforts of the governments as per their capacity and in a useful way. Their role in helping the schools in spreading consumer education and in running consumer clubs is well recognised. Further, the national awareness programmes like "*Jago Grahak Jago*" requires to be launched aggressively at the district levels with the help of local VCOs for the most vulnerable categories of consumers such as: (1) Farmers and Rural Families, (2) Women and Children, (3) Students, and (4) Middle and Working Class.[2] The report also mentions that selected VCOs are identified as lead institutions to build capacity to produce materials which can be used by schools in consumer education activity. The government is thinking in terms of constituting multimedia committee for continuous monitoring of "*Jago Grahak Jago*" campaign by representation of members of VCOs. The government wants helplines at the state-level to run in partnership with VCOs. It wants consumer advisory centres in the district to run with the help of VCOs.[3] Thus, the role of Consumer Organisations or VCOs in the rural areas in raising consumer awareness and education and also consumer protection is very much required. Given this importance this chapter discusses aspects like what are Consumer Organisations, what roles they play in increasing consumer awareness and education to protect consumers, importance of Consumer Organisations in Rural India, what methods they adopt to increase the consumer education in rural areas and what should be an action agenda for them in the context of rural Indian society.

What are Consumer Organisations?

Consumer Organisations are those organisations which are formed and framed by consumers to fight for their rights, to create awareness among fellow consumers about their responsibility, to enhance consumer welfare through proper coordination with the government and institutions. The Consumer Organisations are formed: (1) to provide consumer education which includes their rights and responsibilities; (2) to share and exchange consumer related information; (3) to promote co-operation and collaboration of all activities related to consumer protection and interests; (4) to conduct research and product testing; (5) to ensure the basic needs such as Food, Housing, Health Care and Clean Environment to every consumer; (6) to develop the spirit and confidence among the consumers to represent their grievances; (7) to educate consumers to think critically to make their own decisions and to gain strength to resist hazardous trends and practices; (8) to work with communities to help them to solve their problems; (9) to provide counselling and guidance in case of grievances; and (10) to organise programmes of public interest.[4]

Role of Consumer Organisations

Given this nature of Consumer Organisations, theoretically they have two roles: (1) the organisations deal with individual consumers, handling consumer complaints and at times acting as a facilitator between the consumers and the service provider; and (2) the organisations focus on policy issues like economic, legal and social and environmental issues affected by various consumer policies of the government. In specific, the role of Consumer Organisations in India both in rural and urban areas has so far been the following:

- Consumer Organisations by organising consumers and encourage them to safeguard their rights are playing vital role to enhance the consumer consciousness.
- Consumer Organisations by exerting legal, moral and economic pressure on producers and providers, consumer consciousness is being enhanced.
- Consumer Organisations play the role of helping individual consumers to fight with malpractices of traders.
- Consumer Organisations by doing research on competitive testing are equipping the consumers with knowledge and awareness.
- Consumer Organisations are taking-up the issues of wrong business practices.
- Consumer Organisations are spreading the awareness especially in the villages by putting posters and stalls at the time of village fairs.
- Consumer Organisations spread the awareness by distributing the material of government at street corners and public places.
- Consumer Organisations help the cause of consumers by helping them to file cases in the consumer courts.[5]

Importance of Consumer Organisations in Rural India

The changing face of rural Indian economy in the entrenching rural market with the given consumer oriented Indian economy, the need for active role by Consumer Organisations in rural India becomes imminent to increase the consumer awareness and education for the rural masses and rural middle classes to protect themselves from unfair and unethical malpractices adopted in the market like black marketing, food alteration, under-weight, misleading advertisement, raising prices, false claims, lucky draws and zero per cent finance schemes etc.[6]

The role of Consumer Organisations becomes further more important because the rural market is widening due to pull factors like increasing rural population with increasing per capita income by nearly 50 per cent in the last 10 years, growing number of financial schemes, development of infrastructure like roads, power, tele-communications, and growing awareness of consumer goods. The push factors like saturated urban market, matching competitions, corporate social responsibility initiatives of the companies are also responsible for growing rural market.[7] The Fast Moving Consumer Goods (FMCG) and retail market is major market economy in rural India now.[8] It is in this context of changing rural economy and widening rural market, role of Consumer Organisations to protect consumers becomes important.

Methods to enhance Consumer Education and Awareness

The consumer movement in India has different phases. Initially, the movement was confined to inform and educate consumers on the quality of goods and services in 1960s. In 1970s and 1980s the movement by Consumer Organisations focused on problems of inflations, food adulteration and public distribution system. The period from 1981 to 1990 signifies the expansion and consolidation of the consumer movement of India especially after the enactment of Consumer Protection Act, 1986. The period from 1991 to 2000 A.D. and till now is being considered as a period that empowered the Indian consumer. The Consumer Organisations activated consumer education, product testing, product safety and promotion. Beginning with less than 10 organisations in 1965, 1996 established over 900 consumer organisations and today there are more than 2000 Consumer Organisations all over the country.[9] Some of the NGOs which are actively working in the area of consumer protection in rural India are VOICE, CERC, Common Cause, Upbhokta Sewa Samithi, Bihar, NOCER, Kerala, Consumer Protection Council, Visakhapatnam, Andhra Pradesh.

If we analyse, on the basis of the activities of Consumer Organisations in rural India, the following various methods/practices are adopted by the Voluntary Consumer Organisations in rural India to increase the awareness and education of rural consumers.

1. Through spreading the literature and publishing the literature, making CDs and Videos on consumer related problems.

2. Through conducting hunger strikes to attract the consumers to solve their problems after failing through all the efforts.
3. Through conducting workshops, seminars, street corner meetings and street plays.
4. Through forming women clubs among women to solve their consumer related problems.
5. Through consumer youth clubs to empower youth.
6. By forming consumer groups in all section of the society like students, women, employees, farmers etc.
7. Through forming student's centres, consumer clubs in schools and colleges.
8. Through providing platform for mediation for amicable solving various cases.
9. By making consumerism as part of subject in adult education centres and primary schools.
10. Through training the elected representatives' rite from panchayat level to district-level on consumer rights.
11. Through public relations departments of State Government, cultural programmes on consumer rights are organised.[10]

The changing face of rural India and complex problems of rural consumers in the context of expanding rural markets as consequence of globalisation, the roles and responsibilities of Consumer Organisations have become more challenging in this new milieu of rural consumer environment. The consumer organisations have to adopt the following action agenda to effectively safeguard the interest of consumers:

- Since, the consumers in the country are unaware of the existence of consumer forums to which they can make their grievances, there is a need to use the institution of PRIs at the village-level to solve their problems. The *gram panchayats* are there in all the villages which are the available Constitutional mechanism across the country spreading in all 627 districts. It is only through this Constitutional mechanism that the consumer movement can get a boost on consumer awareness. Hence, there is an urgent need to take initiatives by the Consumer Organisations to make the Central and State Department of Consumer Affairs to involve and make use of Panchayati Raj Institutions in various Programmes related to consumer awareness. The Consumer Organisations should pressurise the government to make necessary arrangements to be made to set-up consumer protection council at block and *gram panchayat* as well and to make the PRIs integral part of councils. PRIs are to be given the responsibility to coordinate with Consumer Affairs Department. A mechanism has to be worked out in terms of opening complaints handling cell in each of the *gram panchayat* office to dissolve the cases at local level instead of going to district consumer forums to reduce the burden of district forums.[11]

- Consumer Organisations in order to protect the rural farmers have to take-up consumer awareness programmes on fraudulent methods used by the traders while hoarding the fertilisers and black marketing them with high prices. The awareness also has to be increased on how the traders supply low quality seeds and pesticides. They have to impart knowledge of automobile industry to farmers so as not to be cheated while buying tractors etc.
- The governance system in India to provide food items to poor labour classes in India is generally fraught with loopholes and deficiencies and hence labour classes are made to suffer with problems while supplying food material through ration cards by dealers. Hence, Consumer Organisations have to educate rural labour classes about their rights to utilise their quota of essential commodities supplied by ration shops.
- According to the NCAER study, there are twice as many lower middle income households in rural areas as in the urban areas. At the highest income level there are 2.3 million urban households as against 1.6 million households in rural areas. Forty per cent of consumer packaged goods industry revenues are from rural India.[12] Hence, Consumer Organisations have to educate rural middle classes about the market exploitation such as selling in higher prices, expiry dates etc.
- The service providers of government in Health, Education, Power, Tele-Communications through PHCs, Anganwadis, Mid-Day Meals in Schools, Electricity Boards, and Telecoms suffer the rural people through improper governance. The Consumer Organisations have to raise the consciousness of consumers through awareness programmes on medical negligence and how to represent their problems to the government.
- Forty per cent of 826.93 million mobile phones are from rural India and half of the Indian Pharma market is from rural India.[13]

Hence, the consumers are to be guarded against the cheating practices of private mobile telephone companies and Pharma companies by Consumer Organisations.

- Insurance education and credit card utilisation education is must to rural consumers as Life Insurance Corporation of India (LIC) sold 55 per cent of its policies in rural areas in 2010; 41 million Kisan Credit Cards have been issued as against 22 million credit-*cum*-debit cards in urban areas.[14] Consumer Organisations have to help to increase insurance literacy and loan mechanism details.
- The Consumer Organisations have to raise the consciousness of consumer on how liquor traders increase the rates of liquors as against the rates fixed through the tenders.
- Consumer Organisations have to educate the rural and semi-urban consumers on how to file complaints in district courts, when the builders and contractors make deficiencies in the construction of houses.
- The Consumer Organisations should pressurise the Department of Consumer Affairs to launch awareness programmes in local languages to teach the consumers to avoid being duped by the traders.
- Since, the rural youth are open to fresh concepts as against their elderly family members, so, it is better for the Consumer Organisations to build awareness at a very young age.
- The Consumer Organisations have work through opinion leaders who play important roles in communicating a message to rural consumers.
- Consumer Organisations have to educate the rural masses to take a receipt after purchase and check the expiry date of the item.
- The Consumer Organisations have to protect the consumers from misleading advertisements especially of cosmetics and drug industry to take care of the welfare of the women and children. The rural middle class women have to be educated on Hall Mark Trade Practice of gold so as not to be exploited by gold traders in the country side.
- The Consumer Organisations have to proactively involved in State Commissioned Helpline centres and monitor the *"Jago Grahak Jago"* campaigns.
- Consumer Organisations have to impress the Department of Consumer Affairs to institute some more Awards to best

Consumer Organisations in recognising their services to enhance consumer awareness because so far Awards are given only by Bureau of Indian Standards.

- The environment protection has become big movement in the world and also in India. The consumer organisations through its activists have to make this movement as part of consumer movement and educate the rural masses sustainable consumption and production.
- The Consumer Organisations have to lobby with the government to start consumer advisory centres in the districts immediately as the government is also thinking on those lines.
- Report of working group on consumer protection, Twelfth Five Year Plan (2012-17) has mentioned that there is a need to make media campaign more broad based and dynamic by introducing a scheme to support experienced VCOs in running their own media units on different areas of specialisations like print, radio, TV, folk media etc., so as to integrate the campaign at Central and State/UT levels.[15] Hence, the Consumer Organisations have to work towards this direction.
- Report of working group on consumer protection, Twelfth Five year Plan (2012-17) has mentioned that there is a need to identify selected VCOs as lead institutions to build capacity to be able to produce materials which can be used by schools in consumer education activity.[16] So, Consumer Organisations have to work towards this direction.
- Report of working group on consumer protection, Twelfth Five Year Plan (2012-17) has mentioned that there is a need to keep the list of all genuine registered consumer organisations of all the states on the website of the Ministry. Hence, consumer organisations have to work with the Department of the Consumer Affairs and see that list is placed in the website which will be useful for all Consumer Organisations in the country.[17]

To conclude, taking into consideration the changing face of rural India and fast growing rural market, in future, consumer movement by Consumer Organisations has to focus in the rural areas by adopting the above action agenda.

Notes

1. Government of India, *Report of the Working Group on Consumer Protection*, Twelfth Five Year Plan (2012-17), Volume I, Department of Consumer Affairs, Ministry of Consumer Affairs, Food and Public Distribution, New Delhi, 2012, p.187.
2. *Ibid.*, p.119.
3. *Ibid.*, p.179.
4. Neelakanta, Bettadalli C., (2006), *The Wider Concept of Globalisation, VRF Series No. 408*, p. 3.
5. Report of the Group work submitted in 4th Training Programme for Heads/Presidents/Secretaries/Directors of NGOs/VCOs on Consumer Protection and Consumer Welfare (November 22-26, 2010).
6. Siwach, Meena and Dahiya, A.S. (2009), *J. Hum. Ecol.* 25(1), pp. 41- 44.
7. Bhasin, Rohit and Gupta, Akash, (2012), *A Week in Retail & Consumer*, p. 3.
8. Cheriyan, George (2012), *Rural Consumers and Role of Local Bodies in Consumer Protection*, p. 3.
9. Neelakanta, Bettadalli C. (2006), *op. cit.*, p. 8.
10. Report of the Group Work submitted in 4th Training Programme for Heads/Presidents/Secretaries/Directors of NGOs/VCOs on Consumer Protection and Consumer Welfare, IIPA, New Delhi, November 22-26, 2010.
11. Cheriyan, George (2012), *op. cit.*, p. 5.
12. *Ibid.*, p. 2.
13. Kumra, Gautam, (2007), *India Pharma 2015*, p. 14.
14. Cheriyan, George, (2012), *op. cit.*, p. 2.
15. Government of India, *Report of the Working Group on Consumer Protection*, *op. cit.*, p. 165.
16. *Ibid.*, p. 190.
17. *Ibid.*, p. 188.

References

Amarnatha, B. and Vijayudub, (2009). Brand Awareness in Rural Area– A Case Study of Fast Moving Consumer Goods in Chittoor District of Andhra Pradesh, *Asia-Pacific Journal of Social Sciences*, ISSN: 0975-5942, Vol.I (2), June-December, pp.230-240.

Balachandran, M.K. (2008). *Consumer Protection Act and Medical Profession*, New Delhi: IIPA.

Banerji, Pranab (2008). *Environment and Consumer*, Global Quest for Sustainable Consumption, New Delhi: IIPA.

Bhasin, Rohit and Gupta, Akash, (2012). "*A Week in Retail & Consumer*", July 16 to 20, Internal Publication, PwC, Kolkota, p. 3.

Cheriyan, George (2012). *Rural Consumers and Role of Local Bodies in Consumer Protection,* CUTS Publication.

Government of India, (2012). *Report of the Working Group on Consumer Protection, Twelfth Five Year Plan (2012-17),* Vol. I, Department of Consumer Affairs, Ministry of Consumer Affairs, Food and Public Distribution, New Delhi.

Kapoor, Sheetal (2008). *Consumer and the Market*, New Delhi: IIPA.

Kumra, Gautam, *et al.*, *India Pharma 2015, unlocking the Potential of the Indian Pharmaceuticals Market 2007*, p. 14.

Misra, Suresh and Sapna Chadah (2010). *Competition and Law,* Centre for Consumer Study, New Delhi: IIPA.

Neelakanta, Bettadalli C. (2006). An Assessment of the Need for Effective Consumer Organisations in India and Japan within *The Wider Concept of Globalisation, VRF Series No. 408*, March.

Report of the Group Work submitted in 4th Training Programme for Heads/ Presidents/Secretaries/Directors of NGOs/VCOs on *Consumer Protection and Consumer Welfare*, IIPA, New Delhi, November 22-26, 2010.

Siwach, Meena and Dahiya, A.S. (2009). Knowledge and Utilization of Consumer Education by Rural and Urban Women, *J. Hum. Ecol.*, 25(1), pp. 41-44.

9
Menace of Food Adulteration in Rural India

Need to Empower Women

Amit Kumar Singh and *Pankaj Kumar Singh*

Introduction

Food is essential for life. Unfortunately, the problem of food adulteration has become rampant in India. From raw-vegetables, fruits, meat item, milk, edible oil to sweets and spices, every single item is mixed with cheap and dangerous ingredients for the purpose of making more profit. Consumers not only are being cheated by these unethical and unfair trade practices, but the adulterated and impure food items are putting their life in danger and raising the risk of cancer, paralysis, liver, heart damage, body ache, anaemia, abortion, abnormality of skin and eyes and many more diseases. In a recent report, the Public Health Foundation of India attributed 80 per cent of all premature deaths to contaminated food and water. The greed of unethical businessmen who are involved in the adulteration activities, voraciously exploiting the people, both from the top to grassroots. The market is literally overflowing with adulterated food items. It is very difficult for the consumers to protect themselves from adulterated food.

In recent years, the purchasing power of the Indian consumers has increased considerably which has given rise to many choices. As a result of this and also due to the impact of globalisation the eating habits and pattern of the consumers has considerably changed. Now, consumers are becoming more and more demanding. They tend to experiment with new variety of food products. To exploit this situation more-and-more food chains, companies and businessmen are entering into the food market with the intention to make huge profits. While some of them are making improvements in production, processing and packaging techniques in the food industry, many of them are taking shortcut routes. They are reducing the quality of food commodities through addition of lower quality substance and/or removing vital elements from the food commodities. Now-a-days, adulteration is a health menace. It is a social evil. Food adulteration takes place in many forms: mixing, substitution, concealing the quality, putting-up decomposed foods for sale, misbranding or giving false labels and addition of toxicants.

This chapter focuses on how knowledge enhancement and skill development helps rural consumers especially women in minimising adulteration practices in rural areas. It is based on a case study which has been carried out in the five districts of Tamil Nadu, where rural women especially the members of Self-Help Groups (SHG) have been trained to detect adulteration in food items. The outcome of the training programme was impressive and this chapter will discuss in detail the importance of such type of awareness programmes in enhancing the skills of the women in fighting the menace of food adulteration.

What is Food Adulteration?

Before we analyse the ground realities let us come to a common understanding of What is Adulteration of Food? It is commonly defined as "the addition or subtraction of any substances to or from food, so that, the natural composition and quality of food is affected. At some times food items are adulterated unintentionally or naturally. Food additives may be classified into two categories:

1. *Intentional food adulteration*: It includes colouring agents, flavouring agents, preservatives, acidity imparting agents etc.
2. *Unintentional food adulteration*: This category is strictly speaking, contaminants, incidental through packing, processing steps, farming practices or other environmental conditions."

Now-a-days intentional food adulteration is quite more prevalent in many places in the country. It can be found from the simple stones in rice to the more harmful brick in chilli powder. In general, any article of food is adulterated if:

1. If any inferior or cheaper substance has been substituted wholly or in part.
2. If any constituent of the article has been wholly or in part abstracted.
3. If the article has been prepared, packed or kept under insanitary conditions.
4. If the article consists in part filthy, rotten, decomposed or diseased animal or vegetable or is infested with insects.
5. If the article is obtained from diseased animal.
6. If the article contains any poisonous ingredient.
7. If the article has unprescribed colouring substance or the colouring substance is in excess of the prescribed limits.

Scale of Food Adulteration Problem in India

Food Adulteration occurs in rural as well as urban areas. Studies have shown that the percentage of adulterated food in various parts of the country varies from 30 to 35 per cent. The most frequently used food adulterant is colouring matter. Colour is used in many food products such as milk products, confectionery (including Indian sweetness), soft drinks, alcoholic beverages, tea and spices. Studies have also shown that a wide range of foodstuffs from urban and rural markets exceeds the permissible level on these permitted colours. Apart from this the problem of adulteration of mustard oil stills exists as evidenced by dropsy at Delhi in 1998, Gwalior in 2000, Kannauj in 2002 and Lucknow in 2005.

According to Dr. Arvind Shenoy, an expert in food analysis and testing as much as 25-30 per cent of edibles sold in the market are intentionally adulterated. It is believed that 90 per cent of the vanaspati being sold in the market violates the specifications of the Prevention of Food Adulteration Act (PFA). During festival seasons, tons of adulterated sweets, bakery products, dairy products, and processed foods have to be thrown away by shopkeepers after the raids of health officials. For example, in September-October 2011 the Punjab, Department of Health and Family Welfare seized 2,000 litres of synthetic milk in Patiala. In Chandigarh, the administration destroyed 30 tons of sweets and this 30 tons means 30,000 boxes of one kilo each.

Sreedevi Lakshmi Kutty says that the rampant and indiscriminate use (out of ignorance and desperation) of toxic pesticides and synthetic fertilisers is an unfortunate reality in Indian agriculture. Many pesticides used in agriculture are endocrine disrupters (that interfere with the hormone system) or carcinogens (cancer causing) or mutagens (causes change in genetic material) or cholinesterase inhibitors (that interfere with an enzyme required for the proper functioning of the nervous system), teratogens (capable of causing birth defects) or embryo toxins. This makes many of the food items that come to our table toxic and unsafe and causes enormous damage to the health of the food consumers and farmers as well. The tragedy in India is that we continue to use at least 67 pesticides that are banned in one or more countries.

Table 9.1: National Survey on Adulteration of Milk: An Overview

Per cent of Sample Found Adulterated	*States and UTs*
Below 20	Goa, Tamil Nadu, Andhra Pradesh, and Puducherry,
20-40	Karnataka, and Kerela
40-60	Assam, Madhya Pradesh, Dadra & Nagar Haveli, Himachal Pradesh, and Chandigarh
60-80	Arunachal Pradesh, Delhi, Haryana, Maharashtra, and Rajasthan
80-100	Bihar, Chhattisgarh, Daman & Diu, Gujarat, J & K, Jharkhand, Manipur, Meghalaya, Mizoram, Nagaland, Odisha, Punjab, Sikkim, Tripura, Uttarakhand, Uttar Pradesh and West Bengal.

Source: Food Safety and Standard Authority of India.

In 2011, Food Safety and Standards Authority of India conducted a national survey to ascertain the quality of milk and identify different type of adulteration in the liquid milk throughout the country. Just 31.5 per cent of the samples tested (565) conformed to the FSSAI standards while the rest 1,226 (68.4%) failed the test. In the case of Delhi of the 71 samples randomly taken for testing by the Food Safety Standards Authority of India (FSSAI), 50 were found to be contaminated with glucose and skim milk powder (SMP), which is usually added to milk in the lean season to enhance volumes. Across the country, 68.4 per cent of the samples were found contaminated with detergent, fat and even urea, besides the age-old dilution with water. Detergent found in over 8 per cent of tested milk.

Measures to Control Food Adulteration

It is not that Government of India has not made efforts to control and stop the problem of food adulteration in India. There are certain laws made especially to deal with different food products and standards, such as (i) Agricultural Produce Act; (ii) Agmark specifications; (iii) Prevention of Food Adulteration Act (PFA), 1954; (iv) Meat Food Products Order MFPO, 1973; (v) Bureau of Indian Standards Act, 1986; (vi) Environmental Protection Act, 1986; (vii) Milk Products Order, 1992; (viii) Food Products Order (FPO), 1995; (ix) Essential Commodities Act, 1995; and (x) Vegetable Oil Products Order, 1998. Among them the Prevention of Food Adulteration Act is very important. It was enacted with the objective of ensuring pure and wholesome food to the consumers and to protect them fraudulent and deceptive trade practices. The Prevention of Food Adulteration Act was amended in 1964, 1976, and the lately in 1986 to make the Act more stringent. Though, the Act provides for protection against adulteration or contamination of food that may have deleterious effects on consumer's health, but somehow we have been failed to solve this problem. Till now, we have neither been able to engage appropriate number of well qualified Food Inspectors, Public Analysts, Food (Health) Authorities, Local (Health) nor been able to established quality food testing laboratory at grassroots level.

For a common man it is very difficult to detect the incidence and also the extent of adulteration in food items. The Indian consumers, particularly in the rural areas have become accustomed to live with adulteration, mainly due to ignorance, lack of awareness and choice. Therefore, there is a need to build the capacity of the consumers as well as the community to fight this menace. Educating the consumers about food safety and hygiene, food adulteration and the way to detect food adulteration is the best way to protect them. In this regard, Food Safety and Standard Authority of India has published and circulated a simple and quick test which can easily performed to ascertain the purity of a food product "Quick Test for some Adulterants in Food" to protect the consumers in the country against food adulteration. Unfortunately, it has also not been able to reach to the consumers at local level.

To meet these challenges consumers must arm themselves against these problems since, they are not automatically protected by the working of the market. Therefore, a consumer's best defence is knowledge of his/her rights as a consumer and of the remedies which exist to resolve these problems when they occur. "Knowledge and awareness about adulterated foods, laws and its rights related to adulterated food is crucial in a society where technology heightens opportunities for perpetrators of fraud deception and misrepresentation." The various stakeholders in the consumer protection movement need to workout a strategy to address this problem. Creating awareness and educating the consumers will go a long way in helping the consumers to understand what constitutes food adulteration and how they can save themselves from this.

Food Adulteration in Rural Areas

In India about 70 per cent of the population lives in about 6,40,867 lakh villages. There are states like Uttar Pradesh, Madhya Pradesh, Bihar and Odisha, where rural population varies from 80 to 90 per cent. Though, the level of poverty along with the level of illiteracy is very high in rural areas, rural market contributes to 56 per cent of the country's GDP. But now up to some extent the tempo of development is accelerating in rural India which is increasing the purchasing power its inhabitants. Therefore, for manufacturers, traders and retailers, rural markets have become new opportunities which are opening-up for most of the FMCG products. As mentioned earlier, the percentage of poor and uneducated people is still very high in rural areas; hence, the rural consumers are still purchasing loose products. They prefer unbranded products rather than the branded variety.

Even today 50-60 per cent of edible oils are sold in loose form and loose oils are prone to adulteration. Despite this the Government of India has in 1998 issued directions to all the State Governments to implement compulsory packing of edible oils to avoid adulteration and related health problems. So far, no State Government has implemented the order. Almost every household, hotel and restaurant uses loose spices, vanaspati ghee, tea, milk, pulses, rise, flour etc. and most of these items are prone to adulteration. Quality control of these items is of prime concern from the point of view of personal and public health. Roday (2002) in his study found that in small cities of Maharashtra like, Jalgaon, Nanded and Jalna the percentage of adulteration was very high compared to Nagpur, Pune, Amravati, Solapur etc. According to the report of Food Technology and Quality Control Department, over 66 per cent of the mustard samples were found contaminated with Argemone Mexicana. Similarly, 27 per cent of vegetable ghee in the market was contaminated due to use of low quality raw-materials.

Women can make a Difference

It is highly unlikely that more legislation or increasing fines and jail terms alone will help reduce adulteration, particularly given the corruption that exists in the enforcement area and the low conviction rate. Greater consumer vigilance and action alone can help improve the situation. But, such efforts are not fruitful unless consumers themselves are aware of their rights and responsibilities. Under these circumstances, consumer literacy is the need of the hour, with special attention to low income groups particularly living in the rural areas who suffer the most.

There are a number of studies conducted which reveals that housewives (home-makers) are the actual buyers for food in the family. Pande (2000) reveals that home-makers take independent decision in all the areas of food buying except financial aspect. Studies have also highlighted that "availability of money resource and availability of the product" in the market were the most important factors, whereas "food habit" and "nutritional requirements" were the least important factors while buying a product. On the other hand low income group (LIG)-home-makers preferred ration stores, and independent stores for the groceries and miscellaneous items. For the selection of stores low income group-home-makers gave more importance to credit facilities, lowest price and location of the store. Majority of the housewives (home-makers) from low income groups collect all information from friends and neighbours. Among housewives (home-makers) retail shops are more used than wholesale shops for purchasing grains, monthly purchasing was most common among the employed and unemployed home-makers for grains and grocery.

If we want this movement to grow, more women will have to come in. Consumer movement has to move towards pro-poor, pro-rural and pro-women. Although efforts have been made to detect the percentage of food adulteration in a number of big and small cities, none of the study deals with knowledge and awareness of women (home-maker) about food adulteration. That is why it is necessary to generate awareness among the housewives (home-makers) about the existing food adulteration practices of the retailers and manufacturers and equip them with simple household test for detecting adulteration.

Case Study – Empowering Housewives to Detect Adulteration in Food

It is well said that education is one of the most important tool which leads to economic, social and political empowerment of women. By imparting training and knowledge to women, we can make them active partners in the consumer movement. There is no doubt that empowered women can transform the developmental scenario of the nation. Women are the nation's most precious human resource which needs to be explored to its fullest extent for creating awareness particularly in the rural areas. In view of that on an experiment basis, Department of Consumer Affairs, Government of India has organised several training programme with the help of an NGO from Chennai to build the capacity of the housewives of select districts of Tamil Nadu to detect adulteration in food items.

The expected outcome was that housewives would be trained and made aware about food adulteration, food safety, PFA Act and the Consumer Protection Act. For detection of the adulteration in the food items they were provided a kit known as Annam Spot Test Kit, which was especially meant to detect food adulteration at the household-level. It was based on the presumption that the best way to prevent wilful adulteration is to create a people's movement through awareness and social consciousness. The training programmes focused on knowledge enhancement and skill development. The methodology used in the programmes was mainly lecture and demonstration method. Women participants were taught about the issues like, health and nutrition, food adulteration and food contamination, food hygiene and safety, detection of food adulteration using the Annam Spot Test Kit, Consumer Protection Act and Rules, PFA Act, label reading and detection of adulterants. The women participants were required to take this message and skill down to the village level and also educate their neighbours, fellow relatives and other members of the villagers.

The authors were a part of the research team of IIPA that evaluated the outcome and impact of the pilot project on behalf of Department of Consumer Affairs, Government of India. The training programmes were conducted in 11 districts of Tamil Nadu. However, due to time constrain the study was conducted in 5 districts of the State covering all the regions of the State. Some of the findings of the study have been analysed and presented here in the following sections. The objective is to see as to what extent the trained housewives could spread awareness and educate the villages about food safety measures and detect adulteration in food items. The other objective was to assess the benefit of the training programmes organised to educate the housewives about food adulteration and other issues related to food safety.

Awareness Programmes: Level of Satisfaction

Trainees' satisfaction level has been found to be one of the factors that affects the quality and overall effectiveness of the programme. For our purpose trainees satisfaction refers to the attraction, pride, or positive feeling that the trainees develop towards the programmes or the institution that organises the programmes. The housewives who were trained are largely satisfied by the training that they received. The overall majority of 70 per cent of them were satisfied to a large extent, 29 per cent were satisfied to some extent (Table 9.2). District-wise analysis reveals that in Thanjavur only 40 per cent of the respondents were satisfied to a large extent and majority of them (55%) were satisfied to some extent.

Table 9.2: District-wise Analysis of Satisfaction Level

Districts	*Housewives' Satisfaction Level*		
	Satisfied to large extent	*Satisfied to some extent*	*Not at all*
Thiruvallur	77.0	23.0	0.0
Cuddalore	74.0	26.0	0.0
Thanjavur	40.0	55.0	5.0
Madurai	85.0	15.0	0.0
Tuticorin	74.0	26.0	0.0
Total	**70.0**	**29.0**	**1.0**

Source: Field Survey conducted by CCS, IIPA, 2010.

Follow-up Programmes at Village Level

The objective of imparting training to the housewives was that they would organise follow-up programmes in their community/village to create awareness among the residents regarding food adulteration and also test food items for adulteration.

The survey results show that only 68 per cent of the trainees organised follow-up programmes and 32 per cent did not organise any such programme. Only 30 per cent of the respondents organised follow-up programmes in Thanjvur district while 65 per cent did so in Madurai district. In Tuticorin district 85 per cent of the respondents had organised follow-up programmes to educate people in their community/village level. Unless follow-up programmes are organised it will not have the multiplier effect as far as awareness is concerned.

Table 9.3: Responses on Conducting Follow-Up Programmes

Districts	*Yes*	*No*
Thiruvallur	75.0	25.0
Cuddalore	85.0	15.0
Thanjavur	30.0	70.0
Madurai	65.0	35.0
Tuticorin	85.0	15.0
Total	**68.0**	**32.0**

Source: Field Survey conducted by CCS, IIPA, 2010.

Usefulness of ANNAM SPOT KIT

Table 9.4: Trainee's Opinion on Usefulness of Annam Spot Test Kit

Districts	*Trainees Opinion*	*Usefulness of Annam Spot Test Kit*			
		Simple and handy	*Useful in testing adulterated and unhygienic consumable food items*	*Worthiness of buying or having it*	*Useful at village level*
Thiruvallur	Very useful	80.0	85.0	90.0	90.0
	Up to some extent	20.0	15.0	10.0	10.0
Cuddalore	Very useful	90.0	70.0	80.0	70.0
	Up to some extent	10.0	30.0	20.0	30.0
Thanjavur	Very useful	65.0	55.0	70.0	55.0
	Up to some extent	35.0	45.0	30.0	45.0
Madurai	Very useful	95.0	85.0	95.0	90.0
	Up to some extent	5.0	15.0	5.0	0.0
Tuticorin	Very useful	85.0	90.0	85.0	15.0
	Up to some extent	15.0	10.0	15.0	85.0
Total	**Very useful**	**83.0**	**77.0**	**84.0**	**64.0**
	Up to some extent	**17.0**	**23.0**	**16.0**	**34.0**

Source: Field Survey conducted by CCS, IIPA, 2010.

The kit has been developed to test food adulteration on the spot. The next question was to what extent was the kit useful. The Trainees found the Annam Spot Test Kit to be very useful in detection of food adulteration. Eighty three per cent of the respondents found it to be very useful and only 17 per cent found it to be useful to some extent. They found it to be useful because it was simple and easy to handle. Seventy seven per cent felt that it was useful in testing adulterated and unhygienic food items. Eighty four per cent of the respondents replied that it was worth buying and 64 per cent of them said it was useful at the village level, where the level of food adulteration was high.

Change in Buying Behaviour of the Trainees

After undergoing the training, the trainees buying behaviour has undergone a perceptible change, which they revealed during the discussions. Before the training as they were not aware about food adulteration, label reading etc., and they did not bother much on these issues while making a purchase. However, after the training they seem to be aware about basics as far as purchasing a product in concerned.

Sixty seven per cent of them said that they find out the available options about the product (Graph 9.1). Seventy two per cent of them also check the maximum retail price, 78 per cent of the trainees check the quality of the product before they purchase, 78 per cent of them check the expiry date, 72 per cent always check the contents and 69 per cent always find out about the nutritional value of the product. Standardisation marks are quite popular and 83 per cent of the respondents see the standardisation mark on the product to ensure its quality. As far as the bill/receipt are concerned 78 per cent of them always demand bill/receipt. However, during the discussions it was also revealed that many times the shop keepers make an issue and do not give the bill. This is because consumers by and large do not demand the bill so if someone demands a bill they do not like it. This culture needs to be changed both the consumers as well as the shop-keepers need to be sensitised on this issue. This can only be done through awareness programmes and active participation of all stakeholders in the consumer movement.

Reaction of Business Community

It is a general perception that the business community in the area does not appreciate the efforts of the VCOs in educating the consumers. The

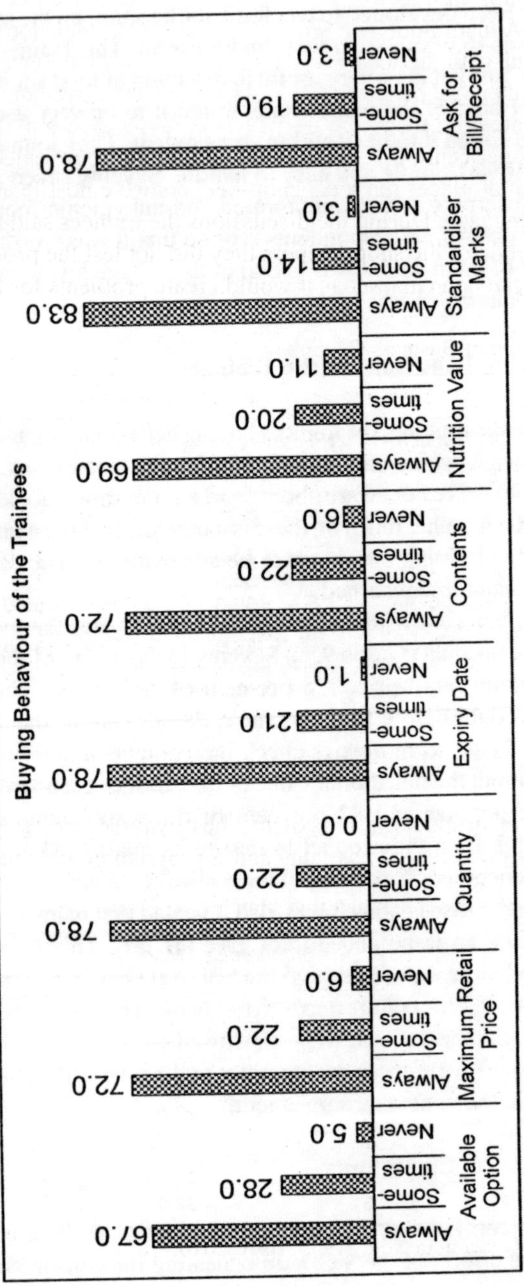

Graph 9.1: Consumer Alertness before buying the food items

Source: Field Survey Conducted by CCS, IIPA, 2010.

same is true in this case as well as they were hostile to such initiatives. The use of the Annam Spot Test Kit by the trainees in their locality has not found favour with the local business community/shop-keepers. The trainees revealed that 37 per cent of the business community/shop-keepers did not cooperate with them and 36 per cent cooperated only to some extent. Only 27 per cent of them cooperated. It was also revealed by the respondents that at places the local shop-keepers were hostile and even used abusive language. During the discussions the trainees said that due to negative attitude of the shop-keepers they did not test the product for adulteration in the open market as it would create problems for them.

Table 9.5: Reaction of Business Community

Districts	*Reaction of Business Community*		
	Very much cooperative	*Cooperative up to some extent*	*Not at all*
Thiruvallur	10.0	25.0	65.0
Cuddalore	20.0	55.0	25.0
Thanjavur	40.0	35.0	25.0
Madurai	50.0	35.0	15.0
Tuticorin	15.0	30.0	55.0
Total	**27.0**	**36.0**	**37.0**

Source: Field Survey conducted by CCS, IIPA, 2010.

Awareness about Standard Marks

Standarisation of products is one of the best ways of protecting the consumers. The government has launched a programme to standardise

Table 9.6: Awareness about Standardised Mark

Districts	*Standardised Mark*			
	ISI	*AGMARK*	*FPO*	*Veg/ Non-Veg Mark*
Thiruvallur	90.0	80.0	70.0	40.0
Cuddalore	80.0	65.0	10.0	30.0
Thanjavur	70.0	60.0	20.0	35.0
Madurai	90.0	70.0	55.0	30.0
Tuticorin	60.0	60.0	5.0	30.0
Total	**78.0**	**67.0**	**32.0**	**33.0**

Source: Field Survey conducted by CCS, IIPA, 2010.

products to ensure its quality and reliability. As far as awareness about the standardisation marks is concerned 88 per cent knew about the ISI mark, 67 knew AGMARK, 40 per cent were aware about the Veg/Non-veg marking and surprising only 32 per cent knew about FPO mark. It is very low in Cuddalore, Thanjavur and Tuticorin districts which are very surprising as FPO relates to food product.

Awareness about PFA Act etc.

The awareness level among the trainees about the Food Adulteration Act is high. Seventy five per cent of them are aware about the PFA Act, 58 per cent knew the address of local Food Testing Laboratory, 67 per cent are aware about the Penalty Structure under the PFA Act and 67 per cent are aware about the Food Safety and Standards Authority of India.

Table 9.7: Awareness about Aspect of Prevention of Food Adulteration

Districts	*PFA Act*	*Address of Local Food Testing Laboratory*	*Penalty Structure under PFA Act*	*Aware about FSSAI*
Thiruvallur	50.0	30.0	75.0	50.0
Cuddalore	60.0	75.0	75.0	60.0
Thanjavur	65.0	75.0	55.0	50.0
Madurai	75.0	60.0	70.0	65.0
Tuticorin	70.0	50.0	60.0	60.0
Total	**64.0**	**58.0**	**67.0**	**57.0**

Source: Field Survey conducted by CCS, IIPA, 2010.

Awareness about CP Act

The Consumer Protection Act was enacted in 1986 and a number of studies have revealed that the level of awareness has been low more so in the rural areas. However, as a result of the training the trainees are aware about the Act. One of the objectives of the project was to create awareness about the Consumer Protection Act. The survey data reveals that sixty per cent of the trainees are aware about the Act and during the interaction they could enumerate a number of provisions of the Act. Sixty eight per cent of the trainees could state as to who is a consumer as defined in the CP Act. The district-wise variation is quite negligible as far as the level of awareness is concerned.

Table 9.8: Awareness about Consumer Protection Act

Districts	*Aware about CP Act*		*Who is Consumer*	
	Yes	*No*	*Yes*	*No*
Thiruvallur	65.0	35.0	70.0	35.0
Cuddalore	55.0	45.0	75.0	45.0
Thanjavur	50.0	50.0	65.0	50.0
Madurai	70.0	30.0	75.0	30.0
Tuticorin	65.0	35.0	70.0	35.0
Total	**61.0**	**39.0**	**71.0**	**39.0**

Source: Field Survey conducted by CCS, IIPA, 2010.

Conclusion

Food adulteration is common in India, whether it is urban or rural area, no place is spared and no food item is left. Most worrying factor is the growing prevalence of such practices in rural India where more than half of the people are already in distress condition. They are not well equipped, both economically as well as educationally, to fight with the unethical practices of the mighty business class. Therefore, we have to think about the newer strategies to fight with the threat of adulteration and contamination in food products. In this, we have to focus on our women consumers, who not only constitute 50 per cent of the total consumer population, but also make 80 per cent of all purchase decisions. We have to make them aware about the type of malpractices that is being practiced in rural areas. The strategies for women's empowerment should cut across the welfare efficiency and equity approaches and ensure that women are accorded opportunities and their contributions put to good use by society. Therefore, the focus must be on the empowerment and capacity building of women, especially rural women so as to build public awareness about the hazardous effects of consumption of adulterated food.

Since, government cannot do this work itself and cannot reach to the every person at the grassroots, here the job of consumer organisations becomes very important. This study finds that they can play a crucial role in advocacy of food safety, quality, nutritional and related matters and assist greatly in providing education and information. Efforts should be made to subsidies the kits with the financial assistance from the Central/ State Governments so that more consumers could purchase it. At present the cost of detection kit is a deterrent. The business community/shop-keepers of the locality should also be sensitised. This can be done through rallies/pamphlets with the active involvement of the local VCOs working in the area.

References

Centre for Consumer Studies, (2010), *Evaluation Report of Phase II the Project on Workshop*-cum-*Training Programme for Housewives on Detection of Adulteration in Foods by CONCERT*, Chennai.

Clean India: Preventing Food Adulteration, http://www.cleanindia.org/resoucewatch/foodaduteration.htm

Devendra Sharma: http://devinder-sharma.blogspot.in/2011/10/india-where-food-adulteration-is-most.html

Food Safety Authority of India: *State Milk Survey*, 2011.

Food Safety Issues – Residues, Contaminants: Scenario in India, (2012): http://foodsafetyauthorityindia. blogspot.in/2012/01/food-safety-issues-residues.

Gupta, N., and Panchal, P., (2009), *Extent of Awareness and Food Adulteration Detection in Selected Food Items, Purchased by Home-Makers*.

Kutty, Sreedevi Lakshmi (2012). *Is Our Food Safe*? http://www.yentha.com/news/view/5/is-our-food-safe?

Money Life: http://www.moneylife.in/article/25-30-of-the-food-items-in-india-are-intentionally-adulterated-says-dr-arvind-shenoy/27527.html

Patel, Nishika (2010). *Slow Poisoning*, July 3, 2010, *Times of India*, http://indiatoday.intoday.in/story/slow-poisoning/1/103954.html

Roday, S. (2002). *Food Hygiene and Sanitation*, New Delhi: Tata McGraw Hill Publication Ltd., pp. 248-49.

Shakuntala Manay, N. & M. Shadaksharaswamy (2005). *Food – Facts and Principles*, New Delhi: New Age International (P) Ltd., p. 448.

10
Role of Civil Society Organisations in Promoting Awareness among Rural Consumers
Challenges and Strategies

Sapna Chadah

Introduction

Globalisation, liberalisation and privatisation have enabled the entry of several private traders, including large multinationals, who have transformed the Indian economy into a vibrant, rapidly growing consumer market. They have flooded the market with different kinds of goods and services, substantially effecting and changing the purchasing pattern of the consumers. The rural markets, which were earlier ignored by most of the big international market players, are now being seen as a land of great business opportunity. As the disposable income of the masses is growing, more and more corporate houses are entering into the rural markets with their new goods and products. Due to this marketing for rural consumers is becoming more complex.

In a country like India, where a substantial number of the rural people are living below the poverty line (BPL), having high level of unemployment and poor literacy level; consumer awareness continues to remain low. Several studies have shown that rural consumers are generally ignorant and they are also unorganised. Under these circumstances, the sellers or the manufacturers, exploit the consumers. Though, the consumers in India have been provided with various safety measures against their exploitation, still the sellers and producers are hoarding and black-marketing the essential goods, involving economic corruption and frequently cheating the consumers. Rural markets are full of sub-standard goods and duplicity of branded goods is another major problem in rural areas. Spurious goods are very common in these markets. As there is no check on production and sale of such products in the rural markets, many consumers of these goods and products also sustain injuries. The expansion of service sector has added to the problem. Services like insurance, banking, electricity, medical have expanded in the rural areas without any checks and balances and the rural consumers continue to be exploited by the service providers. Deficiency in services is a major area of concern. Spurious drugs are causing major health hazards. The vulnerable sections are generally women, children and farmers. It is common to find that farmers are supplied defective seeds, adulterated pesticides and other commodities. The expansion of mass media has further given impetus to consumerism in the rural areas.

Consumer Education and Awareness

As today the consumers operate in an increasingly complex marketplace and are faced with increasing amounts of information and an expanding choice of complex products and services, the need for consumer education has increased over time. As a consequence they are more exposed to fraud and require a wider range of skills and knowledge than ever before. Consumer education is a potent tool for empowering consumers as it equips consumers with information and skills necessary to meet challenges posed by the markets. Through education, consumers obtain information that protects and empowers them and makes them aware of their rights and responsibilities and helps to ensure their welfare. Consumer education improves the position of the consumers in the marketplace, help them make informed choice and thereby enhance their welfare. It also contributes to the well-functioning of the markets by promoting effective competition. It is thus in the common interest of governments, consumers and businesses to empower the individual consumer as much as possible with an awareness of his/her rights, knowledge of how to defend himself against various pitfalls and to cope with the subsequent consequences, as well as the ability to act proactively in the marketplace. According to Wells and Atherton consumer education can be defined as:

> "... a process of gaining skills, knowledge and understanding needed by individuals in a consumer society such that they can make full use of consumer opportunities presented in today's complex marketplace."[1]

As a tool for empowerment, consumer education is central to make markets work well for consumers. Business can reap real benefits from an active involvement in consumer education, improved communication with more discerning customers and quicker, easier, and less expensive solutions to problems where they arise. For this the consumer protection law should set minimum standards for quality and safety and ensure that consumers have access to updated and quality information. Thus, to be effective, consumer education initiatives should be focused on clear priorities and targeted at those most in need. By deciding priorities in this way, consumer education can bring real benefits for vulnerable and socially excluded consumer by offering the opportunity to gain valuable life skills.

There is general agreement among those working in the consumer field that all people should be skilled and informed consumers, so that, they can understand their rights and, as importantly, their responsibilities, within an increasingly complex market place. There is also broad agreement as to the core skills required to achieve this among key organisations involved in educating consumers. The problem occurs in deciding where and how consumer education should take place. Therefore, the various stakeholders in the consumer protection movement need to work out a strategy to address the problems of the consumers. Creating awareness and educating the consumers will go a long way in helping the consumer to understand what constitutes consumer protection, what is the need to know about one's rights and how to redress one's grievances, if anything goes wrong. Moreover, an educated and informed consumer will be able to take a rational decision while buying a product or availing a service.

Need for Awareness among Rural Consumers

A change in consumption patterns and access to communication media have made rural market a vital cog in the sales-growth wheel, especially with the plateau in demand for many categories of products and services in the urban markets. In spite of increasing number of rural consumers, provisions for consumer protection and welfare are often based on the general standard and circumstances of those living in big cities and towns. Although consumers as a whole are in an equal bargaining position, there are certain recognizable groups which are disadvantaged in more ways than the others. Disadvantaged consumers are those who are less able to assert their rights and rural consumers comprise one such group. Rural consumers remain disadvantaged as their right to information, choice, redress, and consumer education are not sufficiently fulfilled. Consequently, such consumers need support in maintaining their rights, so that, they can bargain equally with the producers or the service providers.

There are significant differences in the levels of awareness and literacy among the rural and urban consumers. Per capita income in rural area is half of that of urban areas. Value for money is more important to rural people. They buy small quantities and more frequently. Urban people often do not display brand loyalty, whereas rural people display brand stickiness. Due to lower literacy levels and less exposure among rural people, touch and feel, seeing is believing and one-on-one communication works well. The most common below-the-line communication platforms in rural markets include *haats*, *melas*, *mandis* and other places of public gathering. While communicating with the rural masses it is required that the message delivered should be simple and direct to be effective.

As a result of globalisation and liberalisation the rural market in India is the largest potential market in the world. Thus, there are vast opportunities for rural marketing. With the growth in rural markets and due to poor knowledge about their rights and lack of skills to take a rational decision based on information about the product or services, the rural consumers in India are being exploited in many ways. The manufacturers and traders take advantage of the condition of the rural consumers. It has been observed that the condition of the rural consumers is deplorable, because they are largely exploited in the rural markets on account of lack of competition among the sellers, low level of awareness and limited choice. The rural consumer has been made to endure sub-standard products and services, adulterated foods, short weights and measures, spurious and hazardous drugs, exorbitant prices, unfulfilled manufacturing guarantees, lack of safety and quality control in appliances and equipment's, electrical and mechanical, unfair warranties and guarantees, imitation, sales gimmicks and unreasonable pricing and host of other ills. The rural consumers who generally depend on weekly markets to purchase essential things are often cheated due to lack of choice.

The rural consumers in India are generally ignorant and they are also unorganised. Thus, they are exploited by the manufacturers, traders and the service providers in different way. They are not only scattered but also diverse and heterogeneous. The government and its various agencies need to counter the misleading claims of the producers/service providers. *"Jago Grahak Jago"* is an important mean to communicate with the consumers. However, to communicate effectively with the rural audiences, we need to move further. It is important to understand the aspirations, fears and hopes of rural consumers.

Role of NGOs/VCOs in Consumer Education

There are three main players in the society—Government, Business, and Civil Society which need to be proactive and interface with each other to bring consumer empowerment. The civil society, which includes class organisations, educational organisations, non-profit non-governmental organisation (NGOs), media etc., cannot only play an important role in protecting people's rights and interests, but also can be a major contributor in educating the masses regarding their rights. If the civil society is strong the government will try to become more democratic and people's welfare oriented. Similarly, the business sector will also become more responsible and sensitive. Therefore, civil society including NGOs is inseparable component of the democratic society. The main mission for the NGOs/VCOs should be to provide service to the most venerable section of the society to make them empowered, capable and organised, so that, they become able to defend their right and to enhance their quality of life and living standard. They are required to go where the government is not adequately reaching and the areas where the government has not paid adequate attention. Their objective is not to substitute the government, but to show the example of service to draw attention of the responsible agencies and to help the local people to be self-reliant.

The NGOs have an important role to play in consumer education and empowerment. The utility of Voluntary Consumer Organisations (VCOs) in the area of consumer protection is second to none by virtue of their operational domain at the grassroots level. They are useful in many ways. They can effectively contribute in promotion and propagation of the programmes and schemes relating to consumer education and awareness especially in rural areas. Thus, they can play the role of the catalyst in generating consumer awareness. They can also help the consumers in filing complaints in the consumer fora or can take up the issues which affect the consumers in general. They can be very effective in dealing with the menace of hazardous products, spurious goods and can take up such complaints before the quasi-judicial machinery. These organisations can through specialised activities such as comparative testing of consumer products can disseminate information regarding products and services which can be very helpful for the consumers. However, the task is gigantic and therefore, it is time to involve the local level institutions/organisations to reach the rural consumers. As the largest consumer base is in the rural areas, protecting the rural consumer has to be a priority in any strategy to protect the consumers.

This chapter is based on an evaluation study carried out by the Centre for Consumer Studies, IIPA of a project sanctioned to an NGO, for organising information, education and communication programme in Kathiar and Kishanganj districts of Bihar for strengthening consumer movement at grassroots. The objective of the project was to enhance awareness among consumers in the two districts by organising information, education and communication programmes and also to set up consumer counselling committees at village and block levels to serve as resource centres for consumers seeking information and guidance. Under the project, 285 awareness programmes were organised at Panchayat, Block and District levels.

Research Methodology of the Evaluation Study

The evaluation study has been carried out with the help of both primary and secondary sources. The major target groups of the awareness programmes were the villagers, panchayat officials, students, teachers and headmasters of the school where programmes were conducted. The interviews were conducted with the help of structured questionnaire consisting of close ended questions. Two separate questionnaires were prepared one for the villagers and another for government/panchayat officials. Discussions were also held with the local village and block officials. District officials were also approached for information. The information collected through the questionnaire was analysed with the help of simple statistical techniques, tabulated and interpreted and is presented in a report form.

Study Area of the Evaluation Study

Under the Project the programmes were organised in all the 19 Blocks of the two Districts. Therefore, to collect the primary data, random sampling technique was used and 5 blocks of each district were chosen for the study. The Blocks were selected keeping in view the geographical spread of the sample area so as to cover all the parts of respected Districts. Thus, more than 50 per cent of the Blocks constituted the sample size. In the second step four villages from each Block were selected randomly. Again at the village level samples were selected from two categories:

(i) 20 villagers were approached to collect information through one set of structured schedules; and (ii) 5 village representatives from each village, preferably panchayat officials and school teachers who attended the programmes were also interviewed with the second set of questionnaire to have their opinion about the quality and requirements of this type of awareness programmes. Therefore, a total of 1000 persons were interviewed from the two districts. Apart from this focus group discussions were also held with a large number of students, women and consumers from the villages to assess the level of awareness about consumer protection issues achieved as a result of the consumer awareness programmes and also to gather information about the programmes organised in their area. Discussions were also held with various officials at the block level and district level for assertion of their views about the programmes in particular and the project in general.

Response of Villagers towards the Awareness Programmes

Rural India constitutes a huge consumer base. Due to ignorance, low literacy level as well as lack of consumer education and awareness the consumers are exploited by the marketers. The exploitation is in various forms. With the rise in rural prosperity and the changing consumption pattern in the rural areas there is a need to enhance the awareness of the rural consumers on various issues. The main objective of the Project was to take the consumer movement to the grassroots level and impart consumer education to the village residents so as to enhance awareness about their consumer rights. The success of a project depends on the fact as to what extent it has been able to achieve its objectives in terms of its effectiveness and usefulness. An awareness programme should be able to reinforce knowledge and also help develop skills that would change the buying behaviour of the consumers, help them seek information and take rational buying decision. Therefore, an attempt was made to gather the perception of villagers regarding the organisation and the effectiveness and usefulness of the programmes organised by the said agency at village level.

Techniques Adopted to Disseminate Consumer Awareness

To achieve the objectives the techniques/methods used by the NGO were *Prabhat Pheri* (rally), lecture, screening of documentary film, street play (*nukkad natak*), and organising cultural programmes. Duration of the programme was of half day in each village. The villagers were informed in advance about the date and time of the half day consumer awareness camp to be organised in their villages and all the villagers were requested to attend the programme. Representatives of panchayat, schools and local officials were also requested to attend the programme. Women and school children were especially encouraged to participate in the programme in large number.

In most of the villages, the programme started with a consumer awareness rally and the participants of this rally were mostly school children, women and NGO personnel. Usually, the rally started from the schools and passed through the lanes of the village. In most of the villages the school was chosen as the venue for the programmes. The choice of the school as the venue was a good idea mainly because of its accessibility and also that most of the villagers knew about its location. The rally was followed by lectures. The topics of the lectures related to the various issues of consumer protection and awareness. The topics covered in the programmes related to basic information about Consumer Protection Act and Rules, defective goods and deficient services, deceptive practices by traders, general mistakes made by common man and tips for being a smart and alert consumer. After the lectures, cultural programmes were organised for the benefit of the participants. Through the medium of singing and other cultural activities the message of Consumer Welfare was passed on to the villagers. Artists in these programmes were mostly locals who used local dialects to spread the consumer awareness messages. It was an easy form of communications. Subsequently, villagers were also shown documentary films prepared by the organisation titled "*Jagruk Upabhokta Surakshit Upabhokta*". The documentary depicted the day-to-day common problems faced by the consumers and provided remedies available to the consumers. The documentary was in Hindi with Bhojpuri dialect. Local problems and issues were highlighted in the documentary. The documentary has been seen by the research team and is well made, informative, educative and effective. At some places *Nukkad Nataks* and Puppet shows were also used to spread the message. A Pamphlet in Hindi published containing information on consumer awareness was also distributed to the villagers. It contained relevant information regarding consumer rights, machinery for redressal of consumer grievances and where to approach in case of problem. It provided relevant information to consumers.

Out of the above mentioned activities, consumer awareness documentary "*Jagruk Upabhokta Surakshit Upabhokta*" was screened in most of the villages as 92.6 per cent of the respondents confirmed that (Table 10.1). The documentary is a good medium to generate awareness as the audio-visual medium leaves a lot of impact on the mind of the people particularly those with low levels of literacy. The documentary was found to be informative and effective as it was in Hindi language with title in local dialect, which could be easily understood by the local community and was filmed in local backdrop with which the people could easily correlate. Common problems like defective goods, medical negligence etc. have been depicted and beautifully dealt in the documentary. The documentary has left an impact on the consumers.

The next main programme to be organised was Speech/Debate as 66.1 per cent of the respondents confirmed that speech/debate was organised in their village. At number of places the organisation organised *nukkad nataks* enacting consumer problems and how CPA provides redressal for the same. About 63.1 per cent of the respondents confirmed the organisation of Public Street Play, followed by Rally (57.1%) and cultural programmes (49.7%) highlighting consumer issues through songs in local dialect were organised. As far as Rally is concerned, it was organised only in the morning when school children were available. Therefore, rallies could not be organised in those villages where programmes were conducted in the afternoon.

Participation of Villagers in the Programmes

The survey indicates that the programmes were largely well attended. Majority of the respondents said that these programmes were attended by about 100-300 villagers on an average. 26.3 per cent said it was attended by 100-200 people. 34.8 per cent of the respondents opined that about 200-300 villagers had attended the programmes, and 14.2 per cent said 300-400 villagers attended the programme.

The lowest response (4%) was found in the category of below 100 (Table 10.2). It indicates that proper publicity was provided to the programmes. Villagers were informed in advance and the topic generated lot of enthusiasm among them to participate in the awareness programmes. In such programmes the audience is not constant. Inflow and outflow is a constant phenomenon; therefore, the number varies during the programmes.

Level of Participation in Activities

The objective of the campaign at village level was to make the villagers

Table 10.1: Programmes Conducted under the Project

Districts	*Blocks*	*Programme Conducted*									
		Rally		*Cultural Programme*		*Street Play*		*Screening of Documentary*		*Speech/Debate*	
		Yes	*No*	*Yes*	*No*	*Yes*	*No*	*Yes*	*No*	*Yes*	*No*
Katihar	Barari	45.8	54.2	43.8	56.3	65.4	34.6	93.8	6.3	70.4	29.6
	Kadwa	43.8	56.3	64.6	35.4	55	45	79.2	20.8	51.7	48.3
	Katihar	45.8	54.2	55.1	44.9	65.4	34.6	93.8	6.3	76.7	23.3
	Kordha	64.6	35.4	47.9	52.1	67.5	32.5	93.8	6.3	70.4	29.6
	Pranpur	62.5	37.5	37.5	62.5	63.3	36.7	98.3	1.7	74.6	25.4
	Total	**52.5**	**47.5**	**49.8**	**50.2**	**63.3**	**36.7**	**91.8**	**8.3**	**68.8**	**31.2**
Kishanganj	Bahadurgarh	54.2	45.8	56.3	43.8	65.4	34.6	91.7	8.3	70.4	29.6
	Dighalbank	54.2	45.8	52.1	47.9	48.8	51.3	97.9	2.1	53.8	46.3
	Kishanganj	70.8	29.2	37.5	62.5	65.4	34.6	85.4	14.6	49.6	50.4
	Pothiya	70.8	29.2	58.3	41.7	71.7	28.3	97.9	2.1	68.3	31.7
	Thakurga	58.3	41.7	43.8	56.3	63.3	36.7	93.8	6.3	74.6	25.4
	Total	**61.7**	**38.3**	**49.6**	**50.4**	**62.9**	**37.1**	**93.3**	**6.7**	**63.3**	**36.7**
	Grand Total	**57.1**	**42.9**	**49.7**	**50.3**	**63.1**	**36.9**	**92.6**	**7.5**	**66.1**	**34**

Source: Field Survey, CCS, IIPA.

Table 10.2: Number of Villagers Attended the Programme

Districts	*Blocks*	*Number of People*					
		50-100	*100-200*	*200-300*	*300-400*	*400-500*	*Above 500*
Katihar	Barari	8.3	18.8	29.2	18.8	6.3	18.8
	Kadwa	4.2	33.3	27.1	10.4	14.6	10.4
	Katihar	0.0	29.2	39.6	10.4	20.8	0.0
	Kordha	0.0	14.6	27.1	22.9	20.8	14.6
	Pranpur	0.0	29.2	41.7	6.3	12.5	10.4
	Total	**2.5**	**25.0**	**32.9**	**13.8**	**15.0**	**10.8**
Kishanganj	Bahadurgarh	12.5	43.8	27.1	10.4	2.1	4.2
	Dighalbank	6.3	20.8	33.3	10.4	18.8	10.4
	Kishanganj	8.3	20.8	35.4	12.5	14.6	8.3
	Pothiya	0.0	35.4	37.5	14.6	6.3	6.3
	Thakurga	0.0	16.7	50.0	25.0	6.3	2.1
	Total	**5.4**	**27.5**	**36.7**	**14.6**	**9.6**	**6.3**
	Grand Total	**4.0**	**26.3**	**34.8**	**14.2**	**12.3**	**8.6**

Source: Field Survey, CCS, IIPA.

aware about their consumer rights and to educate them about consumer issues such as quality, quantity and utility of contemporary products or services. The same would not have been achieved if the villagers had not attended the programmes. Therefore, it was imperative to know the level of participation of the villagers in the programmes organised. In response to the question on participation in the programmes, Table 10.3 indicates that 81.9 per cent of the respondents said that they had seen the documentary film screened. The advantage with the documentary films was that it was screened mainly in the afternoon when all the villagers are relatively free and relaxed. Therefore, the participation was high when compared with other forms of programmes.

It is also apparent that programmes held in the late evening had a higher participation. 60.2 per cent of the respondent had seen the Street Play, 66 per cent had attended Public Talk/Speech and 48.8 per cent saw Cultural programmes. The lowest participation of villagers was found in the rally as only 45.4 per cent of respondents confirmed their participation in the same. It is notable that most of the participants in the rallies were school children as the NGO has organised the rallies only in the morning when only the school children were available.

Table 10.3: Level of Participation in Programmes

Districts	Block	Programme attended by Villagers									
		Rally		Cultural Programme		Street Play		Screening of Documentary		Speech/Debate	
		Yes	No	Yes	No	Yes	No	Yes	No	Yes	No
Katihar	Barari	33.3	66.7	48.8	51.3	63.3	36.7	79.2	20.8	75.4	24.6
	Kadwa	31.3	68.8	34.2	65.8	36.3	63.8	64.6	35.4	42.1	57.9
	Katihar	29.2	70.8	57.1	42.9	48.8	51.3	77.1	22.9	77.5	22.5
	Kordha	68.8	31.3	59.2	40.8	71.7	28.3	85.4	14.6	52.5	47.5
	Pranpur	56.3	43.8	61.3	38.8	63.3	36.7	87.5	12.5	75.4	24.6
	Total	**43.8**	**56.3**	**52.1**	**47.9**	**56.7**	**43.4**	**78.8**	**21.2**	**64.6**	**35.4**
Kishanganj	Bahadurgarh	39.6	60.4	50.8	49.2	65.4	34.6	91.7	8.3	79.6	20.4
	Dighalbank	43.8	56.3	38.3	61.7	57.1	42.9	83.3	16.7	48.3	51.7
	Kishanganj	50	50	40.4	59.6	61.3	38.8	70.8	29.2	54.6	45.4
	Pothiya	54.2	45.8	32.1	67.9	65.4	34.6	91.7	8.3	75.4	24.6
	Thakurga	47.9	52.1	65.4	34.6	69.6	30.4	87.5	12.5	79.6	20.4
	Total	**47.1**	**52.9**	**45.4**	**54.6**	**63.8**	**36.3**	**85**	**15**	**67.5**	**32.5**
	Grand Total	**45.4**	**54.6**	**48.8**	**51.3**	**60.2**	**39.8**	**81.9**	**18.1**	**66.0**	**34.0**

Source: Field Survey, CCS, IIPA.

Perception about the Quality of the Programmes

Organising programmes in villages is an important step to disseminate information and generate awareness among masses at grassroots level. In this endeavour, the consumer organisations can play a crucial and important role by educating and informing the villagers on crucial consumer issues. Therefore, opinion of villagers was sought on the quality and effectiveness of the awareness programmes conducted. Accordingly 55.4 per cent of the respondents agreed that the quality of the awareness programmes was very good. 35.6 per cent found the programmes to be good and only 9 per cent opined that the programmes were of average standard (Table 10.4). During the discussions it was revealed that the issues highlighted were of common interest to all the villagers and it touched their problems. They could also understand the medium used and the documentary and the cultural programmes made it very interesting and the message was conveyed.

Table 10.4: Perception about Quality of the Programmes

Districts	*Block*	*Perception of Villagers*		
		Very Good	*Good*	*Average*
Katihar	Barari	62.4	27.5	10.1
	Kadwa	54.1	33.7	12.2
	Katihar	64.5	27.5	8.0
	Kordha	33.3	56.6	10.1
	Pranpur	60.3	31.7	8.0
	Total	**54.9**	**35.4**	**9.7**
Kishanganj	Bahadurgarh	45.0	43.0	12.0
	Dighalbank	62.7	27.2	10.1
	Kishanganj	52.5	37.4	10.1
	Pothiya	54.1	37.9	8.0
	Thakurga	55.4	30.7	13.9
	Total	**55.8**	**35.7**	**10.8**
Grand Total		**55.4**	**35.6**	**10.3**

Source: Field Survey, CCS, IIPA.

Usefulness of the Programmes

The objective of the programmes organised was to enhance the villagers' knowledge about consumer related problems, create awareness about consumer welfare and educate them about consumer rights and redressal mechanism available to them. Therefore, it was imperative to find out the effectiveness and usefulness of the programmes for the villagers. When the respondents were asked about the usefulness of the programmes, they were of the opinion that overall the programmes were useful in enhancing consumer awareness and the message was effective. 30.4 per cent of the respondents found it to be useful to a large extent. 48.5 per cent of them said that these programmes were helpful only to some extent. About 21 per cent of respondents did not find the programmes useful at all as per Table 10.5. They said that the programmes would have been more useful if they were organised on a regular basis as common man has a tendency to forget the information and knowledge imparted after sometimes. The major problem with the programmes was that they were organised once in each village and there was no provision for regular follow-ups. They were mostly one time episodes which left some impact on the people. There is a need to organise such programmes at regular intervals to keep the villagers updated on the issues.

Table 10.5: Usefulness of the Programmes

Districts	*Blocks*	*Programme Helpful to Village Consumers*		
		To large extent	*To some extent*	*Not at all*
Katihar	Barari	27.1	54.2	18.8
	Kadwa	37.5	47.9	14.6
	Katihar	31.3	45.8	22.9
	Kordha	33.3	39.6	27.1
	Pranpur	29.2	54.2	16.7
	Total	**31.7**	**48.3**	**20.0**
Kishanganj	Bahadurgarh	25.0	54.2	20.8
	Dighalbank	27.1	50.0	22.9
	Kishanganj	33.3	52.1	14.6
	Pothiya	29.2	45.8	25.0
	Thakurga	31.3	41.7	27.1
	Total	**29.2**	**48.8**	**22.1**
Grand Total		**30.4**	**48.5**	**21.0**

Source: Field Survey, CCS, IIPA.

Effectiveness of Documentary Film on Consumer Awareness

The organisation made a documentary "*Jagruk Upabhokta Surakshit*

Upabhokta" on consumer related issues and had screened the same during their awareness campaigns. The survey results reveal that the documentary was informative and effective in making people aware about their rights as consumers and the redressal mechanisms available to them in case of grievance. An audio-visual presentation through the documentary has left a lot of impact on the villagers. As per the data (Table 10.6), 77.6 per cent of the respondents found the film to be very effective and useful and 16.7 per cent of the respondents found them to be effective and useful. While 5.7 per cent respondents found the film to be effective and useful only to some extent.

Table 10.6: Effectiveness of Documentary Film on Consumer Awareness

Districts	*Blocks*	*Opinion about Documentary Film*		
		Very Effective and Useful	*Effective and Useful*	*Effective to some extent*
Katihar	Barari	77.1	18.8	4.2
	Kadwa	79.2	12.5	8.3
	Katihar	79.2	12.5	8.3
	Kordha	68.8	18.8	12.5
	Pranpur	72.9	20.8	6.3
	Total	**77.5**	**16.7**	**5.8**
Kishanganj	Bahadurgarh	68.8	29.2	2.1
	Dighalbank	87.5	8.3	4.2
	Kishanganj	68.8	18.8	12.5
	Pothiya	77.1	20.8	2.1
	Thakurga	91.7	6.3	2.1
	Total	**78.8**	**16.7**	**4.6**
Grand Total		**78.2**	**16.7**	**5.2**

Source: Field Survey, CCS, IIPA.

Extent of Knowledge Gained by the Villagers

However, as a result of the programmes, no substantial change in the buying behaviour of the respondents was seen. 61.9 per cent of the respondents checked the weight of the product they purchased, 13.1 per cent read the MRP on the packet, 8.5 per cent always checked the manufacturing date and only 11.3 per cent checked the manufacturing date sometimes (Figure 10.1). 72.5 per cent of the respondents always bargained on the price. Lack of literacy and purchase of loose items on credit was cited as a major reason for not checking the above markings.

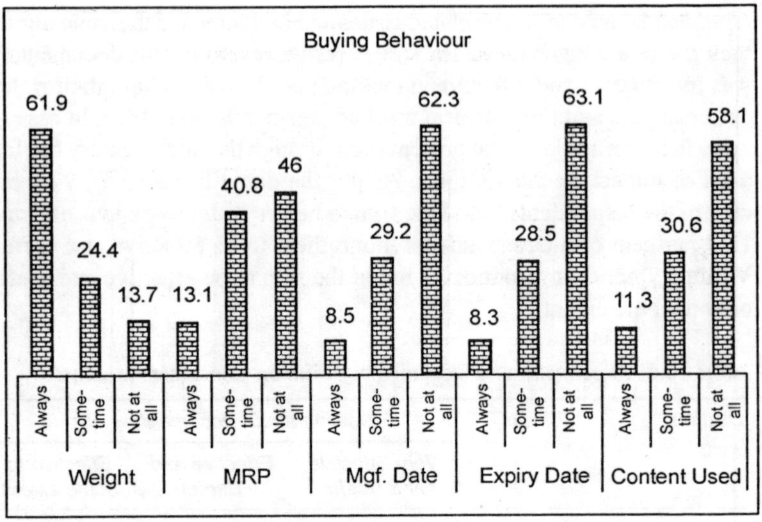

Figure 10.1: Buying Behaviour of Villagers

Source: Field Survey, CCS, IIPA.

Only 6.8 per cent knew about ISI mark. 26.3 per cent had seen veg/non-veg marking and 24.1 per cent knew about Agmark (Figure 10.2). Students constituted the bulk of the respondents who knew about these markings. Awareness about CP Act is lacking as only 4.31 per cent of the respondents knew about the CP Act. 79.6 per cent did not know the definition of consumer as per the Act and only 16.07 per cent had some idea. 76.5 per cent knew about "*Jago Grahak Jago*" advertisement and the main source of information was radio (59.8%).

Village Consumer Counselling Committees

As informed by the organisation, a committee has been set-up consisting of a group of 10 villagers. At many places it involved Panchayat officials and other representatives of the village. When the villagers were asked about the existence of the village consumer counselling committees, 58.8 per cent of the respondents confirmed that they know about these committees in the villages. However, only few villagers have contacted these committees with problems relating to adulteration, black-marketing of kerosene, poor quality of fertilisers, substandard products being sold by the local shop-keepers. Few issues have been resolved by the committee

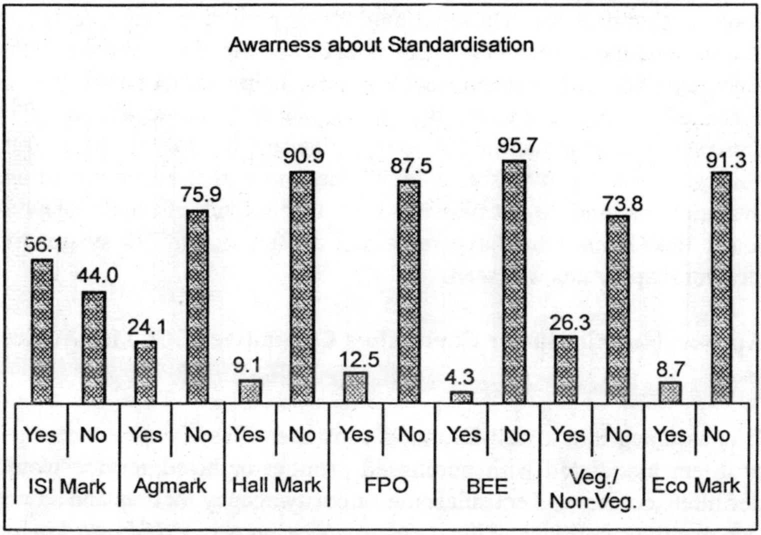

Source: Field Survey, CCS, IIPA.

Figure 10.2: Awareness about Standardisation Marks

through mediation where local shop-keeper was involved. However, the committee lacked expertise on technical issues like adulteration, black-marketing etc. and had very limited knowledge about the CPA, therefore,

Table 10.7: Village Consumer Counselling Committee

Districts	*Block*	*Yes*	*No*
Katihar	Barari	64.2	46.4
	Kadwa	61.7	41.2
	Katihar	58.8	38.3
	Kordha	60.5	39.5
	Pranpur	53.6	35.8
	Total	**59.7**	**40.3**
Kishanganj	Bahadurgarh	61.8	45.6
	Dighalbank	58.9	41.1
	Kishanganj	62.4	47.7
	Pothiya	54.4	38.2
	Thakurga	52.3	37.6
	Total	**57.9**	**42.1**
Grand Total		**58.8**	**41.2**

Source: Field Survey, CCS, IIPA

could not advice properly regarding appropriate redressal mechanism available to the consumers. There is need for capacity building of the members of the committee to enable them to help and advice villagers in a more effective, efficient and appropriate manner. However, as said earlier these committees are formed but do not play an effective role. Moreover, during the survey it was also found that most of the Committee are dysfunctional and do not play any role. Due to lack of regular flow of funds the Committees have remained dysfunctional. No systematic structural apparatus was seen.

Approaching Consumer Counselling Committee (CCC) for Advice/ Help

It is assumed that a well-informed consumer if confronted with some problem associated with purchased product or hired service would definitely contact and consult some authority/agency for help and advice to solve their problems. Since, the organisation was a NGO working at the grassroots level and has organised awareness programmes in the villages, therefore, it was expected that villagers would approach the NGO or any committee set up by it for help, advice and assistance. As per the objective of the project, the NGO was to set up Consumer Counselling Committees at village and block levels which can serve as the resource

Table 10.8: Approaching CCC for Advice/Help

Block	*Districts*	*Help from the NGO*	
		Yes	No
Katihar	Barari	4.2	95.8
	Kadwa	6.3	93.8
	Katihar	16.7	83.3
	Kordha	8.3	91.7
	Pranpur	4.2	95.8
	Total	**7.9**	**92.1**
Kishanganj	Bahadurgarh	2.1	97.9
	Dighalbank	10.4	89.6
	Kishanganj	4.2	95.8
	Pothiya	6.3	93.8
	Thakurga	8.3	91.7
	Total	**6.3**	**93.8**
Grand Total		**7.1**	**92.9**

Source: Field Survey, CCS, IIPA.

centres for consumers seeking information and guidance. Thus, one of the functions of the NGO was to advice and help the villages on specific consumer issues through these committees.

To judge the functionality of these committees and the initiatives taken by the NGO to resolve the problems of the consumers, the study tried to find out how many villagers actually tried to contact consumer committees and the NGO for advice and help. Unfortunately, according to the data (Table 10.8) only 7.1 per cent of the respondents had consulted the organisation for help after the programme. Rest 92.9 per cent of the respondents had never consulted the organisation, though many of them had problems relating to purchased commodity or hired services.

Reaction of Business Community

Educating common man about their rights and to make them aware about various dimensions of consumer protection is only one of the aspects for the success of the consumer movement in this country. There is a need for action on the part of all the major stakeholders of the movement, viz. the government, consumer and the business. This makes it imperative to motivate the manufacturers, traders and retailers to adopt ethical market practices, particularly in rural areas where people are very poor, uneducated, and underprivileged. There is a need for the business to understand their social and moral responsibility towards consumers and implement it in letter and spirit. It is a general perception that the business community does not appreciate the efforts of the VCOs in educating the consumers. The same is true in this case as well. They were also found to be hostile to such initiatives.

Table 10.9 indicates the opinion of the respondents about the impact of programmes on local shopkeepers. It can be seen that the responses were not encouraging. Only 12.3 per cent of the respondents said that these programmes were able to make an impact and curb the unethical marketing practices of local shopkeepers for some time. Majority of the respondents (70.4%) have confirmed that no changes were found in the behaviour of local shopkeepers despite having consumer awareness programmes in their villages.

Suggestions

(1) The project is important as the bulk of the consumers live in rural areas and is exploited in various forms. There is a need to educate

Table 10.9: Reaction of Business Community

Districts	*Block*	*Behavioural Change of Shopkeepers*		
		To large Extent	*To some extent*	*Not at all*
Katihar	Barari	31.3	6.3	62.5
	Kadwa	8.3	14.6	77.1
	Katihar	4.2	20.8	75.0
	Kordha	22.9	14.6	62.5
	Pranpur	16.7	20.8	62.5
	Total	**16.7**	**15.4**	**67.9**
Kishanganj	Bahadurgarh	14.6	12.5	72.9
	Dighalbank	4.2	25.0	70.8
	Kishanga	10.4	20.8	68.8
	Pothiya	6.3	14.6	79.2
	Thakurga	4.2	22.9	72.9
	Total	**7.9**	**19.2**	**72.9**
G. Total		**12.3**	**17.3**	**70.4**

Source: Field Survey, CCS, IIPA.

the rural consumers and also to involve the Panchayati Raj Institutions in the consumer movement. Hence, such programmes may be continued with appropriate checks and balances.

(2) The monitoring mechanism provided in the project did not function effectively hence delay in dispatch of the reports which led to delay in the implementation of the project. The involvement of the Department of Food, Civil Supplies and Consumer Affairs, Government of Bihar will be useful. The Director, Consumer Affairs in the State Government can be made the nodal officer instead of the District Magistrate to monitor the project, inspect and send reports to Department of Consumer Affairs, Government of India.

(3) A project of high value like the present one should have a provision for mid-term review based on field data.

(4) The number of participants at places increased many fold due to the involvement of local politicians hence, the programmes lost its educational value. There is a need to fix a range of participants say 100-150 per programme.

(5) The quality of resource persons/trainers needs to be improved. A list of resource persons should be prepared and training should be imparted to them well in advance. A Trainer Manual/Guide

Book should be prepared and adequate training imparted to the resource persons.

(6) The duration of each programmes should be increased. It could be at least a half day programmes, but preferably a full day programmes. In the morning rallies should be organised followed by a general awareness programmes. In the evening documentary and cultural programmes be organised followed by focus group interaction. Gathering a mass of people and lecturing will have limited effect.

(7) School children should be involved in large numbers in the programmes. The schools should become the central point. Activities like debates, poster/painting competition should also be organised for school children.

(8) The Village Consumer Counselling Committees are more or less dysfunctional and have not played an effective role. They need to be revived and strengthened, so that, the consumers can seek advice and help. A nodal person should be in-charge of each committee with knowledge of consumer issues. He should be trained. The location, time and other details of the committee should be published. These committees could be linked to the state helpline and consumer advice centres being set-up in the state.

(9) The President and Members of the District Forums should be involved as they can play a role in such awareness programmes.

(10) A Booklet on Consumer Protection must be prepared along with pamphlets and these be distributed in large numbers.

(11) Panchayati Raj Institutions should be involved to educate the rural masses and generate awareness. Consumer Awareness programmes can be organised during the Gram Sabha Meetings.

Conclusion

Consumer education should foster mutual awareness and understanding between the urban and rural sectors as well as rich and poor sections of society. Consumer education can strengthen the bonds that exist between various social segments and minimise the divisive factors. The market and the industry seek to widen the gaps that exist and seek to rule consumers through fostering divisions. The consumer education programmes whether at school and college levels or through government or NGO channels should seek to remove these distances. An aware consumer of any age, gender, class and background has certain rights as well as responsibilities. Each segment has certain responsibility towards others. All-round sustainable development is possible only if each consumer segment fulfils its duties and responsibilities sincerely. If we want this movement to grow, more people will have to come in. Greater consumer vigilance and action alone can help improve the situation. But, such efforts are not fruitful unless consumers themselves are aware of their rights and responsibilities. Under these circumstances, consumer literacy is the need of the hour, with special attention to low income groups particularly living in the rural areas who suffer the most.

The role played by the civil society organisations especially the VCOs in consumer protection is second to none. However, at present these organisations are riddled with many problems. They lack both functionaries and finances. Further, there is need for accreditation and professionalisation of VCOs to raise their credibility. These VCOs should attract and involve professionally qualified people retain them and motivate them to work for community. There is also need for creating some mechanism to identify credible VCOs which if supported could effectively contribute towards strengthening the consumer protection. Training and skill development of those who are working with VCOs will no doubt make them more effective to take up the cause of consumers.

Note

1. Wells, J. and Atherton, M., (1998). "Consumer Education : Learning for Life", *Consumer 21*, Autumn, pp. 15-20.

References

Atherton, Margaret; Wells, Juliet, (1998). "Consumer Education: Learning for Life", *Consumer Policy Review*; July/August; 8, 4: 127-131.

Bannister, R. and C. Monsma, (1982). "Classification of Concepts in Consumer Education", *NASSP Bulletin*.

Beatrice Fihn, *The Role of Civil Society in Building Awareness —Engaging Critical Actors,* http://www.unidir.ch/pdf/conferences/pdf-conf1055.pdf.

Department of Consumer Affairs, *Report of the Working Group on Consumer Protection,* Vol. I, pp. 28-31, Department of Consumer Affairs, Government of India.

European Commission, (2010). *The Role of Civil Society in Global Governance*, Brussels, 1 October.

George Cheriyan, "*Rural Consumers and Role of Local Bodies in Consumer Protection*", CUTS, Centre for Consumer Action, Research & Training.

Ina Zharkevich, (2010). *The Role of Civil Society in Promoting Political Accountability in Fragile States: the Case of Tajikistan*, INTRAC.

OECD, (2009). *Consumer Education: Policy Recommendations of the OECD's Committee on Consumer Policy.*

OECD, (2009). *Promoting Consumer Education – Trends, Policies and Good Practices*, OECD, pp. 11-31.

Suresh Misra, Sapna Chadah (2010). *Consumer Awareness in Rural India—An Empirical Study*, New Delhi: CCS, IIPA.

Wells, J. and Atherton, M., (1998). "Consumer Education: Learning for Life", *Consumer 21,* Autumn, pp. 15-20.

11
The Role of VCOs in Consumer Protection
An Empirical Study in Rural Karnataka

Abbokar Siddiq

"Consumer Organisations should not only ask what the government can do for them, they should also tell government what they can do for their consumers." —**John, F. Kennedy**

Introduction

Consumers are the pillars of economic development of any country as the entire economy revolves around them. They are the basis for building the economy and responsible for the transformation of resources into productive assets. They are also responsible for the production of goods and services which are the index of economic growth. They are the directors and dictators of the economic world and the kings of the market. But the reality is something very different which contradicts these assumptions. The consumers are relegated to the back seat rather than given any commanding supremacy in the business world.

Problems

The developing countries and many underdeveloped countries at present feel a new 'ism' known as 'Consumerism' to protect consumers since they have become victims of various types of exploitation. In spite of various provisions providing protection to the consumers, very little could be achieved in the field of Consumer Protection. The enactment of the laws alone is not the solution for consumer problems unless legislation is supplemented by effective enforcement. There should be an effective linkage between the law and the consumers, so that, quick and inexpensive justice could be taken to their doorsteps. For this purpose, the need for Voluntary Consumer Organisations (VCOs) is gaining momentum to play a vital role to help and to render assistance to the ill-fated consumers in protecting their rights and interests.

Literature Review

Srivastava, P.N. & Sakhivel (1990) pointed out some of the basic problems faced by the VCOs; the defensive attitude of erring businessmen, limited financial resources and the non-availability of dedicated professionals. It is suggested that more vigorous efforts are needed on the part of VCOs in order to solve the problems in the various fields such as consumer education, consumer advocacy, government regulation and policy etc.

Kalpana (1992) in her article "Making Consumerism a Movement" stressed the establishment of VCOs to safeguard the consumers against the malpractices and exploitation by the businessmen. She concluded that only legislation cannot solve the problems of consumers.

Dutt, S.K. (1998), a member of Consumer Forum, New Delhi, conducted a survey, which showed that there were no VCOs in 60 per cent of the districts out of the 532 districts in India. In a large number of districts, the number of VCOs is not more than one or two. The number of VCOs functioning in the districts is not equitable in relation to the area of population. Out of a total of 610 VCOs, 203 are concentrated in Andhra Pradesh alone. Even considering large cities on an All-India basis, VCOs are functioning only in 40 per cent of these cities while there is none in the remaining 60 per cent. Thus, the growth of VCOs is not balanced and need-based.

Objectives of the Study

The present study has been carried out with the following objectives:

1. To understand the level of awareness among the complainant consumers about Consumer Protection Legislations and Consumer Rights in the study area.
2. To know the expectations of Complainant Consumers from the various Voluntary Consumer Organisations in the study area.

3. To understand the activities of different Voluntary Consumer Organisations in the study area.
4. To suggest measures to improve the functioning of VCOs to provide better protection to the consumers based on the findings of the study.

Study Design and Methodology

The primary data for the present study was collected from complainant consumers and VCOs of the study area through personal interviews with different sets of questionnaires. The study area comprises two districts of coastal Karnataka, viz. Dakshina Kannada and Udupi. There are a total of 23,600 complainant consumers put together in both the districts, who have approached the VCOs with complaints for settlement in the ten year period between 2000 and 2010. Due to time, distance and resource constraints only 472 complainant consumers have been selected as sample respondents, and it works out to 2 per cent of the total complainant Consumers. These consumers were selected on the basis of convenience sampling method. The researcher has taken care to see that the respondents represent gender, age, literacy, income, occupation and area of the population under study.

There are in total 40 VCOs in both the districts. All the VCOs were selected as samples to give 100 per cent representation. But 2 VCOs did not respond and as a result the response rate is 95.12 per cent. The primary data collected from the sample respondents on various aspects has been organised in the tabular form. Such organised data has been analysed with the help of different statistical tools like average, percentage, chi-square etc. for easy understanding of the data and for drawing meaningful conclusion. Along with the primary data, secondary data has been collected from various published sources like books, journals, reports of Department of Consumer Affairs, Food and Civil Supplies, District Fora etc. and by visiting libraries, institutes of consumer education and management institutes. The ideas drawn from these sources have been incorporated wherever necessary to substantiate the primary data.

Data Analysis

Awareness of Consumer Rights among Complainant Consumers

The Consumer Protection Act has given the consumers—the Right to

Safety, Right to be Informed, Right to Choose, Right to be Heard, Right to Redressal, Right to Consumer Education and Right to Healthy environment. The study of the awareness of Consumer Rights is important to understand the role played by the VCOs in creating awareness among consumers about their rights and protection. The relevant data have been collected and presented in Table 11.1:

Table 11.1: Awareness of Consumer Rights among Complainant Consumers

Awareness	*No. of Consumers*	*Percentage*
Aware	148	31.4
Unaware	324	68.6
Total	**472**	**100.0**

Binomial, p = 0.000 h
Source: Survey Data.

An analysis of Table 11.1 reveals that out of the 472 complainant consumers, only 148 (31.4%) were aware of "Consumer Rights". The respondents who had heard and knew something about "Consumer Rights" were considered 'Aware' for the purpose of study. A majority of (68.6%) complainant consumers were unaware of "Consumer Rights". The respondents who had not even heard about "Consumer Rights" were considered 'Unaware'. The binomial value shows that there is a highly significant difference in the awareness of consumers about "Consumer Rights" in the study region. Therefore, from the table it is found that a majority of complainant consumers are unaware of "Consumer Rights" in the study region.

Awareness of Consumer Rights among Complainant Consumers

The enactment of Consumer Protection Act, 1986 is a boon to consumers. Consumer Rights are the instruments in the hands of the consumers to protect themselves against the deception and exploitation by the business community. In order to know the awareness of complainant consumers about the different types of their rights, the data has been gathered and presented in Table 11.2.

An analysis of Table 11.2 shows that out of the 148 complainant consumers who were aware of "Consumer Rights", a majority (77.7%) knew about the "Right to be Informed". Seventy Two (48.6%) consumers knew about the "Right to Redressal", while 64 (43.2%) of them were aware of the "Right to Safety". But, a few (27.7%) complainant consumers

Table 11.2: Awareness of Consumer Rights Among Complainant Consumers

Consumer Rights	*No. of Consumers*	*Percentage*
Right to Choose	51	34.5
Right to Safety	64	43.2
Right to be Informed	115	77.7
Right to be Heard	28	18.9
Right to Redressal	72	48.6
Right to Consumer Education	41	27.7
Right to Healthy environment	56	37.8

χ^2 (6) = 76.065, ρ = 0.000 hs

Notes:

1. Percentage is not equal to 100 because of multiple responses.
2. Multiple Response Rate is equal to total number of responses divided by the number of respondents.

Source: Survey Data.

were aware of the "Right to Consumer Education". The χ^2 value calculated for the table reveals that there is a highly significant difference in the awareness of complainant consumers about the different types of Consumer Rights. Therefore, it is found from Table that out of the complainant consumers who know about Consumer Rights, a majority are aware of only the "Right to be Informed". The reason may be that the "Right to Information Act" is passed recently in India.

Awareness of Complainant Consumers about Consumer Protection Legislations

The Government of India has implemented number of legislations to protect the interests of the consumers. For any legislation to be successful the awareness among the population should be high and the people should be aware of the law and also aware of how it can protect their rights and interests. The data have been gathered and presented in Table 11.3 to know the awareness of complainant consumers about Consumer Protection Legislations.

It is evident from Table 11.3 that out of the 472 respondents, only 176 (37.3%) respondents were aware of the Consumer Protection Legislations existing in India. A majority of (62.7%) respondents did not know about the existence of Consumer Protection Legislations. The

Table 11.3: Awareness of Complainant Consumers about Consumer Protection Legislations

Awareness	*No. of Consumers*	*Percentage*
Aware	176	37.3
Unaware	296	62.7
Total	**472**	**100.0**

Binomial, ρ = 0.000 hs.
Source: Survey Data.

binomial value calculated for table shows that there is a highly significant difference in the awareness of complainant consumers about Consumer Protection Legislations. Therefore, it is found from table that most of the consumers who have complained to the VCOs in the study region did not know about Consumer Protection Legislations.

Degree of Awareness of Consumer Protection Legislations

The degree of awareness among Complainant Consumers about Consumer Protection Legislations varies from individual to individual. The consumers who had heard the name of the legislations were considered as "Least Aware" and the consumers who knew the important aspects of the legislations were considered as "Aware". Accordingly, the consumers who knew the contents of the legislations were treated as "Fully Aware". The data has been gathered and presented in Table 11.4 to know the degree of awareness of complainant consumers about consumer protection legislations.

An analysis of Table 11.4 reveals that out of 176 complainant consumers who knew about consumer protection legislations, 104 (59.1%) had the awareness of Drugs and Cosmetics Act, 1940. Out of the 104, only 7 (6.7%) were "Fully Aware" and 52 (50.0%) respondents were "Least Aware". Among 113 (64.2%) respondents who knew about Prevention of Food Adulteration Act, 1954, a majority of (58.4%) respondents were "Least Aware" of the Act. The Essential Commodities Act, 1955 was known to 121 (68.8%) respondents. But, it is noted that only 3 (2.5%) of them were "Fully Aware" of it. A small number of (58.0%) respondents knew about MRTP Act, 1969. Among them only 2 (2.0%) were "Fully Aware" and 53 (52.0%) were "Least Aware" of it. Out of the 115 (65.3%) respondents who knew about Standards of Weights and Measures Act, 1976, 5 (4.4%) respondents were "Fully Aware" and 58 (50.4%) were "Least Aware" of it. The Consumer Protection Act, 1986 and Right to Information Act, 2005 were known to 132 (75.0%) and 153 (87.0%) respondents respectively. Only 10 (7.6%) respondents were "Fully Aware" of Consumer Protection Act and 06 (3.9%) respondents were "Fully Aware" of Right to Information Act. The mean value calculated shows that the complainant consumers who knew about different consumer protection legislations were on an average aware of these legislations. The χ^2 value also justifies that there is only a significant difference in the awareness of different consumer protection legislations among the complainant consumers.

Table 11.4: Degree of Awareness of Consumer Protection Legislations

Consumer Protection Legislations	*Degree of Awareness*			*Total*	*Mean*	*Standard Deviation*
	Fully Aware	*Aware*	*Least Aware*			
Drugs and Cosmetics Act, 1940	7 (6.7)	45 (43.3)	52 (50.0)	104 [59.1] (100.0)	1.6357	0.61158
Prevention of Food Adulteration Act, 1954	7 (6.2)	40 (35.4)	66 (58.4)	113 [64.2] (100.0)	1.7071	0.58144
Essential Commodities Act, 1955	3 (2.5)	57 (47.1)	61 (50.4)	121 [68.8] (100.0)	1.5200	0.55224
MRTP Act, 1969	2 (2.0)	47 (46.0)	53 (52.0)	102 [58.0] (100.0)	1.5079	0.54766
Standards of Weights and Measures Act, 1976	5 (4.4)	52 (45.2)	58 (50.4)	115 [65.3] (100.0)	1.5874	0.57321
Consumer Protection Act, 1986	10 (7.6)	57 (43.2)	65 (49.2)	132 [75.0] (100.0)	1.6503	0.62394
Right to Information Act, 2005	6 (3.9)	60 (39.2)	87 (56.9)	153 [87.0] (100.0)	1.5684	0.56956

χ^2 (12) = 24.650, ρ = 0.017; N = 176

Note: Figures in the parentheses denote percentages to the total.

Source: Survey Data.

Expectations of Consumers and Activities of VCOs

The consumers expect a variety of activities from VCOs for the protection of their interests. Due to this, the VCOs have responsibilities to structure their programmes according to the expectations of the consumers and monitor these in that direction on a continual basis. Since, the consumers' perceptions and satisfaction are always sourced out from the benefits that they generally expect from the VCOs, a study of the major activities, the respondents generally expected from the VCOs was felt necessary. Keeping this objective in mind, the data has been collected and presented in Table 11.5.

Table 11.5 shows the activities expected by the consumers from the VCOs and the activities actually undertaken by the VCOs. The expected activities are arranged rank-wise after collecting the data from the consumers. An analysis of the table reveals that out of the 472 complainant consumer respondents, all (100%) expected the VCOs to settle consumer complaints and they ranked it first. In turn, out of the 38 VCOs, all the VCOs (100%) are settling consumer complaints daily. Out of the 472 respondents, a majority of 471 (99.8%) expected the VCOs to give consumer advocacy, i.e. the advice and guidance to fight the case in the CDRAs, and all the VCOs (100%) are performing this activity. Publication of newsletters, periodicals and magazines related to consumer affairs is the source of information to consumers. Out of the 472 respondents, a majority (99.6%) expect this activity from the VCOs. But only 18 (47.4%) VCOs are contributing to this publication either weekly, fortnightly, annually or occasionally and a majority (52.6%) of VCOs are not interested in the publication of articles in the newsletters, periodicals and magazines. Among 472 respondents, a fair number of 390 (82.6%) expect the VCOs to organise meetings, training programmes, conferences, workshops and street plays. In turn, out of the 38 VCOs, 33 (86.8%) are conducting meetings, training programmes, conferences, workshops and street plays either monthly, quarterly, half yearly, annually or occasionally. Out of the 472 respondents, majority (81.1%) expect the VCOs to organise talks in schools and at colleges to train the young generation on consumer related issues and to create awareness about their rights. But only a small number of 25 (65.8%) VCOs are performing this activity on weekly, monthly, quarterly, half yearly and annual basis or occasionally. A majority of (71.2%) consumers opine that the VCOs should conduct consumer surveys. But only 07 (18.4%) VCOs are conducting surveys, that too occasionally. The consumers expect that the VCOs should give talk on radio or TV on consumer affairs for their benefit. Out of the 472, a majority (69.7%) expect this activity. But only a small number of 10 (26.3%) VCOs are performing this activity either monthly, quarterly, half yearly, annually or occasionally. Conducting competitions, debates and contests are the activities expected by the consumers from the VCOs.

A majority (64.4%) out of the 472 consumers expect this from the VCOs. But, a small number of 7 (18.4%) VCOs organise competitions,

Table 11.5: The Expectations of Consumers and the Activities of Voluntary Consumer Organisations

Activities	*Activities expected by consumers*		*Activities undertaken by VCOs*									*Total*
	No. of consumers	*Rank*	*Daily*	*Weekly*	*Fortnightly*	*Monthly*	*Quarterly*	*Half yearly*	*Annually*	*Occasi-onally*	*Never*	
Settlements of consumer complaints	472 (100.0)	1	38 (100.0)	0 (0)	0 (0)	0 (0)	0 (0)	0 (0)	0 (0)	0 (0)	0 (0)	38 (100.0)
Consumer advocacy	471 (99.8)	2	38 (100.0)	0 (0)	0 (0)	0 (0)	0 (0)	0 (0)	0 (0)	0 (0)	0 (0)	38 (100.0)
Publication of news letters / periodicals / magazines	470 (99.6)	3	0 (0)	7 (18.5)	6 (15.8)	0 (0)	0 (0)	0 (0)	1 (2.6)	4 (10.5)	20 (52.6)	38 (100.0)
Organising meetings / training programmes / conferences / workshops / street plays	390 (82.6)	4	0 (0)	0 (0)	0 (0)	3 (7.9)	3 (7.9)	5 (13.2)	4 (10.5)	18 (47.3)	5 (13.2)	38 (100.0)
Organising talks in schools / colleges	383 (81.1)	5	0 (0)	1 (2.6)	0 (0)	2 (5.3)	2 (5.3)	3 (7.9)	2 (5.3)	15 (39.4)	13 (34.2)	38 (100.0)
Conducting Consumer Surveys	336 (71.2)	6	0 (0)	0 (0)	0 (0)	0 (0)	0 (0)	0 (0)	0 (0)	7 (18.4)	31 (81.6)	38 (100.0)
Giving talk in radio / giving TV Interviews	329 (69.7)	7	0 (0)	0 (0)	0 (0)	1 (2.6)	1 (2.6)	1 (2.6)	3 (7.9)	4 (10.6)	28 (73.7)	38 (100.0)
Conducting competitions, debates, contests etc.	304 (64.4)	8	0 (0)	0 (0)	0 (0)	0 (0)	0 (0)	0 (0)	2 (5.3)	5 (13.1)	31 (81.6)	38 (100.0)
Organizing demonstration-*cum*-exhibition	213 (45.1)	9	0 (0)	0 (0)	0 (0)	0 (0)	0 (0)	0 (0)	0 (0)	4 (10.5)	34 (89.5)	38 (100.0)
Product Testing	121 (25.6)	10	0 (0)	0 (0)	0 (0)	0 (0)	0 (0)	0 (0)	0 (0)	2 (5.3)	36 (94.7)	38 (100.0)

χ^2 (7) = 141.171, ρ = 0.000, hs

Source: Survey Data.

debates and contests annually and some VCOs occasionally. The consumers opine that the VCOs should organise demonstration-*cum*-exhibition on food adulteration etc. Out of the 472 respondents, 213 (45.1%) expect the VCOs to conduct this activity. But, a small number of 04 (10.5%) VCOs conduct this activity occasionally. Regarding product testing activity, out of the 472 respondents, only 121 (25.6%) have such expectations. But, only 2 (5.3%) VCOs are conducting product testing activity occasionally. It is evident from table that the settlement of consumer complaints, consumer advocacy and organising meetings, training programmes, conferences, workshops and street plays are the only activities conducted by the VCOs according to the expectations of the consumers.

The VCOs are not conducting other activities up to the expectations of the consumers and a majority of VCOs are concentrating only on complaint settlement. The χ^2 value calculated for table shows that there is a highly significant difference between the expectations of the consumers and the performance of the VCOs. It shows that the VCOs are not performing their activities as per the expectations of the consumers.

Suggestions and Implications

On the basis of the findings of the study and observation, the following suggestions are made to improve the functioning of VCOs and to popularise the VCOs to protect the interests of the consumers and to strengthen the consumer movement:

1. The Government at the Centre and the State should feel the necessity of consumer education and awareness programmes. It is observed that the level of consumer awareness is very low in the rural areas. The government should encourage the consumers to establish the VCOs in the district, taluk and village levels and it should provide them grants every year for their functioning and conduct of their activities. This will provide an opportunity to the consumers and their organisations to fight for their rights and interests.
2. The government should give publicity about the existence and functioning of VCOs through electronic and print media. It will encourage the aggrieved consumers to file their complaints against exploitation by the businessmen.
3. The government should include consumer education in the curricula of Schools and Colleges. They should also take the services of NCC, Scouts and NSS for creating consumer

awareness, so that, the future generation will be more vigilant and aware about consumer protection.

4. There should be a separate Department with full-fledged Secretary for Consumer Affairs in states to deal with Consumer Protection and Legislations. The government should make it compulsory for all the VCOs, government departments, schools and colleges to celebrate the World and National "Consumer Rights Day" on 15th March and 24th December respectively. This will create more awareness among consumers.
5. It should be made mandatory for the traders to display the address and telephone numbers of the nearest VCO at prominent places in the shop. It would be ideal, if a system could be evolved whereby manufacturers, traders and service providers could, after due verification by VCOs, obtain a "Consumer Friendly Certificate" from them which would assist consumers in their easy identification of such business enterprises.
6. The VCOs should conduct their activities according to the expectations of the consumers. They should conduct varieties of activities instead of concentrating only on complaint settlement. It helps the consumers to involve themselves in consumer protection programmes.
7. Adequate infrastructural facilities should be provided to the VCOs. The vacant posts of President/Members must be filled up to make non-functional Consumer Fora functional. This will serve the purpose of the establishment of CDRAs.
8. The VCOs with the help of the Department of Weights and Measures, Drugs and Cosmetics and Ministry of Food and Civil Supplies should organise seminars and workshops to overcome the menace of short weights and measures, adulterated, duplicate, hazardous and sub-standard goods and spurious drugs. The government should set-up product testing laboratories in the headquarters of each district to enable the VCOs to test the products. This will help in protecting the interests of the consumers against all kinds of unfair trade practices undertaken by some of the traders.

Conclusion

Consumer Movement should become Peoples' Movement. There must be total commitment from the Government, Businessmen, Voluntary

Consumer Organisations, Consumer Activists, NGOs, Educational Institutions, Consumers and the Media to play an important role in disseminating information related to Consumer Protection to the common consumers of the country and to make Consumer Movement a great success.

References

Sharma, Chandrakant (1995), *Role of Consumer Organisations in Consumer Protection,* New Delhi: Kanishka Publishers.

Dhyani, A.K. and Saklani, A. (1994), "Awareness of Rights among Indian Consumers", *Indian Journal of Marketing*, XXIII (7-8), July-August.

Himachalam, D. (1998), "Consumer Protection in India – A Brief Analysis", *Consumer Protection and the Law*, New Delhi: APH Publishing Corporation.

Lalita Khurana (1995), "Consumer Protection – The Growing Concern", *Yojana*, 39(5), March 31.

Narayana Reddy, P. and Anil Ramesh, M. (1998), "The Role of an Independent Agency to Protect the Consumer Interest: An Empirical Study", *Indian Journal of Marketing*, XXVIII (8-12), August-December.

Narender Kumar & Neena Batra (1990), "Consumer Rights: Awareness and Actions—In Small Cities", *Indian Journal of Marketing*, XXI (1-4), September-December.

Neelakanta, B.C. and Anand, H.B. (1985), "Consumerism in Karnataka: An Overlook", *Southern Economist*, 24 (13), November 1.

Ralph, M. Gaedeke (1970), "What Business, Government and Consumer Spokesmen Think about Consumerism", *The Journal of Consumer Affairs*, 4 (1), Summer.

Srinivasa, Narayanaswamy (1990), "Role of Government Agencies in Consumer Protection", *Consumer Confrontation*, 10 (4), July-August.

Srivastava, P.N. & Sakhivel (1990), "Role of Voluntary Organisations in Promoting Consumerism", *Indian Management*, 29 (10), October.

Subramanyam, D.A.R., Ram Prasad and Anil Kumar (1982), "Need for Consumer Organisations ", *Indian Journal of Marketing*, XII (9-10), May-June.

Thanulingam, N. and Kochadai, M. (1989), "An Evaluation of Consumer Awareness", *Indian Journal of Marketing*, XIX (8-9-10), April-May-June.

Vyas, H.D. (2003), "Consumer Protection: Role of Voluntary Organisations of Bhavnagar District", *Indian Journal of Marketing*, XXXIII (7), July.

Webster, F.E. (1973), "Business and Consumerism?" *Harvard Business Review*, September-October.

Will Straver (1977), "The International Consumerist Movement: Theory and Practical Implications for Marketing Strategy", *European Journal of Marketing*, 11(2).

SECTION III
Grassroots Democracy and Consumer Empowerment

12
Grassroots Democracy and Empowerment of Rural Consumers through PRIs

Mohammad Azvar Khan

Introduction

Rural consumers continue to attach a high degree of importance to value for money; both manufacturers and traders would be compelled to explore every conceivable method to improve operational efficiencies, in order to achieve substantial and profitable business growth. The Indian rural consumer durables market has undergone a major transformation since the liberalisation process, initiated in 1991. The market size, product penetration, the variety and technology of products sold, have all experienced a quantum leap. Improved product choice and decline in real prices, matched by increased consumer incomes have driven the market growth rate to dizzy heights. The annual market for consumer durables in India (excluding computers and communication products) is currently of the order of Rs. 25,000 crore. The rural market is growing at a much faster rate than its urban counterpart, and the former offers encouraging potential for further growth as well. The penetration of durables and home appliances is quite low in India, compared to several other developing countries.[1]

The consumer groups in rural areas differ by occupation, income, social and cultural groupings. The rural marketer will find it useful to identify consumer groups that require products purchased from the urban market. The rural market has significant group in the service sector, either the Government or the organised sector, and this group is ready market for urban products.[2] The rural consumer is less literate/communicative, conservative/ utility oriented, loves traditional values/serious and adheres to socio-cultural customs/practices, simple, brand loyal, emotional, adopts savings oriented lifestyle, the family decision making rests with the eldest male member only.They are price sensitive, looks for reliable products, heterogeneous in grouping on income and wealth, loves finance/credit facility in purchases, not brand loyal, limited infrastructure facilities with large geographic area, warmer social connectivity and cultural ethnicity, lesser information dissemination on products and festival oriented purchases season.[3]

Exploitation of Rural Consumers

With the growth in rural markets and due to poor knowledge about their rights and also the lack of skills to take a rational decision based on information about the product or services, the rural consumer of India is exploited in many ways. The rural consumer has been made to endure sub-standard products and services adulterated food, short weights and measures, spurious and hazardous drugs, exorbitant process endemic shortages leading to black marketing and profiteering, unfulfilled manufacturing guarantees and host of other ills.The rural consumer who generally depend on weekly markets to purchase essential things are often cheated due to lack of choices.

The rural consumers in India are generally ignorant and they are also unorganised. Thus, they are exploited by the manufactures, traders and the service providers in different ways.The rural consumer are not only scattered, but also diverse and heterogeneous. As a result of Globalisation and liberalisation the rural market in India is the largest potential market in the world. Hence, there are vast opportunities for rural marketing.The manufacturers and the traders take advantage of the condition of the rural consumers. It has been observed that the condition of the rural markets on account of lack of completion among the sellers. The rural consumers face various problems like adulteration, short weighing and measuring, lack of safety and quality control in appliances and equipment, electrical and mechanical, unfair warranties and guarantees, imitation sales gimmicks and unreasonable pricing.[4]

Panchayati Raj Institutions: Boost to Grassroots Democracy

The 73rd Constitutional Amendment Act contains provisions for devolution of powers and responsibilities upon panchayats at the appropriate level with reference to (a) the preparation of plans for economic development and social justice; and (b) the implementation of such schemes for economic development and social justice, as may be entrusted to them. The Provision of the Panchayat (Extension to Scheduled Areas) Act, 1996 (PESA) extends panchayats to tribal areas in nine States. It enables the tribal society to shape their own development, preserve and conserve their traditional rights over natural resources. The status of PRIs in a State can be reviewed in terms of the following parameters: (i) Conduct of Panchayat Elections; (ii) Devolution of Financial Powers; (iii) Devolution of Functions and Functionaries; (iv) Constitution of District Planning Committees (DPCs); (v) Act 40 of 1996 – Provision of the Panchayat (Extension to Scheduled Areas) Act, 1996 (PESA); and (vi) Status and Empowerment of Gram Sabha. The Union Cabinet of the Government of India, on 27 August, 2009, approved 50 per cent reservation for women in PRIs. The Indian states which have already implemented 50 per cent reservation for women in PRIs are Madhya Pradesh, Bihar, Uttarakhand and Himachal Pradesh.[5] As of 25 November, 2011; the states of Andhra Pradesh, Chhattisgarh, Jharkhand, Kerala, Maharashtra, Odisha, Rajasthan and Tripura also reserve 50 per cent of their posts for women.[6]

At the village level, the most important provisions relating to participation and accountability are those governing reservations and the Gram Sabha. Under the 73rd Amendment, one-third of all seats must be reserved for women. Likewise, reservations for Scheduled Castes (SCs) and Scheduled Tribes (STs) are made in proportion to their population.[7] At the village level, the Gram Sabha, which constitutes all eligible voters within a Gram Panchayat area, is meant to serve as a principal mechanism for transparency and accountability.

The "Eleventh Schedule" of the 73rd Amendment identifies 29 areas over which Panchayats can legitimately have jurisdiction. Many of these – such as agriculture, minor irrigation, animal husbandry, fisheries, social forestry, small-scale industries, and implementation of land reforms – focus on particular sectors within the rural economy. Others such as rural housing, rural electrification, transportation and communication linkages are primarily concerned with the provision and maintenance of rural infrastructure. Some cover the provision of key rural services, such as health, sanitation and primary, secondary and vocational education. Others still governs the provision of targeted welfare benefits such as the PDS, and benefits for scheduled castes and tribes, women and children and the handicapped. In short, the 73rd Amendment covers many areas that would enable the Panchayats to improve the lives and wellbeing of poor and vulnerable groups.[8] Moreover, it contains specific provisions that guarantee the participation of traditionally excluded groups, such as women, SCs and STs, and transparency for local institutions such as the Gram Panchayats and the Gram Sabha.

Problems of Rural Consumers

When the rural market grows in such a rapid pace, the quantum of consumer grievances also increase simultaneously. The main problems faced by rural consumers are related to adulteration, short weighing and measuring, lack of safety and quality in appliances and equipment, unfair warranties and guarantees, imitation and sales gimmick, unreasonable pricing etc. The Indian Consumer Protection Act (CPA), 1986 ensures better protection of rights and interest of people who are consumers in one way or the other form the exploitation of trade and industries. According to the Act, anyone who buys goods and services for his/her use is a consumer. A user of such goods and services with the permission of the buyer is also a consumer.[9] The Department of Consumer Affairs of the Government of India and various State Governments have undertaken a number of innovative measures to protect rights of rural consumers. Consumer disputes redressal mechanism (popularly known as consumer forums) are set-up under the Act at district, state and national level to provide simple and inexpensive quick redressal against consumer complaints.[10]

A consumer can file complaint in the consumer court against any defective goods purchased or deficient service rendered including restrictive/unfair trade practice adopted by any trader/person.[11] The Consumer Forum has power to order removal/replacement of defects/deficiencies in goods and services, refund of price paid, compensation for loss/injury suffered, discontinuation of unfair/restrictive trade practice, withdrawal of hazardous or unsafe goods or award of adequate cost to the parties etc.[12] However, the three-tier consumer forums, set-up under the Act are in urban areas. This makes it difficult for rural consumers to approach the forum. Moreover, though the forum have been set-up as special courts, the non-extension of their benches in rural areas makes accessibility a big problem and leading to poor public participation. A web-based system for lodging and monitoring of complaints is also in place. However, only 6.9 per cent of the Indian population are internet users. Hence, unfortunately very few have availed this excellent mechanism due to lack of awareness and accessibility, particularly amongst rural and semi-urban populations. While experts and consumer activists believe that redressal platforms can forge consumer activism in rural areas, the government is undecided about setting-up such a mechanism below the district level. The Department of Consumer Affairs has been organising consumer rights' awareness events in all *talukas*. As of now, there are no plans to extend the sittings of the *lok adalats* to villages or to set-up redressal platforms there. Experts attribute the lack of participation by the rural population in consumer fora to the failure of the government to form protection councils as per the Act, at the state and district levels, to promote and protect consumer rights. The absence of laboratories at district level to test disputed products further makes the process delayed. In this context, the local administrative bodies in the country can play an important role in protecting the rural consumers.

Empowerment of Rural Consumer and Role of PRIs

Like in many other countries, consumer movement in India as a social force originated with the necessity of protecting and promoting the interest of consumers' against fraudulent, unethical and unfair trade practices. The movement initially reflected a common perception, which characterised traders and manufacturers as people who were out to maximise profits by means of fair or foul with scant regard for consumers' well-being. Selective shopping could be the only form of consumer resistance at the early stages, the basic tenet governing the legal position of consumers being "buyers beware". The movement gained a momentum after enactment of CPA. Overtime the movement found expression in efforts to bring pressure on business firms as well as government to correct business conduct that may be unfair and against the interest of consumers at large. The movement, which has been confined to the middle class citizens in urban centres by large, is now having a presence in the rural areas as well. But, it has to spread and strengthened further among the masses in rural and semi-urban areas.[13]

The fact is that majority of consumers in the country are even unaware of the existence of consumer forums to which they can make their grievances. A CAG-commissioned survey finding on the status of the CPA conducted in 2006, in connection with 20 years of CPA says, 82 per cent of the consumers are not aware of the CPA and 66 per cent of their rights. The ground reality is that the conditions are not very favourable and conducive for the consumer. He is being exploited and cheated day in and day out. Ignorance is one of the prominent factors contributing in the exploitation of the consumers and is most prevalent amongst the rural masses.[14] The Gram Panchayats are there in all the villages, which is the available constitutional mechanism across the country spread in all 643 districts. It is only through this Constitutional mechanism that the consumer movement can get a boost and consumer awareness can be spread among rural masses. Hence, there is an urgent need to take initiatives by the Central and State Department of Consumer Affairs to involve and make use of PRIs in various programmes related to consumer awareness. In addition publicity/awareness materials on consumer protection need to be brought out in regional languages and distributed among the elected representatives of PRIs.[15]

Gram Sabha is the best forum to educate the rural masses about their rights as consumers as well as the techniques to redress their grievances, which are attended by almost every villager. On occasions like December 24, which is the National Consumer Day, meetings of the Gram Sabha need to be convened, where the villagers could properly be educated about their rights as consumers. Necessary amendments has to be made to set up consumer protection councils at Block and Gram panchayat as well and to make the PRIs integral part of the councils at all the three levels. In addition, the concerned departments mandated to deal with issues related to consumer protection need to be transferred to the PRIs and PRIs to be given the responsibility to coordinate the functioning of these departments.

The *Gram Panchayat* could play a significant role in creating awareness at the grassroots level. Appropriate technology and creative media could be used to raise awareness. The relevant resource materials in regional languages could be made available in hard copies as well as in soft copies through internet. The *Gram Panchayats* also can consider using media such as documentary films, street plays, competitions etc. to spread consumer awareness. The services of government primary school teachers could be utilised in conducting consumer awareness programmes. Complaints Handling, Information and Advisory Services (CHIAS) cell could be opened in each of the *Gram Panchayat* offices. CHIAS can act as an advice giving and complaints handling mechanism between the common consumer and the district consumer fora. This will help in speedy resolution of the complaints without taking it to the consumer forums as well as substantially reduce the burden of district forums. Selected representatives from each of the *Gram Panchayats* can be identified and trained to handle these cells. Issues at local level affecting the consumers can be discussed and disposed of in these CHIAS cell instead of taking each complaint to the district forum. Similar mechanism could be established at *Taluka* (Block) level as well.

A selected group consisting of *Gram Sevak, Sarpanch*, PRI members, teachers, youth, office bearers of Self-Help Groups (SHGs) etc. can be trained as '*barefoot consumer activists*' to assist the rural population to complaint resolution at the prelitigation stage. Personal consumer advice could also be provided not only for legal problems, but also for every day consumer problems. Required budgetary allocations have to be made to PRIs for consumer awareness, capacity building as well as for supporting the functioning of CHIAS.[16] Ministry of Panchayati Raj, Government of India is in the process of establishing Bharat Nirman Rajiv Gandhi Seva Kendras (RGSK) at Block and Panchayat headquarters respectively in each of the states to bring about convergence of techniques, resources and manpower. This RGSK could well support the functioning of CHIAS cell. In addition Ministry of Information and Technology is in the process of connecting every panchayat in the country through internet. By 2012, every panchayat will have an internet equipped service centre, to ensure rural access to various online services. This can provide further boost to CHIAS.[17]

Conclusion

There is an urgent need to address the concerns of the rural consumers and the only way forward is to involve the available Constitutional mechanism of PRIs. PRIs cannot become effective institutions of local self-government unless they have strong financial base with clearly defined sources of revenues. For this, it is suggested that States should have a separate Budget document for PRIs and ULBs respectively indicating transfer of resources under Plan and Non-Plan Head, tied and untied funds to these bodies. PRIs should have enough powers to raise resources from local resources. State Government should provide one-third of the total Plan size to the PRIs as an untied funds. Furthermore, States would be required to earmark resources out of the total plan of the States for decentralised planning; and the State Governments should create a separate Budget Head "Panchayats" under which all the funds from Centrally Sponsored Schemes (CSSs) as well as from the State Budget should be pooled together at least at the district level from where the district panchayats distribute the funds to different tiers as per their felt needs. The PRI – NGO relationship should not be adversial but they should complement each other's efforts. NGOs have to accept the primacy of PRIs, while Panchayats should appreciate the role of NGOs in terms of their access to knowledge, technology and capacity to deliver.

There is a need to conceptualise the relationship between PRIs and NGOs and establish a linkage between them. NGOs should work under the direction and supervision of the PRIs especially if subjects dealt with fall under jurisdiction of the panchayats and are financed by NGOs and PRIs can help each other, keeping in view the larger interests of the poor, will have to be done.the public funds. The delineation of areas where 73rd Constitutional Amendment Act, 1992 aims at to establish democratic decentralised development process through people's participation in decision-making, implementation and delivery. To achieve this, panchayats are required to play an active role in the preparation of plan and its implementation for economic development and social justice. However, State Governments have vested wide powers of suspension and dismissal of elected PRI in the State bureaucracy under their Panchayati Raj Acts. This has placed PRIs at disadvantaged position vis-à-vis State bureaucracy and hurts the concept of democratic decentralised administration and autonomy of the PRIs. Therefore, State Governments are required to repeal all orders/instructions that make PRI subordinate to State bureaucracy and make necessary amendments in the Panchayati Raj Acts so that autonomy of elected panchayati raj bodies can be maintained and they function as a unit of local self-government.

Notes

1. Kumar, N. Anil & Karpagam, J. Joseph, *International Journal of Business and Management Tomorrow,* Vol. 2, No. 4.
2. Choudhry, Rajendra. "Consumer Protection Act—A Boon for Farmers and Rural Consumers", *Kurukshetra*, May 2008.
3. *Supra* note 1.
4. Misra, Suresh (2009). "Market and the Rural Consumer", *Yojana,* February, p. 44.
5. Mullick, Rohit & Raaj, Neelam. "Panchayats turn into Kangaroo Courts", *The Times of India*. (9 September 2007) http://timesofindia.indiatimes.com/Opinion/Sunday_Specials/Panchayats_turn_into_kangaroo_courts/rssarticleshow/2351247.cms
6. India 2007, Publications Division, Ministry of Information and Broadcasting, Government of India, p. 696.
7. Subrata, K. Mitra & Singh, V.B. (1999). *Democracy and Social Change in*

India: A Cross-Sectional Analysis of the National Electorate. New Delhi: Sage Publications.

8. Subrata K. Mitra (2001). "Making Local Government Work: Local Elites, Panchayati Raj and Governance in India", in Kohli, Atul (ed.). *The Success of India's Democracy*. Cambridge: Cambridge University Press.
9. See section 2(1) (d) of Consumer Protection Act, 1986.
10. *Ibid.,* Section 9.
11. *Ibid.,* Section 2(1) (c).
12. *Ibid.,* Section 14.
13. Mehta, S. Pradeep (1998). "How to Survive as a Consumer" *CUTS.*
14. Bijapurkar, Rama & Rajesh Shukla "*Spotlight on Rural Consumers*", December 2008, Livemint.com
15. Bijapurkar, Rama & Shukla, Rajesh (2009). "*The Rural Consumer Myth – II*", March 26, 2009, Livemint.com
16. *History of Panchayati Raj in India,* availableat:*http://en.wikipedia.org/wiki/History_of_panchayati_raj_in_India* CUTS Report of Upabhokta Mitra Training (UMT) Programme, 2000.
17. Cheriyan, George, *Rural Consumers and Role of Local Bodies in Consumer Protection*, CUTS, Centre for Consumer Action, Research & Training.

13

Panchayati Raj Institutions

A Mechanism for Consumer Empowerment

Joseph Benjamin

Introduction

India is one of the biggest consumer markets in the world. But then how the rights of consumers are being protected is the matter of concern. Most of rural consumers being illiterate, ignorant and not fully aware of their exploitation by the manufacturers, producers and shopkeepers are unable to get justice. All these happen because the consumers are unaware of their rights. The success of consumer movement mainly depends upon the level of consumer awareness generated in the country by educating the consumers about their rights and responsibilities. Then, who should be educating the rural mass about their consumer rights? Before one discusses the agency responsible for educating the rural mass about their rights, it would be pertinent to define the meaning of consumer. Who can be considered as consumer? Anyone who consumes certain goods and avails of certain services for which she/he pays is a consumer. At the same time a person who buys goods or avails of services exclusively for the purpose of earning his/her livelihood by means of self-employment, comes under the definition of consumer. In order to protect the consumers, Government has taken a significant step by amending the Consumer Protection Act, 1986.

The new provision incorporated the Mahatma Gandhi's perception that "Consumer is the King," in this Act. The Consumer Protection Act was passed in 1986. This Act extends to the whole of India except the state of Jammu & Kashmir. According to Section 2(1) (d) of 1986 Act, Consumer means any person who buys any goods or hires or avails of any services for a consideration which has been paid or promised or partly paid or partly promised or under any system of different payment, but does not include a person who obtains such goods for resale or for any commercial purpose. The consumer rights includes the following: (i) the right to be protected against the marketing of goods and services which are hazardous to life and property; (ii) the right to be informed about the quality, quantity, potency, purity, standard and price of goods or the services; (iii) the right to be assured, wherever possible, access to a variety of goods and services at competitive prices; (iv) the right to be heard and to be assured that consumers' interests will receive due consideration at appropriate Forums; (v) the right to seek redressal against unfair trade practices or unscrupulous exploitation of consumers; and (vi) the right to consumer education. Who will be able to impart consumer education? In rural India *gram panchayat* will play a very important role in imparting consumer education to masses. The present chapter studies the role of Panchayat in consumer education. Before studying the role of Panchayati raj in imparting consumer education in rural areas, it will be pertinent to study the Panchayati Raj in India.

Panchayats are the backbone of the Indian villages since the advent of history. It is an engine of growth, agent of change and development. The contribution of Lord George Fredrick Samuel Ripon (1827-1909) in starting in the year 1881-84 local self-government is remarkable. Gandhiji's dream of every village being a republic or Panchayats having powers has been translated into reality after Independence. April 24, 1993 is a landmark in the history of Panchayati Raj in India as on this day the Constitution (73rd Amendment) Act, 1992 came into force to provide Constitutional status to the Panchyati Raj Institutions. Since 1993, the Panchayati Raj Institution has been playing a vital role in educating the rural consumers in their rights. The present chapter is an effort to study how the Panchayati Raj Institution will be a catalyst in making rural mass aware about the consumer right in their respective field.

Panchayati Raj and Rural Development

The first Prime Minister of Independent India Pandit Jawaharlal Nehru set in notion Community Development Programme in 1952. Today Panchayats have been the backbone of the Indian villages for its development. Gandhiji's dream of every village being a republic or Panchayats having powers has been translated into reality with the introduction of the three-tier Panchayati Raj system to enlist people's participation in rural reconstruction and development. Seventy third Constitutional Amendment Act, 1992 has been the landmark in the history of *Panchayati Raj in India.* The salient features of the Act are: (i) to provide three-tier system of *Panchayati Raj* for all States having population of over 20 lakh; (ii) to hold *Panchayat* elections regularly every 5 years; (iii) to provide reservation of seats for Scheduled Castes, Scheduled Tribes and women (not less than 33%); (iv) to appoint State Finance Commission to make recommendations regarding financial powers of the Panchayats; and (v) to constitute District Planning Committee to prepare draft development plan for the district as a whole. According to the Constitution, Panchayats shall be given powers and authority to function as institutions of self-governance. The powers and responsibilities to be delegated to Panchayats at the appropriate level are: (a) preparation of plan for economic development and social justice; (b) implementation of schemes for economic development and social justice in relation to 29 subjects given in Eleventh Schedule to the Constitution; and (c) to levy, collect and appropriate taxes, duties, tolls and fees. The 73rd Constitutional Amendment Act gives Constitutional status to the *Gram Sabha.*

Under the Act, *Gram Sabha* has been vested with powers for ownership of minor forest produce, development plans approval, selection of beneficiaries under various programmes, consultation on land acquisition, manage minor water bodies, control mineral leases, regulate/ prohibit sale of intoxicants, prevent alienation of land and restore unlawfully alienated land of Scheduled Tribes, manage village markets, control money lending to Scheduled Tribes, and control institutions and functionaries in all social sectors.

New Face of Rural India

Over the past few years rural India has witnessed an increase in the purchasing power of consumers, accompanied by their desire to upgrade their standard of living. The steps taken by the Government of India to eradicate the poverty have also attempt is made to improve the condition of rural masses. As a result, rural consumers have upgraded their life styles through making changes in their consumption patterns by adding more nutritious food and are purchasing life style products such as cosmetics, mobile phones, cooking gas etc., which have become necessities for them. Besides this, a number of schemes launched by the government have changed the face of rural India. The Governmental schemes like of India especially Mahatma Gandhi National Rural Employment Guarantee Act (MGNREGA) scheme, which has a budget of more than 40,000 crore have given the rural population an opportunity to meet their daily needs. With the initiation of various rural development programmes there have been an upsurge of employment opportunities for the rural poor. NREGS guarantees 100 days employment to a rural household and provides much needed bargaining power to battle the exploitation in the farming sector as a labourer. Also the increased demand for labour in the urban projects such as Jawaharlal Nehru National Urban Renewal Mission (JNNURM) has resulted in more money being sent back home by the immigrant worker. Bharat Nirman, an Indian plan for creating basic rural infrastructure, is having a budget of Rs. 58,000 crore for 2011-12. It is a step towards bridging the gap between rural and urban areas and improving the quality of lives of rural masses. It comprises projects on irrigation, roads (Pradhan Mantri Gram Sadak Yojana), housing (Indira Awaas Yojana), water supply and electrification and telecommunication connectivity.

According to a report by McKinsey & Company named "The Bird of Gold: The Rise of India's Consumer Market", by 2025 India will triple its income level and will become the fifth largest Consumer Market. A lot of this wealth will be created in the urban areas, but even the rural households will benefit. The real annual income for rural households will move from 2.8 per cent in the past two decades to 3.6 per cent in the next two. Rural markets are growing at double the pace of urban markets and for many product categories, rural markets account for well over 60 per cent of the national demand. Companies are realising slowly but surely that the key to gain true market leadership lies in tapping the rural potential.

Government and Consumer Empowerment

Realising the importance of consumer empowerment the Government has accorded top priority to Consumer Education, Consumer Protection and Consumer Awareness. India is a country, which has taken a lead in introducing progressive legislation for consumer protection. The most important milestone in Consumer Movement in the country has been the enactment of the Consumer Protection Act, 1986. The Act has set in motion a revolution in the field of consumer rights that perhaps cannot have any parallel anywhere else in the World. The Act applies to all goods and services unless specially exempted by the Central Government, in all sectors whether Private, Public or Co-operative.

Rights of the Consumers

Consumers' Protection Act, 1986 recognises the following rights of the consumers:

(1) *Right to Safety*: Every consumer has a right to be safeguarded and protected from goods which are dangerous or harmful to life and property, e.g. colours used in food products, toys, home appliances etc.

(2) *Right to Information*: The consumers have the right to be informed about the quality, quantity, potency, purity, standard and the price while choosing a commodity or service for purchase.

(3) *Right to Choose*: The consumers have the right to be assured, wherever possible, an access to a variety of goods at competitive prices. This right will help the consumers to make a choice of selecting goods and services according to their financial ability and preferences.

(4) *Right to be Heard*: Consumers have the right to express their opinions regarding the quality and prices of the commodities or services. Their views should receive due consideration from manufacturers, sellers and traders. Many business houses have their Consumer Affairs Departments to entertain the consumer's feedback about their products and services.

(5) *Right to Seek Redressal*: Every consumer has the right to seek redressal of grievances before the Consumers' Redressal Agencies, namely the District Forum, the State Commission and the National Commission.

(6) *Right to Consumer Education*: Every consumer has the right to receive information about low quality, spurious, adulterated and dangerous goods through posters, exhibitions, literature etc., through whatever other media.

Need for Consumer Education

Consumer education delivers practical skills and knowledge that are relevant to everyone and helps consumers to get the most from today's competitive markets where business works hard for their customers and respond to their needs. The importance of consumer education is increasingly being recognised. It should be an integral part of the formal education and lifelong learning programmes. Consumer education can help markets work well for consumers and also help to protect vulnerable consumers prevent consumer detriment and combat social exclusion. Consumer education is thus, a potent tool for empowering consumers and empowered consumers are knowledgeable, confident, assertive and self-reliant. As a tool for empowerment, consumer education is central to make markets work well for consumers. Business can reap real benefits from an active involvement in consumer education, improved communication with more discerning customers and quicker, easier, and less expensive solutions to problems where they arise. For this the consumer protection law should set minimum standards for quality and safety and ensure that consumers have access to updated and quality information. Thus, to be effective, consumer education initiatives should be focused on clear priorities and targeted at those most in need. By deciding priorities in this way, consumer education can bring real benefits for vulnerable and socially excluded consumer by offering the opportunity to gain valuable life skills.

Need for Consumer Awareness

To meet the challenges, consumers must arm themselves against problems faced in the market since they are not automatically protected by the market. Therefore, a consumer's best defence is knowledge of his/her rights as a consumer and of the remedies which exist to resolve these problems when they occur. The various stakeholders in the consumer protection movement need to work out a strategy to address the problems of the consumers. Creating awareness and educating the consumers will go a long way in helping the consumer to understand what constitutes consumer protection, what is the need to know about one's rights and how to redress one's grievances if anything goes wrong. Moreover, an educated and informed consumer will be able to take a rational decision while buying a product or availing a service.

The rural consumer has to be educated about resource maintenance and environment preservation. The rural consumers have to be educated about the possible exploitation of their resources and the subsequent detrimental changes in their life styles, if they are not protective of their environment and yield to the pressure that booming urban markets exert upon rural areas. Consumer education should foster mutual awareness and understanding between the urban and rural sectors as well as rich and poor sections of society. Consumer education can strengthen the bonds that exist between various social segments and minimise the divisive factors. The market and the industry seek to widen the gaps that exist and seek to rule consumers through fostering divisions. The Consumer education programmes whether at *gram panchayat*, school and college levels or through government or NGO channels should seek to remove these distances.

Governmental Initiatives towards Consumer Awareness and Education

In a country like ours, given the scenario of economic disparity and level of education and ignorance, educating the consumers, remains a gigantic task. This calls for concerted efforts from everyone. Government has takenup number of initiatives for creating consumesr awareness in the country. The Consumer Awareness Scheme for the Eleventh Five Year Plan amounting to a total of Rs. 409 crore has been approved by the Cabinet Committee on Economic Affairs in January 2008.

The slogan "*Jago Grahak Jago*" has now become a household name as a result of the publicity campaign undertaken in the last few years. It can be seen almost everyday in the newspapers. It has been making people aware their rights and tells them that before one buys any goods one must see the expiry dates. Through the increased thrust on consumer awareness in the Eleventh Five Year Plan, the Government has endeavoured to inform the common man of his rights as a consumer. As part of the consumer awareness scheme, the rural and remote areas have been given top priority.

There is a full-fledged Department of Consumer Affairs which tries to provide consumer education through seminars in different educational institutions. Special programmes have also been telecast on Lok Sabha TV and Doordarshan to highlight the issues relating to consumer awareness. Issues pertaining to rural and remote areas have been given prominence in the various advertisement spots.

Consumer awareness messages are also being disseminated through Meghdoot Postcards in consultation with Department of Post to reach far-flung rural areas including North-East States. Posters carrying messages pertaining to consumer awareness have been displayed in 1.55 lakh Rural Post Offices and more than 25,000 Urban Post Offices throughout the country.

The multi-media publicity to educate consumers and make them aware about their rights will have a long lasting impact not only on the end consumers, but also on the entire manufacturing and services sector.

It will go a long way in introducing greater accountability and transparency in the services provided by the public as well as private sector since the end user, i.e. consumer will be educated and will become aware enough to ask for best possible services in return of his hard earned money. Through newspapers the Department of Consumer Affairs has been trying to educate the Indian masses. The day is, therefore, not far off when the consumers will be truly empowered.

Rural India and Consumer Education

Today about 70 per cent of India's population lives in rural areas. Of the 121 crore Indians, 83.3 crore live in rural areas while 37.7 crore stay in urban areas, as per the Census 2011. The National Council of Applied Economic Research (NCAER) survey report says that there are 720 million consumers across the villages in rural India. Hence, the development of the nation largely depends upon the development of the rural population. Majority of the rural population is dependent upon agriculture for their subsistence. Community Development Programmes, Integrated Rural Development Programme, bringing local self-government to the roots of the village through introduction of *Panchayati Raj* system ushered a new era of rural development. Schemes for providing effective rural healthcare, guaranteeing 100 days of job, promoting literacy and adult education, expansion of rural industries are other development programmes that have received the thrust of the government's development approach.

Factors Leading to Consumer Exploitation

In India, consumers generally face a number of problems. They include non-availability of goods, adulteration, hoarding, black marketing, deceptive and misleading selling techniques and false warranties or guarantees etc. There are number factors which are responsible for the exploitation of consumers, viz., High Price, Poor Quality of goods, Lack of Knowledge, Unorganised group of consumer, unorganised group of consumer, Unfair trade practices, Lack of coordination, Intangible services, Multiplicity of weights and measures, Market oriented production.

(1) *High Price:* Sometimes, artificial shortage of commodities is created in the market. Consumers are compelled to buy the commodities at high price. There may not be actually shortage of goods, but they are

kept in the godown so that it can be taken out when goods are completely exhausted. The villagers being ignorant about their consumer rights are exploited frequently.

(2) *Poor quality of Goods:* There is a general feeling that in India especially in rural area, the quality of goods or services has been declining. Manufacturers, in expectation of greater profit, increase production, but neglect the quality aspect of production. Many reputed firms have their own quality control departments, but the number of such firms is very limited. The quality of the products can be deteriorated due to adulterated material used in production. Such adulteration is very dangerous to health.

(3) *Lack of Knowledge:* The Consumer Protection Act confers on the consumer the right to be informed about the quality, quantity, purity, standard and price of goods. Sometimes the goods demanded by the consumers are not available in the market. Consumers are compelled to purchase the unknown substitutes. Consumers do not get the full information about the quality of the product. They have to buy inferior goods at high prices due to lack of information. Because of their ignorance, rural mass fall prey of exploitation.

(4) *Unorganised group of Consumers:* The producers are organised lot. They can determine the prices of their products. Hence, they sell their products at exorbitantly higher prices. The consumers on the other hand are unorganised. He is not in a position to demand justice. In the village rural mass can think of *nyaya panchayat.* They are misled and deceived by the manufacturers and traders while purchasing goods or hiring services. In the villages, people are busy with their cultivation and are not organised. Hence, they become the victim of exploitation.

(5) *Misleading Advertisements: A*dvertisement is a powerful media of mass communication. Consumers get information about the arrival of new products in the market through different advertising media. Sometimes, the consumers are misled by false advertisements. The manufacturers also use advertising as a tool to create artificial demand for undesirable goods. Rural mass being ignorant are attracted by new items in the market. There is not expiry dates on the new goods nor have they branded name.

(6) *Unfair Trade Practices*: Consumers face various problems due to unfair trade practices adopted by the producers. Unfair Trade Practice means a trade practice, which for the purpose of promoting the sale, use or supply of any goods or for the provision of any service, adopts any unfair or deceptive practice. For example one can see the false representation that the goods or services are of a particular standard,

quality, quantity, grades, etc. Sometimes, old goods are sold as new goods by changing the wrappers. Manufacturer gives to the public warranty and guarantee which sellers do not provide.

(7) *Lack of Coordination*: There is no coordination amongst the consumers, traders, manufacturers and the government. That means that there is no interaction between them due to which the interest of the consumer is not protected. In rural areas all are busy with their work. *Sarpanch* has no time to listen to the grievances of consumers in the village. It is the *sarpanch* and *gram sabha* which should coordinate the consumers in the village.

(8) *Intangible Services*: The services offered by producers are intangible. A consumer has a right to see, touch, smell, hear or taste the product before purchasing. But, it is not applicable to services. Therefore, the consumers are cheated while purchasing the services.

(9) *Multiplicity of Weights and Measures:* The illiterate consumers are cheated due to multiplicity of weights and measures. They create

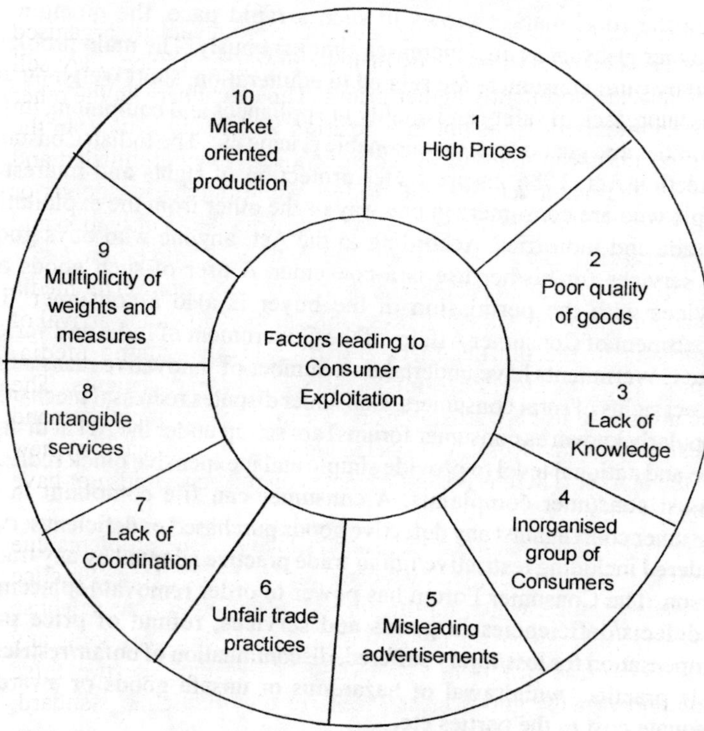

Fig. 13.1: Factors leading to Consumer Exploitation

uncertainty, especially in the rural marketing. Sometime, piece of brick or stone is used to measure the grains in rural areas. The measuring weight are not passed by the passing authority, hence rural people depend on the old weight. Most of them are not aware that measuring weights are to be passed periodically.

(10) *Market oriented Production*: The production of goods is market oriented. The goods produced in the economy satisfy the wants of upper and middle classes. The production should cater to the needs of the people of lower classes. Some traders do not give proper treatment to poor customers. Because any production for poor does not provide enough profit. Therefore, their wants are ignored. Some farmers think of cultivating cash product like sugar cane, soybean etc. There is scanty eatable grain available for rural mass.

Absence of Redressal Mechanism in Rural Areas

When the rural market grows in such a rapid pace, the quantum of consumer grievances also increases simultaneously. The main problems faced by rural consumers are related to adulteration, short weighing and measuring, lack of safety and quality in appliances and equipment, unfair warranties and guarantees, unreasonable pricing etc. The Indian Consumer Protection Act, 1986 ensure better protection of rights and interest of people who are consumers in one way or the other from the exploitation of trade and industries. According to the Act, anyone who buys goods and services for his/her use is a consumer. A user of such goods and services with the permission of the buyer is also a consumer. The Department of Consumer Affairs of the Government of India and various State Governments have undertaken a number of innovative measures to protect rights of rural consumers. Consumer disputes redressal mechanism (popularly known as consumer forums) are set-up under the Act at district, state and national level to provide simple and inexpensive quick redressal against consumer complaints. A consumer can file complaint in the consumer court against any defective goods purchased or deficient service rendered including restrictive/unfair trade practice adopted by any trader/ person. The Consumer Forum has power to order removal/replacement of defects/deficiencies in goods and services, refund of price paid, compensation for loss/injury suffered, discontinuation of unfair/restrictive trade practice, withdrawal of hazardous or unsafe goods or award of adequate cost to the parties etc.

However, the three-tier consumer forums, set-up under the Act are in urban areas. This makes it difficult for rural consumers to approach the forum. Moreover, though the forum have been set-up as special courts, the non-extension of their benches in rural areas makes accessibility a big problem and leading to poor public participation. A web-based system for lodging and monitoring of complaints is also in place. However, only 6.9 per cent of the Indian population is internet users. Hence, unfortunately very few have availed this excellent mechanism due to lack of awareness and accessibility, particularly amongst rural and semi-urban populations.

While experts and consumer activists believe that redressal platforms can forge consumer activism in rural areas, the government is undecided about setting-up such a mechanism below the district level. The Department of Consumer Affairs has been organising consumer rights' awareness events in all *talukas*. As of now, there are no plans to extend the sittings of the *lok adalats* to villages or to set-up redressal platforms there. The absence of laboratories at district level to test disputed products further makes the process delayed. In this context, the local administrative bodies should come forward and protect the rights of the rural consumers.

Consumer Protection and Role of Local Bodies

Like in many other countries, consumer movement in India as a social force originated with the necessity of protecting and promoting the interest of consumers' against fraudulent, unethical and unfair trade practices. The movement initially reflected a common perception, which characterised traders and manufacturers as people who were out to maximise profits by means of fair or foul with scant regard for consumers' well-being. Selective shopping could be the only form of consumer resistance at the early stages, the basic tenet governing the legal position of consumers being "buyers beware". The movement gained a momentum after enactment of Consumer Protection Act in 1986. Over time the movement found expression in efforts to bring pressure on business firms as well as government to correct business conduct that may be unfair and against the interest of consumers at large. The movement, which has been confined to the middle class citizens in urban centres by large, is now having a presence in the rural areas as well. But, it has to spread and strengthened further among the masses in rural and semi-urban areas.

The fact is that majority of consumers in the country are even unaware of the existence of consumer forums to which they can make their grievances. A CAG-commissioned survey finding on the status of the Consumer Protection Act (1986) conducted in 2006, says that 82 per cent of the consumers are not aware of the Consumer Protection Act and 66 per cent of their rights. The ground reality is that the conditions are not very favourable and conducive for the consumer. Ignorance is one of the prominent factors contributing in the exploitation of the consumers and is most prevalent amongst the rural masses. The *Gram Panchayats* are there in all the villages, which is the available Constitutional mechanism across the country spread in all 627 districts. It is only through this Constitutional mechanism that the consumer movement can get a boost and consumer awareness can be spread among rural masses.

Gram Sabha is the best forum to educate the rural masses about their rights as consumers as well as the techniques to redress their grievances, which are attended by almost every villager. On occasions like December 24, which is the National Consumer Day, meetings of the Gram Sabha need to be convened, where the villagers could properly be educated about their rights as consumers.

The *Gram Panchayat* could play a significant role in creating awareness at the grassroots level. Appropriate technology and creative media could be used to raise awareness. The relevant resource materials in regional languages could be made available in hard copies as well as in soft copies through internet. The *gram panchayats* also can consider using media such as documentary films, street plays, competitions etc. to spread consumer awareness. The services of Government primary school teachers could be utilised in conducting consumer awareness programmes. "Complaints Box or Cell" could be opened in each of the Gram Panchayat offices. This can act as an advice giving and complaints handling mechanism between the common consumer and the district consumer forum. This will help in speedy resolution of the complaints without taking it to the consumer forums as well as substantially reduce the burden of district forums. Selected representatives from each of the *gram panchayats* can be identified and be trained to handle these cells. Issues at local level affecting the consumers can be discussed and disposed of at this level only instead of taking each complaint to the district forum. Similar mechanism could be established at *Taluka* (Block) level as well. A selected group consisting of *Gram Sevak, Sarpanch*, teachers, youth, can be trained for this purpose. Personal consumer advice could also be provided not only for legal problems, but also for everyday consumer problems. Required budgetary allocations have to be made to *Gram Sabha* for consumer awareness. The Panchayati Raj can be a mechanism for consumer education for the rural mass. How can they educate the rural mass? The present Figure 13.2 shows how the *gram sabha* can be a catalyst for consumer education.

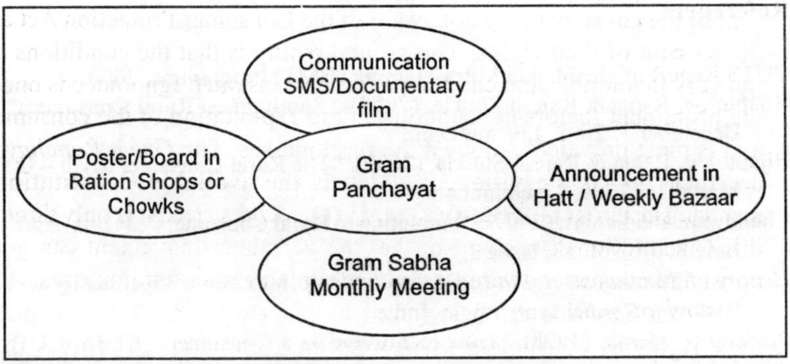

Fig. 13.2: Role of *Gram Sabha* in Consumer Education

Conclusion and Suggestions

It is high time that the *gram panchayat* should take a lead in consumer education in their respective areas. Disadvantaged consumers are not able to assert their rights. Rural consumers remain disadvantaged as their right to information, choice, redress, and consumer education are not sufficiently fulfilled. Consequently, such consumers need support in maintaining their rights, so that, they can bargain equally with the producers and the service providers. There are significant differences in the levels of awareness and literacy among the rural and urban consumers. Per capita income in rural area is half of that of urban areas. Value for money is more important to rural people. They buy small quantities and more frequently. Urban people often do not display brand loyalty whereas rural people display brand stickiness. The most common communication platforms in rural markets include *haats, melas*, *mandis* and other places of public gathering. While communicating with the rural masses it is required that the message delivered should be simple and direct to be effective. The *Gram Sabha* can play a vital role in consumer education. It can promote the right of rural consumer through four different ways (see the Fig. 13.2). It can put poster on the ration shop as given by department of consumer Affair, such as, *Jago Grahak Jago.* During the weekly bazzar, the *gram sabha* could distribute leaflets and show some documentary film on consumer awareness. In every *gram sabha* meeting the *sarpanch* should evaluate the cases of consumer exploitation. Through street play, the *gram sabha* can impart consumer education. If the villagers themselves can provide consumer education in their *panchayat*. It is the need of the hour.

References

CUTS Report of Upabhokta Mitra Training (UMT) Programme, 2000.

Bijapurkar, Rama & Rajesh Shukla, (2008). "Spotlight on Rural Consumers", December 3, 2008, Livemint.com

Bijapurkar, Rama & Rajesh Shukla, (2009). "The Rural Consumer Myth – II", March 26, 2009, Livemint.com

Chandwani and Sanjay, (2009). "Marketing to Rural Consumers", *Vision*, April-June 2009, Vol. 13, Issue 2.

History of Panchayati Raj in India, available at: http://en.wikipedia.org/wiki/History_of_panchayati_raj_in_India

Pradeep S. Mehta, (1998). "How to Survive as a Consumer", *CUTS*, CUTS Publication.

"The Bird of Gold: The Rise of India's Consumer Market", May 2007, McKinsey & Company.

Velayudhan, Sanal Kumar *"Rural Marketing: Targeting the Non-Urban Consumer"*, Response Books, Sage Publications, Second Edition.

14
Rural Consumers and the Panchayats
Case Study of Shimoga District, Karnataka

B.V. Gopalakrishna and C.L. Ramesh

Introduction

Consumerism is an eternal issue to humanity. The consumer movement in India is as old as trade and commerce. In *Arthashastra*, Kautilya long ago stressed that the duty of the King was to prevent malpractices in business. In modern era, consumerism was given stress by Mr. Ralph Nadar, a well known American advocate during eighteenth century. President John F. Kennedy of the United States called upon U.S. Congress to accord approval to the Consumer Bill of Rights on 15th March, 1962 (World Consumer Rights Day).

In the history of development of consumer policy, 9th April, 1985 is an important date as it is on this day the General Assembly of United Nations persuaded its member countries to adopt guidelines through Law. Accordingly, Indian government enacted a landmark legislation called the Consumer Protection Act on 24th December, 1986 (National Consumer Day) to provide better protection and to safeguard the interest of consumers. The Act has been in existence for nearly 32 years now. The structural arrangements to operationalise the Act have been established. Lakhs of consumers have approached the redressal mechanisms set-up under the Act for redressal of their complaints. The success of the Act in protecting the consumers has been a mixed one. Apart from the weaknesses and delay in disposal of complaints, the State Governments have not been very supportive to the consumers. The consumer movement itself has remained weak due to various reasons. Perhaps the major lacunae lies in the fact that large numbers of consumers are not even aware about the existence of such an legislation. Lack of awareness about the consumer rights is the major impediment in the effectiveness of the Act. The situation is much worse in the rural areas.

Problems Faced by Rural Consumers

There are about 6,40,867 villages in India. Seveny per cent of our consumer population, accounting for about 83.3 crore lives in rural areas. Consumerism is still in its infancy in our country, particularly with respect to the rural consumer. In our country a substantial number of rural people are living below the poverty line having high level of unemployment and poor literacy level. As they are illiterate, they are easily vulnerable to the unscrupulous and unethical marketing practices of the greedy marketer. Rural consumers are exploited due to ignorance and lack of unity (unorganised) amongst them. They are largely exploited in the rural market on account of lack of competition among sellers since, there are only one or two petty shops available in rural places and the consumers have no choice. The main problems faced by rural consumers are related to adulteration, short weighs and measures, fake brands and spurious products, lack of safety and quality in appliances and sales gimmicks, unreasonable pricing, misleading advertisements and imitation. They are also facing hardship in reaching semi-urban places for getting good products and better services for want of money and time at their disposal.

MRP – Sky is the Limit

Today most of the products and in particular food products are packed and sold as per the existing statutory rules. Producers have to mention the date of manufacture, contents, expiry date and the maximum retail price (MRP). In the rural areas the exploitation starts from here. The MRP printed and the actual price for which it is sold varies from city/urban/semi-urban/rural places. It is a common experience to find that the price of the product varies from urban to rural. For example the price of a litre of Sesame oil (Gingelly oil) costing a MRP of Rs. 100 per litre is being sold at a price of Rs. 70, 75, or 80 in urban areas, while it is being sold in semi-urban areas like *taluk* headquarters for Rs. 85 or 90. But in the rural areas the same oil is being sold at the stated MRP price of Rs. 100 only.

The question is why the rural consumer is not getting a discount like his urban counterpart. Accordingly, the urban consumers are getting the products at more reasonable prices when compared to semi-urbans and the rural consumers. This is really a sorry state of affairs. It is high time that serious thought has to be given as to how to safeguard the interest of rural consumers who are exploited by the producers and the retailers/ dealers in the guise of MRP. The basis of fixing the MRP is never known to the consumers and the manufactures just fix the price as much as they want.

Consumer Movement in Karnataka

This chapter mainly deals with the consumer movement in Shimoga district of Karnataka, but also gives a bird's eyeview of the growth of consumer movement in the state. Karnataka has 30 districts, 175 *taluks*, 5,650 *grama panchayats* and 37,700 villages. Though there are 30 districts in the state, the consumer movement is active only in a few districts, viz. Udupi, Shimoga, Mysore, Bangaluru, Mangalore, Hubli and Bijapur.

The consumer movement started in erstwhile district of South Canara in a village called Basrur in today's Udupi district. Much before the enactment of the Consumer Protection Act, Mr. Ravindranath Shanbagh guided by his mentor Prof. P. Narayana Rao of Mahatma Gandhi Memorial College, Udupi initiated the movement by regularly writing articles in weekly magazines and other papers about the level of awareness and other issues and also the caution to be taken by the consumers. They are seen as the pioneers of consumer movement in Karnataka. They started this movement in 1970s, and Mr. Shanbagh took this movement forward by continuously awakening the spirit of consumerism through his writings in local language Kannada. This had a great impact on the consumers as they felt empowered through his writings because they could get information about basics that a consumer would like to know.

In District Shimoga, there are 265 *Grama Panchayats* (GP)/Village Panchayats (VP), 7 *Taluks* and about 1450 inhabited villages. The consumer movement was started by Mr. K.M.S. Chandrashekaraiah, a retired Deputy Secretary of Government of Karnataka by registering an NGO called Consumer Forum (Regd.), Shimoga in the year 1990. He was in forefront of the movement for nearly 16 years till his death in 2006. He built-up a strong consumer movement in the district and also developed the capacity of the consumer activists in the district to take-up the task of consumer protection and awareness. Today, the work of the Consumer Forum has been recognised by both the Central and the State Governments.

Exploitation of Rural Consumers

Even though, the consumer movement is active in the district, but still the level of consumer awareness is low due to lack of education and indifference on the part of rural consumers. This is also due to poor knowledge about their rights and lack of skills to take rational decision based on information about the product or service. In the process the rural consumers continue to be exploited in many ways. Negligence on the part of rural consumer is equally responsible for the current condition and hence, they are being cheated day in and day out.

Ignorance is one of the prominent factors contributing to the exploitation of the consumer and is most prevalent amongst rural consumers. These rural consumers remain disadvantaged as their right to information, right to consumer education and right to redress are not being fulfilled because there are no specific programmes and policies to protect these rural consumers. One fact is that majority of the consumers in the country in general, i.e. 82 per cent and more than 95 per cent of rural consumers in particular are even unaware of the existence of consumer forums they can file their complaints. This is the CAG finding on the status of Consumer Protection Act (1986) conducted in 2006. The continued exploitation of the rural consumers due to lack of consumer education and awareness about their rights and redressal mechanism etc. calls for serious debate and discussion and exchange of ideas to device policies, programmes and strategies to meet the challenges being faced by the rural consumers in the country.

Consumer Education and Awareness: Role of NGOs

At present there are six consumer organisations working in various *talukas* of Shimoga. Among them "Shimoga Consumer Organisation, Sagar" and "Shiralakoppa Consumer Organisation" are very much active and involved in consumer welfare activities independently and also with the assistance of Department of Civil Supply and Consumer Affairs in the district. For the larger benefit of the consumers and also to educate the consumers on various issues a monthly periodical paper called "Shivamogga Balakedara" is being brought out in the first week every month which exclusively gives details about consumer movement, rights and awareness programmes, redressal mechanism at the district level besides the number of cases decided in District Forum. These cases educate the people regarding the redressal mechanism available to them and the nature of relief that they can expect from the District Forum. The chapter is being sent to all the village panchayats in the district numbering around 265 and also to all the public libraries in the district. About one thousand copies are being circulated every month. The chapter also has got RNI registration from Registrar of Newspapers of India, New Delhi.

The Consumer Forum has also been entrusted with the work of educating the school children as a nodal agency by the Education Department in about 20 schools identified in the district. Besides programmes in these schools, a number of awareness programmes are also conducted in other schools, B.Ed. Colleges, junior colleges etc. The NGO is also associated with Department of Food and Civil Supply, Consumer Affairs and Legal Metrology while conducting National Consumer Day and World Consumer Rights Day. Further, we are also regularly attending SHG Club of women formed by Women and Child Welfare Department and providing consumer information.

We are also giving exhaustive details regarding the compensation to be given by the service providers as per the Regulatory Commission/ Authority guidance and in accordance with the citizen chartes by the service providers in relation to deficiencies in service among consumers utilities, *viz.* Electricity/Telephone/Insurance/Medical/Transport etc. This information is also published in monthly paper for the information of the rural people.

Since the President of the organisation has also worked as one of the Members in the District Forum, mediation meetings are being conducted by the forum in its forum office located in Zilla Panchayat office. So far, more than half a dozen such cases have been settled. Help is also being provided to the aggrieved complainant to file the petition in District Forum and assist them in the proceedings of District Forum including written statements etc. In one of the cases, Sri Parameswarappa *vs.* KSRTC the relief amount of Rs. 1,500 awarded to him by the District Forum has been graciously donated by him to our Forum to meet the expenses of our monthly paper, "*Shivamogga Balakedara*".

What Role Panchayats can play in Consumer Movement?

The panchayats are the grassroots democratic organisation for the welfare of the rural people. It is a three-tier system with elected bodies at the village, *taluk* and district levels. There are about 30 lakh representatives at all levels and 33 per cent of them are women. There are about 2.4 lakh Gram Panchayats/Village Panchayats in the country. These are constituted as per the 73rd Amendment of the Constitution passed in 1992 which came into force from April 24, 1993. There are Gram Panchayats/Village Panchayats for group of villages, Panchayat Samiti at Taluk/Block level and Zilla Panchayat at District level. These Panchayats have Constitutional mechanism spread across the country.

The Gram Panchayats/Village Panchayats could play a significant role in educating the consumers and creating awareness at grassroots level. There is an urgent need to take initiatives by the Central Government and State Government, Department of Consumer Affairs to involve and make use of Panchayati Raj Institutions (PRIs) in various programmes related to consumer awareness. These Gram Panchayats/Village Panchayats could play a significant role in creating awareness at the grassroots level with the support of voluntary consumer organisations. Panchayats should become the backbone for the success and expansion of the consumer awareness movement in rural areas. It is only through the Constitutional mechanism that the consumer movement can get a boost and consumer awareness can be spread among rural masses.

For the development of rural women the Zilla Panchayats have formed SHGs under SGSY scheme to impart training. In such training programmes consumer awareness and education can be imparted regularly with the help of Voluntary Consumer Organisation activists in the district.

How Panchayats can be involved in Consumer Movement

At present there are three government officials working in Grama Panchayats/Village Panchayats. They are : (i) Panchayat Development Officer, (ii) Village Panchayat Secretary, and (iii) Computer Operator. Direct funds are given to Grama Panchayats/Village Panchayats by the Central Government. Similarly, the Department of Consumer Affairs both at the Central and at State Government level should earmark certain funds towards consumer awareness at Grama Panchayat/Village Panchayat level. The Village Panchayat Secretary should be given training and basic education about consumer awareness. Besides, there is a Co-ordinator/ Facilitator at Taluk/Block Panchayats who should also be trained on consumer issues. Similarly, training should also be given to other officials as well. The Secretary, Village Panchayat and the Co-ordinator, Taluk Panchayat together should also educate the rural people about their consumer rights and the redressal mechanism. Whenever the *Grama Sabhas* are convened they should also be used to spread the message of consumer welfare and also impart consumer education to SHGs.

Grama Sabha is the best institutional arrangement to educate the rural masses about their rights as consumers as well as the techniques to redress their grievances since these meetings are attended by almost every village member. Consumer awareness programmes should be included as an agenda in *Grama Sabha*. Meetings of *Grama Sabha* need to be convened on December 24 on the occasion of National Consumer Day with the objective of education the rural consumers as well. The Village Panchayats can consider using media like screening documentary films, street plays etc. on National and World Consumer Rights Day.

Target Rural Women Consumers

In the rural areas women are perhaps the most exploited among consumers. Be it food adulteration, unfair trade practice or spurious products, they suffer the most. Therefore, there is a need to educate the women consumers living in the rural areas. The Department of Women and Child Welfare also works in unison with Zilla Parishad. Specifically, there are schemes like Stree Shakti Yojana under which Self-Help Groups (SHG) are formed. In such schemes consumer activists can also make them aware about consumer rights and redressal mechanism by giving study material, publicity material etc. in local regional languages. Besides there is a post of Child Development Officer in every *talukas* with a Supervisor working under him. The consumer education training should also be imparted to Supervisor and with the assistance of active VCO they can organise consumer awareness programme in the villages for the benefit of rural consumers.

Catch them Young – Empowering Consumer Clubs

The Education Department in the District works in close cooperation with the Zilla Parishad. In every Grama Panchayat at least one consumer club should be started in schools to impart consumer awareness by giving study materials and lectures. It has to be carried out regularly, i.e. at least once in a month. This scheme should be backed by the Department and have long term financial security. Consumer clubs should develop more activities outside schools such as organising road show, debates, essay competitions, painting competitions at the Village Panchayat level. The service of government primary school teachers could also be utilised in conducting consumer education and awareness Programme. The inclusion of consumerism in the curriculum in school and D.Ed./TCH training institutes will prove to be useful in spreading consumer awareness.

Redressal of Consumer Grievances at Panchayat level

The Panchayats could play a lead role in redressal of consumer complaints as most of the complaints relate to the villages within the Panchayat area. Complaint Handling, Information and Advisory Services (CHIAS) Cell could be opened in each of the Grama Panchayat office. CHIAS can act as an advice giving and complaint handling mechanism between the common rural consumer and the District Forum. Selected representative of each of the Village Panchayat Secretary to whom already training in consumer education is imparted along with office bearers of SHG primary be trained to handle these cells at Grama Panchayat level. Copies of model forms printed in local language need to be made available for the use of rural consumer with the assistance of CHIAS. These model forms can be used for giving notices to opponent parties, submission of petition and the Affidavit in support of complaint etc. to be submitted to District Forum.

District Forum

At present the District Forum functions only at the district headquarters and particularly the rural people are not aware of the District Forum let apart about the Consumer Protection Act and awareness. The District Forums though they are supposed to campaign and spread consumer awareness at the *taluk* and *panchayat* level and not able to do so. This is because they are not vested with specific and sufficient funds to carry out these campaigns and awareness programmes.

At present rural consumer and also semi-urban consumers living in taluk and villages are finding it difficult to approach the District Forum located at the district headquarters due to distance and time constraint. To make them more consumer friendly it is suggested that a sitting of District Forum should be held in every *taluka* headquarters in the district at least once in a month on a particular date of the month. This will take justice to the doorsteps of the rural consumers and they can easily make use of the District Forum to get their disputes redressed with minimum expenses without many difficulties. Further, this is a sort of education to the local people that there is a District Forum which will hear their grievances as per Consumer Protection Act and the rights vested in them may be utilised properly.

Further, it is also suggested that in complaints of certain amount in the District Forum, the proceedings should be conducted without any legal appearance. That amount may be reasonable. By this, immediate and time bound justice will be made available to the small consumers in general and rural consumers in particular with this more and more rural people will be awakened and make use of the District Forum for getting their disputes redressed.

Conclusion

The success of any consumer movement depends on the consciousness and awareness of rural consumers. Consumer Organisations are Voluntary Consumer Organisations (VCOs) established for the purpose of safeguarding interest of consumers in general and rural consumers in particular. Like socialism, communism, capitalism etc., consumerism is a movement to educate consumers about the Consumer Protection Act and other rules. The consumers also need to be educated about their responsibilities as well. Whenever they are cheated while purchasing/ buying any product and are not getting proper services from the utilities (that is deficiency in services) then they have to demand and complain. It is only then that the producers and the service providers will take the consumers seriously.

Another major problem is that at present there is no separate Department of Consumer Affairs exclusively to deal with consumer affairs in the state. A separate Department of Consumer Affairs needs to be created in all the State Governments so that more attention can be given to consumer welfare. At present consumer affairs is attached to Department of Food and Civil Supplies, as this department is burdened with a huge task of Public Distribution System, i.e. PDS and hence they have little time for consumer welfare. If a separate department is created with its own budget and programmes, this will go a long way in strengthening the consumer movement in Karnataka. From the State department down to the panchayat level a institutional mechanism with the active involvement of VCOs should be created to strengthen the consumer movement in the state.

References

George, Cherian, *Rural Consumers and Role of Local Bodies in Consumer Protection*, CUTS International.

Negitara, Bhatt Hema and Upadhyaya, Rajshree, "Knowledge and Utilization of Consumer Education by Rural and Urban Women", *Journal of Advances in Development Research.*

Singh, S.S. and Sapna Chadha, *Consumer Protection in India – Some Reflections,* New Delhi: CCS IIPA.

15

Role of Panchayati Raj Institutions in Consumer Protection

Alok Misra

Introduction

> "The State shall take steps to organise village *panchayats* and endow them with such powers and authority as may be necessary to enable them to function as units of self-government." (Article 40)

The Supreme Court in *State of Uttar Pradesh* vs. *Pradhan Sangh Kshetra Samiti*, AIR 1995 SC 1512, observed that Article 40 does not give guidelines for organising village *panchayats*. All that they require is that the village *panchayats* howsoever organised have to be equipped with such powers and authority as may be necessary to enable them to function as units of self-government. The word *'Panchayat'* literally means assembly or *Ayat* of five or *panch* elderly and wise persons. Panchayati Raj Institutions existed, functioned and contributed significantly throughout the course of Indian History from the Vedic times to present times. It is important to note that the village *panchayats* have always been elected bodies and functioned as units of local self-government. *Gram panchayats* are contrastingly apart and distinct from the unelected *khap* or caste panchayats prevalent in some parts of India.

The details of Panchayati Raj Institutions as political system of local governance are found in abundance in the history of South-East Asia particularly in the countries of subcontinent like India, Pakistan, Bangladesh and Nepal. The Panchayati Raj system was prevalent across the length and breadth of India. In southern India also especially in the kingdom of Chola rulers in Chola Mandalam of present Tamil Nadu the village assembly administration was highly developed. An important inscription in this regard is Uttaramerur inscription of tenth century A.D. found in Tamil Nadu. The inscription gives details of the elections, structure, functions, role of Village Panchayats, qualifications and disqualifications of their members and the rights and duties of the village assemblies etc. Indian social system has tremendous vitality. Since racial, religious, cultural, linguistic, geographical and economic diversity has been co-existing and nurtured since ages, this provides a strong unity to social system. In simple understanding Culture is day-to-day pattern of living. In India the cultural diversity has been maintained as a social policy by the rulers in their polity.

PRI and Consumer Protection: Constitutional and Legal Role

India is a country with extensive topography, vast geography and consequent economic diversity. Largest segment of population which is around 70 per cent of the population lives and works hard in rural India. The people in rural areas are engaged in agricultural and related activities. In Independent India the rural economy has rapidly transformed itself and the economic activities are getting organised very fast. The contribution of rural economy is significant and it sustains a large section of population in India. Agriculture and related activities have grown enormously on scientific and technological lines. Mechanisation of agriculture and irrigation has gone a long way. The economic activities are to be managed and administered in a user friendly manner.

There are more than 72 million consumers in villages and rural India, as per the reports of various government and non-governmental organisations. The protection of consumers in rural areas has become an area of concern. The consumers in the form of farmers and entrepreneurs are using agricultural inputs and technology to a considerable extent. They are to be protected. In this the Panchayati Raj Institutions are required to play a vital role. The powers of these institutions and correlated obligations towards the consumers are required to be emboldened. It will give a new dimension and role to the functioning of these institutions. Panchayati Raj Institutions are required to be oriented towards people and development.

From the second half of the twentieth century law rapidly came to be recognised as a tool of social development and welfare of humanity. The process of social engineering came on priority. The reforms started coming very fast. It was an urgent requirement to emancipate people living in Afro-Asia which had been made slums by the colonial powers. The object of law is to do welfare of humanity, similar to that of all branches of knowledge like science and technology, engineering, medical sciences, social sciences, political science, management science, economics etc. India has been strengthened by various revolutions in co-operative and private sector like the green, yellow, blue, white and pink revolutions. These developments are the result of the hard work of the people of India. There is massive production and consumption of goods and services across India. In all the four sectors of economy there is rapid rise of consumers.

Mahatma Gandhi emphasised on the establishment and organisation of the village *panchayats* for the administration and development of villages as a unit of self-government. He clearly believed that India can have a strong economy only when the villages will be self-reliant. His philosophy came to be known as Gram Swaraj. Article 40 of the Constitution of India stands explicitly inspired by Gandhian philosophy. It is a major directive to the State of India in law and policy-making. In pursuance of this directive, Balwant Rai Mehta Committee in Nehruvian era, Ashok Mehta Committee in Desai era, P.K. Thungan Committee in Rajiv Gandhi era were major milestones. The Constitutional status of Panchayati Raj Institutions by 73rd and 74th Amendments of the Constitution came during Narasimha Rao era in pursuance of the dream of Rajiv Gandhi to take democracy to the grassroots level. In fact the organised establishment and Constitutional status given to the functioning of these institutions had become and urgent requirement in the light of the growth of Indian economy as well as the impact of liberalisation and globalisation of agricultural and related activities.

By 73rd Amendment of the Constitution Part IX dealing with the *Panchayats* (containing Articles 243, 243A to 243O) was inserted. Similarly, Part IXA related to the Municipalities (containing Articles 243P to 243Z, 243ZA to 243ZG) was inserted by the 74th Amendment. For details of the aforesaid provisions Eleventh and Twelfth Schedule were also added in the Constitution. Detailed provisions defining *Gram*, *Gram Sabha*, *Panchayat*, composition of *Panchayats*, *Panchayat* area, Intermediate level, District level, reservation of seats, disqualifications for membership, powers, authority and responsibilities of *Panchayats*, power to impose taxes by, and funds of the *Panchayats*, Constitution of Finance Commission to review financial position, audit of accounts of *Panchayats*, elections to the *Panchayats* etc. have been enshrined. Similar details with regard to the Municipalities have also been provided.

Article 243G mentions powers, authority and responsibilities of *Panchayats* and clearly lays down that the *Panchayats* at appropriate level shall have the responsibilities for the preparation of plans for economic development and social justice, the implementation of schemes for economic development including those in relation to the matters listed in the Eleventh Schedule. Similarly, Article 243W and Twelfth Schedule enshrine the similar role of Municipalities. The Constitution (73rd Amendment) Act, 1992 enshrines a key role for the Panchayati Raj Institutions related to the 29 subjects such as education, health, rural housing, drinking water, agriculture etc., as mentioned in the Eleventh Schedule to the Constitution. States are required to transfer these functions to the Panchayati Raj Institutions and to devolve funds, functions and functionaries upon the Panchayati Raj Institutions for discharging these functions. The Comptroller and Auditor General of India is responsible for exercising control and supervision over the proper maintenance of accounts and the audit of all the three tiers. The format for preparation of budget and for keeping accounts is prescribed by C&AG. The classification of transactions in Panchayati Raj Institutions their budgets and accounts has been structured on a function-*cum*-programme basis to provide uniformity in three levels of governance, i.e. Union, State and Local Government.

The role of the Panchayati Raj Institutions in consumer education and their protection is of prime importance in present times. The evolution of law in the field of consumer protection and the Constitutional status accorded to Panchayati Raj Institutions are closely related. Both of them achieve special significance and meaning in the light of the fact that India is a country with extensive rural base and a large number of consumers are living in rural areas. Rural markets are feeling the impact of globalisation and liberalisation of law and economy. The economic prosperity achieved by the common men in India by their hard and sustained work has gone a long way in pre- and post- green revolution era. This improvement in the economic status has made Panchayati Raj Institutions and consumer protection more meaningful. Education and awareness in rural areas has increased and is to be increased further. The thought process of consumers in rural areas is evolving and getting rationalised resulting into the emergence of better and more rational preferences. The behaviour of consumers in rural areas is becoming systematic and is changing in a positive direction. In this context the innovations in the field of rural management, science and technology have played a crucial role. With the generation of massive requirement in the resurgent nation this is a thrust area in which law related to consumer protection cannot only protect the welfare of masses, but also can work as a tool for social development in conjunction with Panchayati Raj Institutions.

Democracy is incomplete unless the local government and the individual consumers are empowered. There was a time when consumer came last and was least important in the economy, but now the consumer is the mainstay of empowerment. One of the major drawbacks of the present consumer protection movement is that it is restricted to the urban areas. One way to empower the rural population is to empower the members of Panchayati Raj Institutions and through them the masses. On the one side there is growing market and on the other side there is manipulation and exploitation which impairs the interests and rights of the consumers. Consumer protection and business should proceed together. Markets are to be disciplined with orientation towards the satisfaction of the interests of consumers.

Empowerment of Consumers in Rural Areas

India started transforming itself rapidly with the promulgation of the Constitution. The Constitution enshrined the Preamble containing objectives of socio-economic justice, the fundamental rights for the many fold development of the individuals, and the Directive Principles of State Policy to usher the era of welfarism in India. The first Prime Minister Jawaharlal Nehru established the Planning Commission to be *ex-officio* chaired by the Prime Minister, by a Resolution of Cabinet on 15th March, 1950 within 47 days of the promulgation of the Constitution. The Planning Commission got prepared quickly the First Five Year Plan on Harrod-Domar model of developmental economics with top priority to agriculture and irrigation. This plan came into force with effect form 1st April, 1951 and got successfully completed with achievement of targeted growth rate and lowering down of prices. The policy of ceiling, i.e. *hadbandi* on land holdings and bringing scattered peaces of land, i.e. *chakbandi* were major steps of land reforms. Another significant effort in this context was of *Bhudan* and *Gram Dan* movements by Acharya Vinoba Bhave.

The turning point of transformation of agriculture and rural India came with the call of *"Jai Jawan and Jai Kisan"* by Lal Bahadur Shastri, ultimately resulting into the green revolution. Mrs. Indira Gandhi and her government made signal innovations in the empowerment of simple, dedicated and honest people in rural India through Community Development Programmes like Food for Work Programme, National Rural Employment Programme (NREP), National Rural Landless Employment

Guarantee Programme (RLEGP), Integrated Rural Development Programme (IRDP), Training of Rural Youth for Self-Employment (TRYSEM) etc. The legendary Jawahar Rozgar Yojana (JRY) in which the aforesaid programmes got merged and introduction of Perspective Planning were milestones achieved by Rajiv Gandhi Government. Granting of the Constitutional status to Panchayati Raj Institutions was the logical conclusion arrived towards taking democracy to the grassroots level by P.V. Narasimha Rao Government. The empowerment of consumers in rural areas became a visible reality with Insurance of Agricultural Sector under the auspices of General Insurance Corporation (GIC) and making available of historical credit cards, named Kisan Credit Cards by Atal Bihari Vajpayee Government. Mahatma Gandhi National Rural Employment Guarantee Act, 2005 (MGNREGA) is going a long way in empowering the consumers in rural areas.

The welfare measures as mentioned above have contributed to the general well-being, happiness and prosperity in rural India giving vast purchasing power and emergence of rural consumers and markets. The role of the banking industry and of NABARD has helped a lot in this direction. The expansion of cooperative activities in general and of IFFCO, KRIBHCO and NAFED in particular has been beyond imagination. The HBJ (Hazira-Babrala-Jagdishpur) pipeline, rightly named as Gas Ganga has been instrumental in giving and entirely new dimension to rural economy of Northern India.

The philosophy and aim of Co-operative Federalism is proving itself to be the correct objective in nation building. The life and life style of rural India has tremendously changed and getting updated and upgraded. This has narrowed down the gap between Urban and Rural India. Rural Marketing Association of India (RMAI) and MART are providing valuable inputs in this direction. The income in rural areas and of rural consumers is on the rise as is visible from enormous growth in rural marketing operations. The rural share of popular consumer goods and durables is also rapidly rising. The growth and potential in rural markets is enormous and significantly more as compared to urban markets.

The Pharmaceutical Revolution at the dawn of twenty first century popularly came to be known as Pink Revolution has made India the largest manufacturer of medicines in the world. The medical facilities have reached rural India vertically and have spread horizontally making it a thrust area in rural markets. Significantly, Pink Revolution has occurred in private sector. Indian economy is rapidly transforming itself into a global economy with the arrival of patenting in the field of agricultural research and development. The invention of Internet by John Postal led to Information Technology Revolution, ultimately bringing Cell Phone as a necessity in the hands of most of rural consumers. Requirement and availability of mobile phones, computers, internet connectivity, laptops, palm tops and information highways have changed the form, shape, nature and extent of consumer markets in rural India generating remarkable potential changes and growth. Super conductivity and Optical Fiber Technology has contributed a lot towards Rapid Transit Transportation Systems and Tele Communication Technology. The construction of extensive road networks has generated usage of automobiles on a large scale in rural India. Automobiles have given wheels to the people of rural India. Their life has become faster and business oriented.

Problems of Consumers in Rural Areas

Rural consumers in emerging market countries are among the largest and fastest growing segments of the world's population. Rural India is growing at a fast speed and is a potential market for the goods and services. The extent of rural markets in rural India is expected to be double than that of urban India. Liberalisation resulting into Globalisation, rise in income, expansion of media and information technology in rural areas, women empowerment, improvement in infrastructure etc. are some of the catalysts for the growth of rural markets. With the growth and expansion of rural market at such a fast pace there is a consequential and simultaneous rise in the problems and grievances. The major difficulties and problems of consumers in rural areas are lack of awareness, adulteration, less and incorrect weighing and measuring, quite often absence of safety and quality in equipments, defective goods and deficient services, misrepresentation and unfair assurances, misleading warranties and guarantees, high pricing, cheating in the form of spurious and mirror image goods and malpractices like selling on more than prescribed maximum retail price, faulty weights and measures, deficiency in services, misrepresenting advertisements etc. The six sensitive areas in consumer protection are related to Credit Cards, Milk production and supply, Banking, Travel, Telecommunication and Consumer goods.

The reality is that the conditions are unfavourable for the consumers. They stand exploited. Ignorance is an important factor in the exploitation of the consumers especially in the rural areas. With economic reforms the market is gradually being transformed from a predominantly sellers market to a buyers market where choice of the consumers depends on their awareness level. Consumer rights could be protected in a competitive economy only when right standards for goods and services are ensured by evolving a network of institutions and legal protection system. To ensure consumer welfare is the responsibility of the Welfare State. Even a manufacturer or provider of a service is a consumer of some other goods or services. If both the producers and consumers realise the need for co-existence, adulterated products, spurious goods and other deficiencies in services will get reduced.

The rural consumer remains disadvantaged as their right to information, choice, redress, education and to be heard are not sufficiently fulfilled. There is need for the improvement in the existing consumer protection and consumer welfare policies for meeting the specific requirements of rural consumers more effectively. Indian consumer is also to be protected from wrong influences which some times come from the media. In fact the Father of the Nation Mahatma Gandhi had rightly said that a consumer is the most important visitor on our premises. He is not dependent on us, we are on him. He is not an interruption to our work; he is the purpose of it. We are not doing a favour to a consumer by giving him an opportunity. He is doing us a favour by giving us opportunity to serve him. As per the Gandhian thought the consumers and producers were not looked as separate individuals. The process of production was supposed to be decentralised and distributed in parity. In consumer protection movement there is need of emphasising and resorting to Gandhian values with decentralisation as a policy for protecting all, including consumers.

The benefits of the decentralisation must be able to reach the poorest of the poor. As Mahatma Gandhi clearly observed, "Whenever you are in doubt or when the self becomes too much with you, apply the following test: Recall the face of the poorest and the weakest man whom you may have seen and ask yourself if the step you contemplate is going to be of any use to him. Will he gain anything by it? Will it restore him to a control over his own life and destiny? In other words, will it lead to *Swaraj* for the hungry and spiritually starving millions? Then you will find your doubts and your self melting away."

Empowerment of Redressal Mechanism in Rural Areas

Protection connotes that someone is there as protector and protected. The Consumer Protection Act, 1986 aimed to provide better protection to the consumers. Consequently, consumer movement acquired momentum. It provides three-tier structure from district to national level for the redressal of consumer grievances. The Act enshrines consumer rights which are internationally accepted. The Act provides for simple, speedy and inexpensive redressal to the consumer grievances against defective goods, deficiency in services including the restrictive and unfair trade practices. An enlightened consumer is an empowered consumer. An aware consumer not only protects himself from exploitation, but brings efficiency, transparency and accountability in the production of goods and services. It is important that top priority be accorded to Consumer Education, Consumer Protection and Consumer Awareness. The Consumer Protection Act, 1986 applies to all goods and services unless specially exempted by the Central Government, in all sectors whether Private, Public or Co-operative.

A person can make a complaint if he is not satisfied with the standard of service which has been provided to him. Anyone who feels that he was provided a poor service or is not satisfied with the product or the service can make a complaint in the Consumer Court. Consumer complaints are legal methods for expressing dissatisfaction with regard to a service or product. It is the legal way of filing a claim. The important rights of consumers are Right to Safety, Right to Information, Right to Choose, Right to be heard, Right to Redress and Right to Consumer Education etc. Everybody is using goods or services in day-to-day life and is a consumer. However, the reality is that the conditions are not favourable and conducive for consumers. They are being exploited and cheated especially in the rural areas. For this the consumers are to be made aware of various aspects and their rights. The best way to educate the rural consumers is to hold the meetings of *Gram Sabha* regularly which are generally attended by most of the villagers.

The task of consumer protection has three basic dimensions. First, to ensure a legal framework of legislations related to consumer protection. Secondly, to evolve standards so that consumers are able to exercise their choice amongst different products. Standards are the essentials for quality and play a key role in consumer protection. Standards are technical specifications of usage of proper terminology, codes of practice and procedures and of management systems. Thirdly, awareness of consumers and their education for protection is very important. How to educate the rural masses still remains a challenging task. Some significant measures are visible in this direction Multi-media publicity campaigns have been launched through print and electronic media on the issues which are very relevant such as putting ISI marks, Hallmark, Labelling, MRP etc. Advertisements are now released through a network of national as well as regional newspapers. The Department of Consumer Affairs has video spots of 30 seconds duration on various consumer related issues, which are being telecast through Cable and Satellite channels. Special Programmes have also been telecast on Lok Sabha TV and Doordarshan to highlight the issues relating to consumer awareness. Issues pertaining to rural and remote areas have been given prominence in the various advertisement spots.

The Consumer Protection Act, 1986 has its own limitations. Although it is providing protection to the rights of consumers yet it requires to be revisited in the light of extensive changes during last two decades. The disputes redressal mechanism related to consumers operates through consumer forums. They exist at district, state and national level to redress the complaints of consumers. The Consumer Forum is bestowed with the power to order replacement of the commodity or removal of deficiencies in goods and services or refund of payment. It can also award compensation for loss suffered. The three-tier system of consumer forums under the Act reaches to urban areas only. It is difficult for rural consumers to reach the forum. The extension of the consumer forum in rural areas will give relief to consumers. Consumer forums and *Lok Adalats* organised by them are required to reach villages. In this regard there is a significant role for the Panchayati Raj Institutions in protecting the rights and interests of rural consumers. Easy and available remedy will ensure further participation of people in rural areas in the growth and change of rural and semi-urban India. The Gram Panchayats are viable Constitutional mechanism present across India. Through this Constitutional mechanism the consumer movement can be made effective and awareness among rural consumers can be spread. In this context required amendments can be made to establish consumer forums at Gram, Block and District level.

The Gram Panchayats can play a crucial role in spreading awareness. Information Technology and both print and electronic media can be used for this purpose. The relevant literature in this regard in languages of the people can be extensively circulated in hard as well as in soft versions. The Gram Panchayats can use media in the form of documentary films. Street plays can also go a long way in spreading awareness. The teachers and students can do wonders in taking the consumer awareness programmes to every door of villages. Involvement of academicians and researchers in consumer movement is of vital importance. Till now there is not much of the involvement of teachers, students, researchers and educational institutions in generating awareness about the problems of consumers and their protection. There is a need to encourage teachers and students to take up this cause in rural areas. Active participation of the consumers in awareness drives can ensure consumer welfare. There is need of improvement in infrastructure of the Consumer Forums, sufficient allocation of funds in budget for their effective functioning and for consumer protection and welfare, provision for training of staff, and members of the Consumer Forums and provision of necessary legal aid to the consumers in order to enable them to defend themselves.

Conclusions and Suggestions

In a democratic system people are required to be made active participants in the process of governance and development. This helps in strengthening the democratic fabric and processes consequently developing the sense of belonging in people. It also ensures utilisation of the knowledge and experience of the people as a human resource. In this way people develop skills also in them to contribute and accelerate the process of development.

Decentralisation and devolution of legislative and executive powers is the primary requirement of resurgent nation. Earlier village assemblies resolved disputes between individuals in villages. Now, the Constitution and law has decentralised and delegated several administrative functions to the local level. This has empowered elected Gram Panchayats. This decentralisation of the aforesaid powers and functions with regard to such a huge population is historical in the history of humanity. C. Rajgopalachari rightly opined "A knitting together of people's hearts makes democracy". The rights of consumers are to be protected in every sector and especially of the rural consumers. The Panchayati Raj Institutions are required to be made the pivotal agencies in educating and protecting the consumers through policy-making.

The active involvement and participation from the Union and State Governments, the Educational Institutions, the NGOs, the print and electronic media and the adoption and observance of a code of professional conduct by the trade and industry and the citizen's charter by the service providers is necessary for the success of the consumer movement. Impact of participation of women as functionaries in Panchayati Raj Institutions is significant. It has enhanced their self-esteem, confidence, decision-making ability, and respect within the family and in community. Their voice has increased in decisions related to economic matters and other issues in their family. Domestic violence is also mitigating. Women who received training have performed better. It should be organised regularly covering rules and regulations, administrative issues, budgeting, finance and the implementation of development schemes.

The need of the hour is for total commitment to the consumer cause and social responsiveness to consumer needs. It is important that this should proceed in a harmonious manner. The majority of consumers in India are not aware of their rights and existence of the consumer forums. The access to consumer forums is not available to them due to numerous factors in general and absence of the network, branches and benches of consumer forums below the district level in particular. Many a times the consumers suffer financial injuries. Although there is Indian Contract Act of 1872 yet there is no comprehensive legislation like Indian Torts Acts till now. The codification and enactment of Indian Torts Act which is pending since British times is urgently required for the fair justice with regard to civil wrongs. The doctrine of caveat emptor and caveat vendor are required to be in balance.

The media initiatives like "*Jago Grahak Jago*" have reached in every household as a result of the awareness campaigns undertaken during the recent past. There is increased emphasis on consumer awareness in Eleventh Five Year Plan. The State has endeavoured to inform the common men of their rights as a consumer. Consumer awareness initiative in rural and remote areas finds top priority in the Eleventh Five Year plan. Now, the Fundamental Right to Education in Article 21A of the Constitution is set to give a further fillip to consumer protection movement. MGNREGA appears to be a movement towards making Right to Work a fundamental right and actualising the directives of law and policy-making as mentioned in Article 41 of the Constitution. Major concern in this direction is of corruption, financial misappropriation of funds and lack of commitment towards the cause.

In reality the problem in India is not of judicial activism, but of academic, legislative, executive and bureaucratic inactivism. In the Post-Constitutional era the hard-working nation has become resurgent and vibrant. It has shown exceptional dynamism of its own. It appears that the people sitting in Constitutional bodies have failed to rapidly adapt themselves with the fast coming changes. The stage has come when the nation requires middle age leadership with relevant experience to lead it. The people operating the Constitutional systems and rule of law are required to be full of commitment and concern. The process of biological and social evolution is always a forward process. New generations are better than the previous ones. The senior generations will remain relevant only if they show adaptability and if they identify themselves with the requirement of the present.

The issue is of humane governance and not simply of good governance. For this socially responsible skilled professionals are to be produced as their end products by universities, which are sanctuaries of the nation, its happiness and prosperity. In the end it is to be appreciated and kept in mind that although Panchayati Raj Institutions can play a crucial role in policy-making and their implementation yet the judicial function in the adjudication of disputes cannot be given to them because that will go against the principles of natural justice. Since huge finances are and will be involved in development, in many cases Panchayati Raj Institutions will be a party in disputes. So, they can and should not be a judge in their own cause. Awareness, expansion and availability of the network of consumer forums below the district level shall be the right mechanism.

References

All India Reporter, Nagpur, All India Reporter Pvt. Ltd.
Economic and Political Weekly, Mumbai.
Nyaya Deep, New Delhi, National Legal Services Authority.
Social Scientist, New Delhi.
www.economictimes.com
www.ilidelhi.org
www.wikipedia.com

16
Gandhian Perspective on Problems of Rural Consumers in India
Issues and Challenges

Anil Dutta Mishra

> *"The real wealth of a nation is its people. And the purpose of development is to create an enabling environment for people to enjoy long, healthy and creative lives. This simple but powerful truth is too often forgotten in the pursuit of material and financial wealth."* —Human Development Report, 1990

Introduction

Census of India defines rural as any habitation with a population density less than 400 per sq. km., where at least 75 per cent of the male working population is engaged in agriculture and where there exits no municipality or board. India lives in villages, close to 72 per cent of Indian population lives in rural areas. In the country we have 6.38 lakh villages out of which only 13 per cent have population above 2000. The rural economy contributes nearly half of the country's GDP (ETIG 2002-03) which is mainly agriculture driven and monsoon dependent. More than 50 per cent of the sales FMCG and Durable companies come from the rural areas.

The McKinsey report (2007) on the rise on consumer market in India predicts that in twenty years the rural Indian market will be larger than the total consumer markets in countries such as South Korea or Canada today, and almost four times the size of today's urban Indian market and estimated the size of the rural market at $577 billion. Rural India is a major part of India's domestic consumption story not just because it has 70 per cent of India's population, but because it already has 56 per cent of India's income, 64 per cent of expenditure and 33 per cent of India's savings. The rural share of popular consumer goods and durables ranges from 30 per cent to 60 per cent and sales to rural India are steadily growing.

Rural markets in India constitute a wide and untapped market for many products and services which are being marketed for the urban masses. There is a demand for all services which are available in cities are to be provided in rural area across country. Till now, it was government which was trying to reach the villages through various initiates, but the rural areas are still untouched and very poor in goods and services and can be improved only through the introduction of modern and suitable technology along with participation from the private players through public private partnership.

The Problem and the Contradictions

The tragedy of modern India is that the important aspects of the Gandhian philosophy are not given serious attention. The ruling elite never realised that Gandhi was much ahead of time. The quest of humanity for social justice and sustainability will remain a dream until and unless humanity realises what Gandhi meant when he said, that economics is untrue which ignores and disregards moral values. Gandhi in his various speeches and in his articles written throughout the freedom struggle spoke highly of rural people and in modern context rural consumer. In the 22nd July, 1946 issue of *Harijan*, Gandhi stated that "Independence must begin at the bottom".

From the time he (Gandhi) arrived in India from South Africa in 1914 till his death on 30th January, 1948, Gandhi had two objectives. One was the perfection of the technique of *satyagraha* in its individual, group and mass forms and to persuade the people of India and through them, the whole world, to accept it as the only method for resolving political, economic, social and religious conflicts. The other was the reconstruction of the Indian village on a self-governing, self-sufficient, egalitarian, self-contained and spiritually oriented basis as the foundation for the political, economic, cultural and spiritual growth of the country. Gandhi held that by serving the villages, *swaraj* could be established. The country's prosperity and progress depends upon the villages. He maintained that if the village perishes, India will perish too. The importance of rural development should be obvious in country where four out of every five citizens live in the countryside. India lives in villages. Unless the socio-economic and political situation of rural India changed, India cannot progress.

This called for a change in the concept and strategy of rural consumer in the era of liberalisation, privatisation and globalisation. Rural consumer are more vulnerable due to various factors like illiteracy, lack of English, not aware about products, expire date, MRP etc. Rural consumers are not aware of their rights as consumers. As a result rural consumers are worst sufferer. In India consumer are still at the receiving end. Consumers are at the mercy of state and corporate houses at the one hand and retailers, distributors and shopkeepers at the other hand. Virtually, everyone is deceiving the rural people. The traditional system of brand name is no longer in existence in rural India. As a result they are at the mercy of market forces. And market forces are always unkind to poor, farmer and rural people or rural consumers. The market is basically unban centric and guided by global trends. As a result, since early 1970s such terms as "redistribution with growth", and "growth with social justice" became very popular and concept of people's participation in the process of development began to be emphasised keeping the need of rural people. The change of emphasis made development more broad-based.

Rural consumer has emerged as a distinctive field of policy and practice and of research, in the last decade and a half. As a strategy it is defined by its concern with equity objectives of various kinds especially the reduction of inequalities distribution systems and services in rural areas. It is this distributional issue which has marked out "Rural Consumer" as a distinct field, because an overwhelming majority of poor people in India like the other developing countries of Asia and Africa live in rural areas.

In view of the enormity, nature, complexities and urgency of the rural people's problems most of the governments initiated development programmes which led to the creation of a number of new institutions—political, economic, social and administrative. While creating these institutions, greater attention was paid to people's institutions. The reason behind this was that the programmes of development were to be carried out not only by the state bureaucracy, but also through active and effective people's participation. Besides, effective people's institutions have to be created to promote political development and social justice. Thus, local institution is a necessity, if not sufficient, condition for the accelerated rural development. The element of participation is central to rural consumer. It responds to the need to mobilise and use more effectively all the resources available or potentiality available in rural areas of labour, skills, saving, land, fisheries, forests, livestock and water.

Development of rural areas and rural people has been the central concern of development planning in India. Rural India which encompasses three-fourths of the country's population is characterised, by low income levels, not even adequate to ensure a quality of life compatible with physical well-being. The politico-economic and socio-cultural structural disabilities threaten the development of rural poor. This has aggravated the problem of poverty, which has manifested itself in various forms, i.e. unemployment, inequality, malnutrition, growth of slums and ignorance. The growing poverty, which undermines planned development, is much more severe in rural than urban areas and has become the biggest bottleneck in national development.

Gandhi, "the born democrat", wanted to build the structure of the pure democracy 'inch-by-inch' directly from below. He wanted to make each village "a complete republic, independent of its neighbours for its vital wants, and yet interdependent for many others in which dependence is necessity". He was convinced that "if all Indian villages could come up to the ideal, India would be free from most of its worries".

Gandhi, therefore, determined to work for small rural communities wherein people will cooperate with one another and give aid to those who lack the resources for growth and development. He spoke and wrote about village *swaraj*. He said, "the *swaraj* of my dreams is the poor man's *swaraj*. The necessaries of life should be enjoyed by you in common with those enjoyed by the princes and the moneyed men. But, that does not mean that you should have palaces like theirs. They are not necessary for happiness. You or I would be lost in them. But, you ought to get all the ordinary amenities of life that a rich man enjoys. I have not the slightest doubt that *swaraj* is not *Purna Swaraj* until these amenities are guaranteed to you under it."

Revival of the village is indeed the key to the regeneration of India and the fulfilment of the mission in the world, "I want villages to live", says the architect of modern India Pandit Jawaharlal Nehru, "and I do not care what happens to the towns because I am convinced that if village die, there can be no hope for towns. If villages prosper India is also bound to prosper." In fact, the road to the village is the road to the Heaven of India's soul, the road to the cradle of our civilisation, the road to real *yajna*. The village will be barometer of India's progress and prosperity. "Going back to villages", says Dr. Radhakrishnan, "is not to become primitive". It is the only way to keep us in the mode of existence that is instructive to India that supplied him once with purpose, a faith and meaning. It is the only way to keep our species civilised."

Though the income levels overall are still very low there are many pockets of prosperity which have come up in the rural areas in the country. According to NCAER 2002, the number of rural middle class households at 27.4 million is very close to their urban counterpart at 29.5 million. And between, 1981-2001 there has been tremendous improvement in the literacy levels, poverty and rural housing in the villages of the country. Rural literacy levels have improved from 36 per cent to 59 per cent, the number of below poverty houses have declined from close to half to 46 per cent and the number of *pucca* houses have doubled from 22 per cent to 41 per cent.

These figures provide us with a clear picture that rural India with the increase in agricultural income and improving standards is on the verge of becoming a large untapped market which marketers have been aspiring for a very long period of time. Thus, the current status of rural markets makes it an attractive market for marketers. Like contemporary India, Rural Indian is also dominated by the consumerism and market driven agriculture. It is gradually being transformed from a predominantly sellers' market to a buyers' market where exercised choice by the consumers depends on their awareness level. Consumer rights could be protected in a competitive economy only when right standards for goods and services for which one makes payment are ensured by evolving a network of institutions and legal protection system. Ensuring consumer welfare is the responsibility of the government as every citizen of the country is a consumer in one way or the other.

Consumer behaviour has changed in recent years owing to enhanced awareness, information technology and more importantly governmental intervention through legislations. Thus, the manufacturers are more cautious in dealing with consumers of their respective products. The rural consumers in India account for about 73 per cent of the total consumers. In recent years, the life style of a large number of rural consumers in India has changed dramatically and the process of change is on. The buying behaviour of the rural consumers is influenced by several factors such as socio-economic conditions, cultural environment, literacy level, occupation, geographical location, efforts on the part of sellers, exposure to media etc. The consumer movement in India till now has been confined to the middle class citizens in urban areas. It has yet to spread among the masses in rural areas.

The fact is that the rural consumer remains disadvantaged as their right to information, choice, redress, education and the right to be heard are not sufficiently fulfilled. They are exploited in many ways due to poor knowledge about their rights. The rural consumer who depends largely on weekly market especially in the remote areas, to purchase essential things is often cheated in price, weight and measurement. There is a need for the development and adjustment of the existing consumer protection and consumer welfare polices for meeting the specific requirements of rural consumers more effectively. The reality is that to provide service in the rural areas one has to face many challenges:

1. Geographical spread and low population density in the villages.
2. Low purchasing power and limited disposable incomes in the villages.
3. Lack of infrastructure facilities.
4. Lack of education.
5. Lack of awareness.
6. Lack of minimum modern facilities.
7. Lack of market.
8. The mind-set of the people are rigid and not ready to accept new ideas.
9. They are not aware of brands.

What should we do?

In the present context the modern visionary Gandhi rightly said long back: "The earth provides enough for every man's need but not for every man's greed." The real development will take the society from *Vikriti* (perversion) to *Sanskriti* (culture). It is not going back, but going in the right direction. We may emphasised for resorting to Gandhian Values and decentralisation as a vision for protecting all, including consumers. As per the Gandhian thought the consumers and producers were not looked as separate individuals. The process of production was supposed to be decentralised and distributed in parity. Gandhi rightly said:

> **"A customer is the most important person on our premises. He is not dependent on us. We are dependent on him. He is not an interruption to our work. He is the purpose of it. He is not an outsider to our business. He is the part of it. We are not doing him a favour by serving him. He is doing us a favour by giving us an opportunity to do so."**

Unfortunately in the case of rural consumer the shopkeepers take all opportunities to exploit them. The rural consumer is at the receiving ends.

- Firstly, the need of hour is that the efficient and effective programme of Consumer Protection is of special significance to all of us, as we all are consumers. Even a manufacturer or provider of a service is a consumer of some other goods or services. If the producers/service providers and consumers realise the need for co-existence, adulterated products, spurious goods and other deficiencies in services would become a thing of the past.
- Secondly, the active involvement and participation from all stake holder, i.e. the Central and State Governments, the Educational Institutions, the NGOs, the print and electronic media and the adoption and observance of a voluntary code of conduct by the trade and industry and the citizen's charter by the service providers is not only necessary but a *sine qua non* for the success of the Consumer movement.
- Thirdly, the need of the hour is for total commitment to the consumer cause and social responsiveness to consumer needs. This should, however, proceed in a harmonious manner so that, our society becomes a better place for all of us to live in.
- Fourthly, rural consumer needs to be taught, trained and should be made to learn to consume. Consumer should not ask what the government can do for them, but first think what they can do for themselves.
- Fifthly, there is a need of advocating a holistic approach that includes the social, legal, religious and cultural aspects of the consumerism with a view to empower rural consumers.
- Sixthly, in order to deal with the problems of the rural consumers', some institutional back-up system must be put in place within village panchayats.

Summing up

Protection of Rural Consumer has become a buzz word in the era of Liberalisation, Privatisation and Globalisation. LPG can succeed only when we take care of rural people and their needs. In other words rural consumer must be integrated with urban and global consumers.

Protection of Rural Consumer is not as simple as it looks on paper.

Capabilities have to be built-up, suitable structures have to be valued, changes have to be brought about in the administrative, technical and political arena. Equally important is kindling the zeal and enthusiasm of the people. But the most important agents to make rural consumer movement a success are the political and administrative will to decentralise decision making powers to the lower levels on Gandhian line with a clear policy enunciation, full political support, and needed administrative infrastructure, it is expected that the goals of real *swaraj* will be achieved by fulfilling the dream of the Father of the Nation. It is high time for both our policy-makers and the people, to turn the torch within so that they may be inspired to adopt the Gandhian way, if not for any other consideration, but for its pragmatic strength to solve our present day maladies of rural India. There is need to reiterate Gandhian values, and instead of merely garlanding the portraits of Gandhiji, India must translate his ideals into real life and make Rural India free from hunger, poverty and exploitation.

References

Gandhi, M.K. (1962). *India of My Dreams*, Ahmedabad: Navajivan Publishing House, p. 6.

Gandhi, M.K. (1996). *Village Swaraj*, Ahmedabad: Navajivan Publishing House, p. 9.

SECTION IV
Media, Technology and Rural Consumers

17
Role of Traditional Folk Media in Consumer Empowerment

Communicating with the Rural Audience

Suresh Misra, Mamta Pathania and *Virendra Nath Mishra*

Introduction

In a country like India, given the scenario of economic disparity and level of education and ignorance, educating the consumers remains a gigantic task. Consumer education and awareness is the main building block for consumer protection as an enlightened consumer is an empowered consumer. They not only protect themselves from exploitation, but also induce efficiency, accountability and transparency in the entire manufacturing and service sector. With high levels of poverty, unemployment and poor literacy levels, consumer awareness continues to remain low.

The process of development along with the expanding Globalisation and Liberalisation has increased the number of consumer related issues. Thus, in the emerging scenario it is necessary to protect the consumers by educating them about their rights and empowering them to make decisions based on information about the goods and services. So far, the consumer movement has largely been confined to the urban areas, and with the expanding rural markets now the focus has to shift to protect the rural consumer as well. Consumer education has an important role to play in supporting those with less developed consumer knowledge and skills. Consumer education is a potent tool for empowering consumers. Empowered consumers are knowledgeable, confident and assertive. It is a well-known fact that education is a lifelong process of constantly acquiring relevant information, knowledge and skills. However, consumer education is incomplete without the responsibilities and duties of consumers, and this influences individual behaviour to a great extent.

Consumer organisations and similar civil society groups have an important role to play in consumer education. They have the means to provide consumers with information and help them to make informed choices. Consumer information needs to be available at the right time and in the right place before or when purchase decisions are made. Several NGOs are very active in the rural areas in advocating for consumer rights, but due to their limited ability to put enough pressure on policy-makers, they lack consumer support. This is the dilemma of NGO's working in the area of consumer welfare. Regardless of these limitations, consumer empowerment programmes through regular training and education are very crucial.

Building consumer confidence is very important, and in the future, the need to achieve this will raise important challenges. Consequently, consumers will face more complex problems and more rapidly changing choices. With Consumer Protection Act coming in force it has become easy for aggrieved consumers to complain and seek redressal for their problems. Thus, to be most effective, consumer education initiatives should be focused on clear priorities and targeted at those most in need.

Communication and Rural Audience

Rural markets have always been seen as an unmanageable territory, due to its vastness and scattered characteristics. Rural audiences across villages differ with each other. With such a vast difference, it is very difficult to specify who the target audience is. Before doing that, one must remember that rural audience though homogenous, are heterogeneous when it comes to buying value-for-money products.

Rural audience can be broadly categorised into two, when it comes to understanding of advertisements. On one hand, we have the audience who are less literate (even illiterate) and on the other hand we have the educated population. The former group requires a communication message which can be easily understood. While purchasing, this group usually does not specify brand names, because of their inability to read and write. Instead, they choose to demand what they want by mentioning the features or anything that is associated with the brand. They associate their demands (products) with the colours, numerals etc. Hence, while designing the communication strategy, there is a need to take into account their capability to understand information. The youth are more brand conscious due to education, mobility, media exposure etc. because of which they demand the brands of their choices.

Folk Art as a Medium of Communication

Folk Media, as we use the term, is any sort of art or communication created by an individual, a small business, non-profit, or an informal group, created outside of the influence of big media companies or other large institutions. The creations of folk media-makers make our media scape much richer, the artistic frontier more vibrant, and our public dialogue far more diverse, open, and free. Traditional folk media is popular among the rural masses considerably. Traditional media generally, cover folk songs, folk dance drama that depicts the stories of most common rural dwellers. Traditional folk media cannot present what it wants to deliver, in glamorous and colourful manner equally, as compared to other organised sector of mass medium that we have. Traditional folk media cultivates the rural life style and culture specifically, as to match their needs and demand, which are illiterate and backward as well. Further more it goes with rural masses side by side, bringing slower change in their development.

Perhaps the best way to communicate with the rural audience is through folk art. This form is easy to understand and has been used for centuries to educate the masses. Folklore is a medium through which the soul of people expresses itself colourfully. In such creation, they find an artistic fulfilment and entertainment combing with dance which is called Folk art. Folk art differs from primitive art in its outlook and character. The needs and peculiar problems of the village people's life find an expression in folk art. Their daily life is full of religious customs and ceremonies.

Myths and legends are required to be illustrated interestingly and conveyed to the public. While satisfying the needs of the people, folk art attains a certain aesthetic level. It is anonymous and its origin cannot be traced to any particular period of time. The word 'Tradition' implying customs, habits and way of life existed in a society for a long period of continuity from time immemorial and practiced from one generation to another. It can be transmitted through written scriptures or by word of mouth. The nomadic primitive people sharing a common cultural heritage based on oral tradition are generally said to have a folk culture. Folk culture in a society is seen in four different forms—Oral tradition, Material culture, Social folk customs, and Performing arts.

Among these, the Oral tradition and the Performing arts appear to be the main media of communication. Storytellers, singers, minstrels and other kinds of folk entertainers have acted for centuries as sources for the transmission and dissemination of news and information through face-to-face live communication. The values, attitudes, beliefs and culture of the people are propagated, reinforced and perpetuated through these folk forms. The issues in a society are depicted in the form of satire by the Folk artists for curing societal evils.

Hence, the Folk arts have been used for moral, religious and socio-political purposes in India right from the ancient times. Folk media are relatively inexpensive and easily accessible which adds to the popularity of the folk media in rural areas. Their highly spontaneous, participatory and involving quality makes them the media par excellence for any powerful and effective communication. These may be exhibited in different forms such as folk dances, folk music, folk songs and folk theatre. All these are ways to express and entertain and more specifically used to disseminate a specific message to the masses, mediums which are more close to common men at large. The folk theatre is one such medium which communicates messages to the people, which they understand easily and encourage them and also acts as a source of conveying information.

Folk arts when staged as entertainments became folk theatre. Folk theatre performances are closely associated to celebrations. Folk arts and theatres are not only a mode of entertainment, but also a source of conveying information. The folk dramas that originally yielded pleasure to the villagers and the town people alike were transformed into stage. These stage plays have descended into street plays, which deal with the day-to-day problems of people. The street plays being realistic are devoid of the traditional make-up, costumes and screens, and the characters are more life like. Their sole aim is to communicate to the people, which they understand easily and encourage them. The language employed by these media is the common idiom of the society. Hence, it is easily comprehended by both the educated and the uneducated audience. Therefore, the folk dramas were very popular from the medieval period and they are being used as a good media system even today. The folk dramas staged by the rural troupes in all the stages help in promoting mass communication.

Advantages of Folk Media

The appeal of Folk media is quite personal and at an intimate level because it has got direct influence on people. The numerous and different forms of mass media can be exploited to cater to the needs of the people for immediate and direct rapport. Indian folk forms are a mixture of dialogue, dance, song, clowning, moralising and prayer. Though the folk media attracts a small audience, the impact on them is at a much deeper level inviting the audience participation. As the moral instruction campaigned is with entertainment. Being dramatic and lyrical, it satisfies our innate need for self-expression. From a century-wide perspective the folk and traditional media are still the only mass media in the sense that they have their routes in the tradition and experience of a large majority of the population and also that they have a reach much more extensive than any of the modern technological media.

The familiarity, personal contact, common language, intelligibility, credibility and acceptance make the folk media universally acceptable among rural folks. The messages in folk media are far more credible and acceptable than if it were transmitted through the electronic media. In India, folk traditions are used as a vehicle for mass communication. They are local, intimate and establish immediate rapport with the masses in all the regions of the country:

- Their primary appeal is to the emotions rather than to the intellect and they have greater potential for persuasive communication and instant feedback;
- they belong to the community and not to any individual, state or public industry. There are no organised institutions or persons to control either the quality or quantity of these media. There are no authors, or copyrights, but they remain anonymous and can be adapted at will by anyone to suit a particular need;
- they use the language, idiom and symbols of the people. Because of this they can be highly participatory and form part of communal celebrations wherein everyone takes an active part; and
- they command an immense variety of forms and themes to suit the communication requirements of the masses. Themes ranging from myths to current issues can easily find expression through these forms.[1]

A good use of traditional folk media for campaigns like consumer awareness and education, particularly in the rural areas can be very effective. Being ancient forms of art, the folk media is very close to the heart of the people. Its appeal is universal and its understanding is direct and at personal level. So, the folk media can effectively be used as mass communication among ruralities. It has played a very important role in solving several emotional problems and channelising the destructive forces into constructive ones.

In India folk music, folk dances and folk dramas have always played an important role in combating destructive elements and in harmonising emotional outbursts relating to caste, creed, religion and language issues. Various organisations, movements and government bodies can effectively make use of these folk arts for developmental activities. The communication needs in India are much greater than the resources we have today to meet them. While the mass media have been constantly expanding, the folk media have been playing an important role in this field due to our peculiar needs. Apart from these, live programme in face-to-face communication, the folk forms have also been used in programmes over electronic media. India's roles in identifying folk media for communication purposes have been quite positive. While folkway of communication dominates in remote and rural areas, they are present in various forms in urban centres as well. As regard to folk arts, it is very clear that the revival of such forms of arts can very well be utilised for reconstruction of new ideas and building-up of our nation in a better way. Folk media are thus, most effective in changing the unscientific attitudes, superstitions etc. inherited as a part of tradition by the people in rural areas. Thus, it is a great revelation now-a-days that the folk arts are quite sufficient, as a medium to inform and disseminate people to safeguard against superstition and other such beliefs, create awareness on different issues related to the day-to-day life of common man.

Studies have proved that the hold of the folk media on the rural and semi-urban masses is still strong. Each folk art itself is a medium of communication because it is directly linked with the psyche of its audience. It is flexible and it can be modified in regard to its functional relevance to the society to which it belongs. Folk media are closer to the lives of rural audience that is perhaps why it survived.

Apart from the highly organised medium of mass communication that are used in excessive manner presently, like print, audio and audio-visual medium, the traditional folk media is popular among the rural masses considerably well. Traditional folk media cultivate the rural life style and culture specifically, as to match their needs and demand, who are illiterate and backward as well. Traditional folk media go with rural masses side-by-side, bringing slower change in their development. Although, they provide so many messages, that contribute to the rural development significantly. It can command a very strong position in the rural people's mind, as it weaves messages to serve the various needs and purposes as well as entertain the numerous rural people as well.

It generally includes the presentation of different types of programmes like folk song and music, folk dance, *yatra*, drama and theatres, puppetry and street theatre etc. All programmes have the individual criteria and attraction as well, that can render distinctive taste and flavour to the audiences well.

Street Theatre

There are many organisations all over the country which perform folk arts on topics relevant to the society with the purpose of generating awareness for change. They use popular folk form of dance, music and theatre. It shows that the importance of involving the masses at the grassroots level for any change oriented Programme is widely realised as inevitable. Indian street theatre developed as an art form to illustrate the feelings of common people; hence germinated a whole new theatre form, which was then typically categorised as "theatre by the people and theatre for the people". Common people, day-to-day life, problems and the colours of daily life gained a dimension in Indian street theatre whilst making this particular genre of Indian "*natya*" to stand apart amidst the crowd. The Street theatre as an expression of common people was there even in the ancient days of remote past and was ingrained in the age-old Indian traditions. Gradually, Indian street theatre became an effort of communicating the message of the mass; an attempt in illustrating the realities of daily life. Quite ideally, therefore, Indian street theatre became an endeavour in addressing the burning political, social and other communal issues of Independent India. Theatre then was just not a form of entertainment, but evolved as an endearing art form in creating the social awareness. An integral part of various campaigns in India, street theatre is not restricted to issues of any particular ideology; the nature and role of street theatre varies according to different organisational structures and conditions of performance.

West Bengal has Bengali theatre, which primarily refers to theatre performed in the Bengali language. Bengali theatre is produced mainly in West Bengal, and in Bangladesh. Bengali theatre has its origins in British rule. It began as private entertainment in the early nineteenth century. In the pre-Independence period, Bengali theatres played a pivotal role in manifesting dislike of the British Raj. After the Independence of

India in 1947, leftist movements in West Bengal used theatre as a propaganda tool. This added some unique characteristics to the art form that still have strong effects. The many theatres in West Bengal can be broadly divided into Kolkata-based theatres and rural theatres. Outside Bengali-speaking areas, the term "Bengali theatre" primarily refers to Kolkata-based groups, as the rural theatres are less well-known.[2]

Framework of the Research Study

The Department of Consumer Affairs, Government of India has been funding a variety of programmes to empower the rural consumers through consumer education and also enhancing their awareness about their rights and obligations. In West Bengal also a project is being executed by one of the NGOs to educate the consumers by using various traditional mediums to communicate with the rural audience. These were street theatre shows, ventriloquism shows, workshops etc. The mass awareness campaigns targeted at making people aware of consumer rights and the procedure to exercise those rights. A number of theatre based activities were used to reinforce the learning. This study was conducted by the Centre for Consumer Studies, IIPA to evaluate the effectiveness and impact of the Programme on the consumers. The study was conducted in three districts of West Bengal, namely South 24 Parganas, Murshidabad and Hooghly with the following objectives:

1. To evaluate the effectiveness of traditional media in consumer empowerment.
2. To analyse the long and short term impact of communicating with rural consumers' through use of traditional media.
3. To assess the level of awareness among the rural consumers through the use of traditional media.

Research Methodology

The study was carried out with the help of both primary and secondary sources. Discussions were also held with a large number of villagers, students, action group members and district officials to evaluate the various aspects of the project and also assess the level of awareness achieved by them after attending the consumer awareness programmes. In order to ascertain the views of the officials at the village level, block level and district level about the effectiveness of the programmes using traditional media. As far as primary data is concerned, the structured questionnaire consisting of close ended questions was canvassed among the villagers and the students in the respective three districts.

Sample Plan

The study covers three districts, i.e. South 24 Parganas, Murshidabad and Hooghly to assess the impact and outcome of these awareness programmes using traditional media. Three districts were selected by using simple random sampling technique. Subsequently, two blocks from each district were chosen for the study. The blocks were selected keeping in view the geographical spread of the sample area so as to cover most parts of the respective Districts. Finally, three Gram Panchayats were from each block were selected randomly.

The Panchayat level samples were stratified into two categories: (i) first 12 villagers from each Panchayat and 25 students from each school (one school from each block) were randomly selected, in Murshidabad district all 50 (25×2) students were girls while in other two districts students were both girls and boys; and (ii) 10 Action Group members from each Panchayat were selected randomly to have their opinion about the quality and requirements of these types of awareness programmes. As the goal was to create awareness about Consumer Protection Act among masses especially school and college going children and to create consumer protection networks at the various levels for ready redressal of complaints, the school children were included in the sample. Therefore, the sample consists of 546 persons from the three districts.

Time Period of the Awareness Programmes Organised

A programme is said to be achieving its objectives if clientele covered under the programme responds positively as per the objectives of the programme. Similarly, people seem to retain the contents of the awareness programme only if there is continuity in the awareness programmes at regular intervals by keeping the target group updated about the knowledge of the latest developments. For this there is a need to maintain continuity and to ensure a follow-up at regular intervals. As per the project proposal the awareness campaign was designed to be vigorous using different kinds of media. As per the MoU, the project was supposed to complete the aforesaid programmes within a period of six months, covering six districts. The study covered three sample districts to understand the implementation of the projects. It was important to know the time interval of the programmes that were organised in various districts.

Techniques Adopted to Disseminate Consumer Awareness

The purpose of organising the awareness campaigns at the village level was to make the villagers aware about their consumer rights and to educate them about quality, quantity and utility of contemporary products or services. According to the proposal and the agreement between Department of Consumer Affairs and M/s. I-land Informatics Ltd., Kolkata, it was supposed to conduct different types of activities and programmes to educate the rural consumers about their rights, to make them aware about various dimensions of consumer protection and to build capacity of PRI, VCOs and other stakeholders to strengthen access to grievance redressal mechanism. These included street plays, Ventriloquism shows/puppet shows and consumer sensitisation and capacity building workshops. Therefore, it was imperative to know the kind of activities conducted in the programmes.

In response to the question on different activities in the programmes (Table 17.1), 59.8 per cent of the respondents had seen the street plays. Street plays is a good medium of generating awareness among masses as people correlate their own day-to-day consumer decisions and are able to retain it for long. Therefore, the participation was high when compared with other forms of Programmes. 40.2 per cent of the respondents attended the Ventriloquism Shows. The district-wise responses were on the same pattern as 63.1 per cent in Hooghly, 60.7 per cent in Murshidabad and 55.8 per cent in South 24 Parganas attended the street plays while 44.3 per cent in South 24 Parganas, 39.3 per cent in Murshidabad and 36.9 per cent in Hooghly attended the Ventriloquism Shows which were targeted to build awareness among the school children and the youth. The Street theatre shows targeted raising mass awareness and a story line titled "*Sabdhaner Mar Nei* or Helps to be Careful" was developed as a part of the street theatre campaign.

Content of the Awareness Programmes

The data clearly shows that the campaign had effective reach among the rural population in terms of the geographical and mass reach, covering a

Table 17.1: Techniques Adopted in Disseminating Consumer Awareness

Districts	*Blocks*	*Street Play/ Workshop*	*Ventriloquism Show**
Hooghly	Chuchura-Mogra	63.9	36.1
	Dhaniakhali	62.3	37.7
	Total	**63.1**	**36.9**
Murshidabad	Kandi	60.7	39.3
	Beldanga I	60.6	39.4
	Total	**60.7**	**39.4**
South 24 Parganas	Sonarpur	57.4	42.6
	Bhangar II	54.1	45.9
	Total	**55.8**	**44.3**
Grand Total		**59.8**	**40.2**

* Ventriloquism Show was conducted in schools only.
Source: Field Survey, CCS, IIPA.

wide cross-section of people. Therefore, it was imperative to know what the content of the awareness programmes was. According to Table 17.2 more than half of the respondents (53.3%) opined that the programmes stressed on general consumer awareness which was helpful for rural masses in their day-to-day life. 28.7 per cent of the respondents said that the programmes dealt with the Consumer Protection Act/Rights of the consumer while 18 per cent could not understand the content of the

Table 17.2: Content of the Awareness Programmes

Districts	*Blocks*	*CP Act/ Right*	*General Consumer Awareness*	*Both*
Hooghly	Chuchura-Mogra	27.9	52.5	19.7
	Dhaniakhali	19.7	50.8	29.5
	Total	**23.8**	**51.6**	**24.6**
Murshidabad	Kandi	29.5	54.1	16.4
	Beldanga I	37.7	47.5	14.8
	Total	**33.6**	**50.8**	**15.6**
South 24 Parganas	Sonarpur	36.1	52.5	11.5
	Bhangar II	21.3	62.3	16.4
	Total	**28.7**	**57.4**	**13.9**
Grand Total		**28.7**	**53.3**	**18.0**

Source: Field Survey, CCS, IIPA.

awareness programmes. District-wise also majority of the respondents confirmed that the awareness programmes dealt mostly with issues relating to general consumer awareness.

Effectiveness of the Programmes

The purpose of the programmes was to enhance the villagers' knowledge about consumer related problems, create awareness about consumer welfare and educate them about the redressal mechanism available to the consumers. Therefore, it was imperative to find out the effectiveness and usefulness of the programmes for the villagers. When the respondents were asked about the effectiveness of the programmes, they were of the opinion that overall the programmes were effective and helpful in enhancing consumer awareness. As per Table 17.3, 55.2 per cent of the respondents found it to be excellent. 22.4 per cent of them said that these programmes were very good. About 16.1 per cent of respondents found the programmes to be good while 6.3 per cent found the programmes to be fair.

The data shows that the project led to improved understanding of consumer problems at the grassroots level as majority of the respondents at the district level also found it to be excellent.

Table 17.3: Perception about the Effectiveness of the Programmes

Districts	*Block*	*Excellent*	*Very good*	*Good*	*Fair*
Hooghly	Chuchura-Mogra	52.5	24.6	16.4	6.6
	Dhaniakhali	59.0	19.7	13.1	8.2
	Total	**55.7**	**22.1**	**14.8**	**7.4**
Murshidabad	Kandi	59.0	18.0	16.4	6.6
	Beldanga I	57.4	21.3	14.8	6.6
	Total	**58.2**	**19.7**	**15.6**	**6.6**
South 24 Parganas	Sonarpur	50.8	26.2	19.7	3,3
	Bhangar II	52.5	24.6	16.4	6.6
	Total	**51.6**	**25.4**	**18.0**	**4.9**
Grand Total		**55.2**	**22.4**	**16.1**	**6.3**

Source: Field Survey, CCS, IIPA.

Satisfaction about Quality of the Programme

After knowing the usefulness of the programme to the villagers it was quite obvious to know about the satisfaction level of the respondents about the quality of the programme.

When the respondents were asked about the quality of the programmes, majority of them (79.5%) as shown in Table 17.4 were satisfied with the quality of the programmes, while 20.5 per cent were not satisfied with the quality of the programmes. District-wise also majority of the respondents, 83.6 per cent of Murshidabad, 81.1 per cent of Hooghly and 73.8 per cent of the respondents said that they were satisfied with the quality of the programmes.

Table 17.4: Satisfaction about Quality of the Programme

Districts	*Block*	*Satisfied*	*Not satisfied*
Hooghly	Chuchura-Mogra	82.0	18.0
	Dhaniakhali	80.3	19.7
	Total	**81.1**	**18.9**
Murshidabad	Kandi	88.5	11.5
	Beldanga I	78.7	21.3
	Total	**83.6**	**16.4**
South 24 Parganas	Sonarpur	72.1	27.9
	Bhangar II	75.4	24.6
	Total	**73.8**	**26.2**
Grand Total		**79.5**	**20.5**

Source: Field Survey, CCS, IIPA.

Exercising Consumer Rights after Attending the Programme

After attending the programme, the respondents had acquired information and knowledge about issues relating to consumer protection and it was expected that the respondents would use their rights as a consumer and would not compromise on the aspect of quality, quantity of products. It was expected that after attending the programmes the villagers will be more careful while selecting products and would check relevant information on products. The data (Table 17.5) indicates that after attending the awareness programmes, 40.7 per cent of the respondents south 24 Parganas always exercised their rights as a consumer while making purchase decisions, 47.3 per cent used it sometimes and 12 per cent of them said that they never exercise their rights as a consumer.

Table 17.5: Exercising the Consumer Rights after attending the Programme

Districts	*Blocks*	*Always*	*Sometimes*	*Never*
Hooghly	Chuchura-Mogra	34.4	54.1	11.5
	Dhaniakhali	42.6	52.5	4.9
	Total	**38.5**	**53.3**	**8.2**
Murshidabad	Kandi	44.3	42.6	13.1
	Beldanga I	37.7	47.5	14.8
	Total	**41.0**	**45.1**	**13.9**
South 24 Parganas	Sonarpur	39.3	50.8	9.8
	Bhangar II	45.9	36.1	18.0
	Total	**42.6**	**43.4**	**13.9**
Grand Total		**40.7**	**47.3**	**12.0**

Source: Field Survey, CCS, IIPA.

District-wise also 42.6 per cent in South 24 Parganas, 41 per cent in Murshidabad and 38.5 per cent in Hooghly confirmed that they always exercised their Rights as Consumer. While 53.3 per cent in Hooghly, 45.1 per cent in Murshidabad and 43.4 per cent in South 24 Parganas confirmed they exercise their rights only sometimes. This clearly indicates that there is an impact on the buying behaviour of the consumer after attending the programmes. However, there is a need to strive for continuous efforts in this direction and to make people really practice their rights as matter of habit for which continuous programmes needs to be organised in this direction.

Extent of Benefit from the Programmes

To create awareness among the masses different mediums were used. Street plays, Ventriloquism Shows, Puppet shows and workshops for the villagers/students and the action group members were organised. The data reveals in Table 17.6 that a large number of the respondents benefited from the programmes as 56 per cent of the respondents confirmed that they benefited to a large extent from the awareness programmes, 31.7

Table 17.6: Respondents Benefited from the Programme

Districts	*Blocks*	*To large extent*	*To some extent*	*Not at all*
Hooghly	Chuchura-Mogra	72.1	14.8	13.1
	Dhaniakhali	45.9	32.8	21.3
	Total	**59.0**	**23.8**	**17.2**
Murshidabad	Kandi	60.7	29.5	9.8
	Beldanga I	62.3	24.6	13.1
	Total	**61.5**	**27.0**	**11.5**
South 24 Parganas	Sonarpur	39.3	55.7	4.9
	Bhangar II	55.7	32.8	11.5
	Total	**47.5**	**44.3**	**8.2**
Grand Total		**56.0**	**31.7**	**12.3**

Source: Field Survey, CCS, IIPA.

per cent of them said the programmes benefited them to some extent while 12.3 per cent said they did not benefit from the programmes.

District-wise also 61.5 per cent in Murshidabad, 59 per cent in Hooghly and 47.5 per cent in South 24 Parganas confirmed that they have benefited a lot from the programmes organised in their villages. Thus, it is clear that people have benefited from the awareness programmes, but for a better outreach more such programmes at regular intervals need to be organised to make people more vigilant and aware about their rights and responsibilities as a consumer.

Changes in the Buying Behaviour of the Villagers

The study also attempted to find out the change in the buying behaviour of the villagers after the programme, which is indicative of the level of awareness among the villagers as a result of the programme.

Table 17.7 indicates that there is change in the perception and buying behaviour of the respondents after attending the programmes. There is a rise in the level of awareness. Of all the respondents, 46.4 per cent always checked the quantity of the products before purchasing it. As far as MRP is concerned 37.7 per cent of the respondents always read the MRP printed on the product. 49.2 per cent of them do so only sometimes and rest of the respondents, i.e. 13.1 per cent never checked MRP printed on the product. In case of the manufacturing date/expiry date, only 12 per cent

Table 17.7: Buying Behaviour of the Respondents

Particulars	*Response*	*Hooghly*			*Murshidabad*			*South 24 Parganas*			Grand Total
		Chuchura-Mogra	Dhaniakhali	Total	Kandi	Beldanga I	Total	Sonarpur	Bhangar II	Total	
Contents	Always	31.1	37.7	**34.4**	26.2	24.6	**25.4**	29.5	34.4	**32.0**	**30.6**
	Sometimes	50.8	49.2	**50.0**	42.6	41.0	**41.8**	52.5	54.1	**53.3**	**48.4**
	Never	18.0	13.1	**15.6**	31.2	34.4	**32.8**	18.0	11.5	**14.8**	**21.0**
MRP	Always	45.9	41.0	**43.5**	32.8	8.2	**20.5**	59.0	39.3	**49.2**	**37.7**
	Sometimes	41.0	45.9	**43.5**	55.7	82.0	**68.9**	23.0	47.5	**35.3**	**49.2**
	Never	13.1	13.1	**13.1**	11.5	9.8	**10.7**	18.0	13.2	**15.6**	**13.1**
Quantity	Always	60.7	44.2	**52.5**	50.8	13.1	**32.0**	55.7	54.1	**54.9**	**46.4**
	Sometimes	26.2	44.3	**35.3**	41.0	72.1	**56.6**	27.9	36.1	**32.0**	**41.3**
	Never	13.1	11.5	**12.3**	8.2	14.8	**11.5**	16.4	9.8	**13.1**	**12.3**
Quality	Always	34.4	11.5	**23.0**	19.6	21.3	**20.5**	13.1	16.4	**14.8**	**19.4**
	Sometimes	27.9	41.0	**34.5**	27.9	47.4	**37.7**	32.8	47.5	**40.2**	**37.4**
	Never	37.7	47.5	**42.6**	52.5	31.1	**41.8**	54.1	36.1	**45.1**	**43.2**
Expiry Date/ Manufacturing date	Always	11.5	14.8	**13.2**	9.8	8.2	**9.0**	14.8	13.1	**14.0**	**12.0**
	Sometimes	29.5	32.8	**31.2**	24.6	27.9	**26.3**	31.1	29.5	**30.3**	**29.2**
	Never	59.0	52.4	**55.7**	65.6	63.9	**64.8**	54.1	57.4	**55.8**	**58.7**
Standard Mark	Always	26.2	27.9	**27.1**	18.0	14.8	**16.4**	26.2	27.9	**27.1**	**23.5**
	Sometimes	31.2	34.4	**32.8**	24.6	26.2	**25.4**	32.8	27.9	**30.4**	**29.5**
	Never	42.6	37.7	**40.2**	57.4	59.0	**58.2**	41.0	44.2	**42.6**	**47.0**

Source: Field Survey, CCS, IIPA.

respondents always checked before purchasing products. However, majority of the respondents (58.7%) never checked the manufacturing date before purchasing the product. Only 30.6 per cent of the respondents always check the contents, whereas 21 per cent of them never read the content of the product printed on the packet. For quality, only 19.4 per cent always checked the same, 43.2 per cent never check whether the product is of good quality or not. One has to understand the profile of the rural population to understand the impact of a programmes. Lack of literacy, poverty and the struggle for livelihood takes over consumer issues. Lack of choice also forces them to take whatever is available in their village.

Therefore, any programmes will have only partial impact. A slow and sustained effort enhances awareness. In the rural backdrop we should not expect to have a very encouraging result. The project has certainly shown that there is a perceptible change as a result of awareness programmes.

Relevance of the Programmes

Whenever any programme is undertaken it has some or the other objectives which are required to be fulfilled within the time frame. The effectiveness of the programmes can be adjudged if the target group is able to correlate the same with their day-to-day life and are able to practically use the information in their daily purchase decisions. Thus, it was important to know as to whether the programmes had relevance to the local villagers or not. When the respondents were asked whether the awareness programmes conducted were relevant to them, majority of the respondents (75.9%) confirmed that they were relevant and influenced their daily purchase decisions (Table 17.8) while 24.1 per cent of them said that they were not relevant. District-wise also 77.1 per cent respondents in Hooghly, 82 per cent in South 24 Parganas and 73.8 per cent in Murshidabad said that the programmes were relevant and they have benefited from the programmes. During interactions they appreciated the messages being conveyed through the programmes and also said that the medium being used was easy to understand.

Knowledge about Consumer Protection Act, 1986

The Consumer Protection Act was enacted in 1986. However, even after 32 years of its enactment the level of awareness about the Act has been low, more so in the rural areas. Awareness programmes were organised

Table 17.8: Relevance of the Programmes

Districts	*Blocks*	*Yes*	*No*
Hooghly	Chuchura-Mogra	78.7	21.3
	Dhaniakhali	75.4	24.6
	Total	**77.1**	**23.0**
Murshidabad	Kandi	75.4	24.6
	Beldanga I	72.1	27.9
	Total	**73.8**	**26.3**
South 24 Parganas	Sonarpur	86.9	13.1
	Bhangar II	77.0	23.0
	Total	**82.0**	**18.1**
Grand Total		**75.9**	**24.1**

Source: Field Survey, CCS, IIPA.

in villages, markets and Panchayats to make people aware about Consumer Protection Act and various issues related to it. Therefore, the study tried to find out the level of awareness on this aspect among the respondents after the programme. The survey data (Table 17.9) reveal that of all the respondents, 26.5 per cent knew about the Consumer Protection Act. While the rest 73.5 per cent opined that they are not aware about the CP Act. As far as the awareness level in the districts is concerned, 29.5 per cent of the respondents from South 24 Parganas, 27.9 per cent from Hooghly

Table 17.9: Knowledge about Consumer Protection Act, 1986

Districts	*Blocks*	*Yes*	*No*
Hooghly	Chuchura-Mogra	26.2	73.8
	Dhaniakhali	29.5	70.5
	Total	**27.9**	**72.1**
Murshidabad	Kandi	23.0	77.0
	Beldanga I	21.3	78.7
	Total	**22.1**	**77.9**
South 24 Parganas	Sonarpur	31.1	68.9
	Bhangar II	27.9	72.1
	Total	**29.5**	**70.5**
Grand Total		**26.5**	**73.5**

Source: Field Survey, CCS, IIPA.

and 22.1 per cent of respondents from Murshidabad were aware about the CP Act. Majority of the respondents said that they are aware about some of the rights and some basics of consumer protection, but are not aware about what exactly Consumer Protection Act is.

The programme has been able to create an appreciation for consumer issues in the rural areas. During interaction it was revealed that many had at least a vague idea about consumer issues. If nearly 27 per cent have knowledge about the Act as a result of the programmes, it has achieved its objective to a large extent.

Awareness about who is a Consumer

The Consumer Protection Act clearly defines who is a Consumer. After examining the level of awareness regarding the CP Act the villagers were asked about who is a consumer. Accordingly, 54.9 per cent of the respondents said they knew that a consumer is one who buys goods, 38 per cent had no idea about it while 7.1 per cent said a consumer is one who sells goods. The responses (Table 17.10) indicate that for the villagers the term 'consumer' means general meaning as used in day-to-day routine and not as defined in the section 2(1) (d) of the Act. Their knowledge about the definition of consumer as defined under the CP Act is very limited. But more than half of them were aware that if one purchases something he or she is a consumer. District-wise also the results were on

Table 17.10: Awareness about who is a Consumer

Districts	*Blocks*	*Who buys goods*	*Who sells goods*	*Don't know*
Hooghly	Chuchura-Mogra	54.1	11.5	34.4
	Dhaniakhali	49.2	4.9	45.9
	Total	**51.6**	**8.2**	**40.2**
Murshidabad	Kandi	57.4	11.5	31.1
	Beldanga I	42.6	6.6	50.8
	Total	**50.0**	**9.0**	**41.0**
South 24 Parganas	Sonarpur	68.9	3.3	27.9
	Bhangar II	57.4	4.9	37.7
	Total	**63.1**	**4.1**	**32.8**
Grand Total		**54.9**	**7.1**	**38.0**

Source: Field Survey, CCS, IIPA.

the same pattern as 63.1 per cent of the respondents in South 24 Parganas, 51.6 in Hooghly and 50 per cent in Murshidabad said that a consumer is one who buys goods.

However, during interactions many of them said that during the programmes it was communicated to them as to who is a consumer, but they were not able to recall. But they did agree that if they buy something they are a consumer.

Awareness about Number of Consumer Rights

After judging the level of awareness about who is a consumer, the villagers were further asked about the consumer rights guaranteed to every consumer under the CP Act, 1986. As per the survey, 72.40 per cent of the respondents did not know about the total number of consumer rights. Only 7.65 per cent of the respondents were able to tell the correct number of consumer rights (Table 17.11). The district-wise data also indicate the same pattern of responses. In South 24 Parganas 81.97 per cent, 73.77 per cent in Murshidabad and 61.48 per cent in Hooghly did not know about the total number of the consumer rights under the CPA. In the villages due to low level of literacy, it is difficult for respondents of a programme to enumerate the six rights. But, the school children were better aware about consumer issues as a result of the programmes being organised in their school.

Table 17.11: Awareness about Number of Consumer Rights

Districts	*Blocks*	*One*	*Two*	*Three*	*Four*	*Five*	*Six*	*Don't Know*
Hooghly	Chuchura-Mogra	9.8	1.6	0.0	8.2	1.6	29.5	49.2
	Dhaniakhali	3.3	1.6	3.3	8.2	1.6	8.2	73.8
	Total	**6.6**	**1.6**	**1.6**	**8.2**	**1.6**	**18.9**	**61.5**
Murshidabad	Kandi	14.8	1.6	4.9	8.2	8.2	1.6	60.7
	Beldangal	3.3	0.0	1.6	8.2	0.0	0.0	86.9
	Total	**9.0**	**0.8**	**3.3**	**8.2**	**4.1**	**0.8**	**73.8**
South 24 Parganas	Sonarpur	3.3	1.6	0.0	6.6	3.3	1.6	83.6
	Bhangar II	4.9	1.6	0.0	8.2	0.0	4.9	80.3
	Total	**4.1**	**1.6**	**0.0**	**7.4**	**1.6**	**3.3**	**82.0**
Grand Total		**6.6**	**1.4**	**1.6**	**7.9**	**2.5**	**7.7**	**72.4**

Source: Field Survey, CCS, IIPA.

Knowledge about 'Who can file a Complaint'

As the awareness about the rights under the CP Act was quite low among the respondents, the next question of enquiry was the knowledge of villagers about who can file a complaint if anything goes wrong. The data (Table 17.12) reveal that nearly 40 per cent of the respondents were aware that consumers can file a complaint in case something goes wrong. However, 33.1 per cent of them had no idea about filing a complaint. Around 10.1 per cent of them said that businessmen can file a complaint, while 16.9 per cent of the respondents said that both consumers and businessmen can file a complaint. District-wise also 40.2 per cent respondents in Murshidabad, 33.6 per cent in South 24 Parganas and 25.4 per cent in Hooghly were not aware about who can file a complaint.

Table 17.12: Knowledge about who can file a Complaint

Districts	*Blocks*	*Consumer*	*Businessman*	*Both*	*Don't know*
Hooghly	Chuchura-Mogra	36.1	13.1	23.0	27.9
	Dhaniakhali	32.8	14.8	29.5	23.0
	Total	**34.4**	**13.9**	**26.2**	**25.4**
Murshidabad	Kandi	44.3	8.2	9.8	37.7
	Beldanga I	39.3	11.5	6.6	42.6
	Total	**41.8**	**9.8**	**8.2**	**40.2**
South 24 Parganas	Sonarpur	41.0	4.9	19.7	34.4
	Bhangar II	45.9	8.2	13.1	32.8
	Total	**43.4**	**6.6**	**16.4**	**33.6**
Grand Total		**39.9**	**10.1**	**16.9**	**33.1**

Source: Field Survey, CCS, IIPA.

Awareness about Grievance Redressal Machinery

According to the CP Act every consumer has a right to file a complaint before the redressal agencies. Under the Act, the consumer dispute redressal system is well established by setting-up a three tier quasi-judicial mechanism for redressal of consumer grievances. Aggrieved consumers can file a complaint in the appropriate Forum to redress their grievances. To provide adequate, cheap and speedy justice to the consumers at local level is the main objective of establishing a District Forum.

While interacting with the villagers, it was found that quite a good number of the respondents knew about the redressal mechanism under the CP Act. As per the data (Table 17.13), 36.1 per cent of the respondents knew that complaint could be filed in the district forum. 22.7 per cent respondents did not have any idea about the forum to file a complaint. Another 41.3 per cent opined that the complaint could be filed with the Jila Upabhokta Bibhag. This is because most of the villagers of this region have impression that all their problems could be sorted out by the Jila Upabhokta Bibhag. District-wise also 42.6 per cent in Hooghly, 41 per cent in Murshidabad and 40.2 per cent in South 24 Parganas were of the opinion that complaint can be filed in the Jila Upabhokta Bibhag. But the positive aspect is that the villagers knew that a complaint can be filed against the shopkeepers.

Table 17.13: Awareness about Grievance Redressal Machinery

Districts	*Blocks*	*Jila Upbhokta Bibhag*	*District Forum*	*Don't know*
Hooghly	Chuchura-Mogra	45.9	34.4	19.7
	Dhaniakhali	39.3	39.3	21.3
	Total	**42.6**	**36.9**	**20.5**
Murshidabad	Kandi	44.3	36.1	19.7
	Beldanga I	37.7	34.4	27.9
	Total	**41.0**	**35.2**	**23.8**
South 24 Parganas	Sonarpur	41.0	37.7	21.3
	Bhangar II	39.3	34.4	26.2
	Total	**40.2**	**36.1**	**23.8**
Grand Total		**41.3**	**36.1**	**22.7**

Source: Field Survey, CCS, IIPA.

Finding and Conclusions

- More than half of the respondents (63.7%) were of the view that the programme was organised a year back, 34 per cent revealed that it was organised nine months back and only 2.2 per cent of the respondents said that it was organised six months back.
- 53.3 per cent of the respondents opined that the programmes stressed on general consumer awareness which was helpful for

rural masses in their day-to-day life. 28.7 per cent of the respondents said that the programmes dealt with the consumer protection Act/Rights of the consumer while 18 per cent could not understand the content of the awareness programmes.

- Majority of the respondent (70.7%) confirmed that the programmes were conducted for a period of one hour, 22.5 per cent of them said the programmes were conducted for duration of two hours, and only 3.8 per cent said that the programmes took more than three hours.
- More than half of the respondents (51.9%) agreed that around 50-100 villagers attended the programmes, 26 per cent said that it was attended by 100-150 villagers. 9.6 per cent felt it was attended by 150-200 people while 12.6 per cent said more than 200 people attended the programmes.
- 55.2 per cent of the respondents found the programmes to be excellent. 22.4 per cent of them opined that these programmes were very good. About 16.1 per cent of respondents found the programmes to be good while 6.3 per cent found the programmes to be fair.
- As a result of the programme, a marginal change in the behaviour of the shopkeepers is seen. Only 22.4 per cent of the respondents said that these programmes were able to make an impact and curb the unethical marketing practices of local shopkeepers to a large extent. Majority of the respondents (45.9%) have confirmed that no changes were found in the behaviour of local shopkeepers despite having consumer awareness programmes in their villages.
- 27.6 per cent of all the respondents know about ISI mark, 22.1 per cent knew about Agmark, about 19.1 per cent of the respondents knew about Veg/Non-Veg. mark and another 15 per cent knew about the Hallmark which certifies the purity of the gold ornaments. However, there is a higher level of ignorance among the villagers about the other standardised marks. 12.3 per cent of the respondents knew about FPO while the level of awareness regarding BEE was 8.4 per cent and for Eco Mark it was 5.2 per cent.
- The survey data reveals that of all the respondents, 26.5 per cent knew about the Consumer Protection Act. While the rest 73.5 per cent opined that they were not aware about the Consumer Protection Act.

- 96.7 per cent of the total respondents knew about the slogan "*Jago Grahak Jago*" and could actually explain what it meant. In the case of (96.%) respondents who knew about "*Jago Grahak Jago*" advertisements, 71.6 per cent got information from T.V. While 15 per cent got information from the I-land Informatics Limited, 4.6 per cent got information from the newspapers and another 5.5 per cent got the information from radio.
- Regarding placing of grievance redressal boxes in the Panchayat premises of their village, majority of the respondents (79.5%) said that no such boxes were placed in the Panchayat premises, while 20.5 per cent of them confirmed that such boxes were placed in the Panchayat premises. Even during the field visit only a few boxes were seen, but not much purpose was being served by these boxes in grievance redressal.

Recommendations

1. There is a need to educate the rural consumers and create awareness in the rural areas to ensure that the rural consumers are not exploited. Such programmes are useful and important and may be continued.
2. The involvement of the VCOs/NGOs in the consumer movement particularly at the local level is necessary as they have the reach and approach to organise such awareness programmes at the local level.
3. The impact of the programmes enhancing awareness among the masses in the sample districts is visible both at the field level and with the increase in number of complaints suggest that the methodology used is appropriate and may be continued in such project.
4. School Children were part of the programmes as Ventriloquism shows were held in schools only. The schools should be involved for future programmes also and more and more programmes/ activities like poster/painting/slogan writing competitions, debates, and rallies should be organised for the school children to keep the younger generation updated with the latest in consumer awareness.
5. The business community/Shopkeepers should also be sensitised on different aspects of consumer protection through rallies etc. with, the active involvement of VCOs working in that area.

Consumer protection has earned an important place in the political, economic and social agendas of many nations. In India, the Government has taken many steps including legislative, to protect consumers, but still lot needs to be done.

Notes

1. Indian Street Theatre, http://www.indianetzone.com/5/indian_street_theatre.htm
2. Bengali theatre, http://en.wikipedia.org/wiki/Bengali_theatre#Song-and-dance_forms

18

Rural Consumers and the Media

D.S. Poornananda

Introduction

Rural India is changing like never before. The pace of change has accelerated in the last two decades. Social, economic and cultural transformations have made rural India more complex challenging analysis of events and processes only in rural-urban dichotomy. The nature and the type of traditional rural market have been transformed into new versatile modern markets. Rural India is not a single homogenous block. It is heterogeneous. The notion that rural Indians are stuck in the hinterland and unexposed to the developments around them is no longer true. People are engaged in several occupations and travel to towns and cities frequently. With regard to families, just like in urban area there are also small and compact families in rural areas.

Although the contribution of agriculture to total rural income has actually come down the service industry is growing and alternate revenue channels from horticulture, poultry, fisheries and other activities which are less rain-dependant are growing (Bob, 2010). Farmers are switching to new crops and technology. Crop changes and innovative farming techniques are boosting productivity, encouraging new entrepreneurship that has made a huge social impact. The rural market has more than fifty per cent share of total sales of TV sets, Fans, Pressure Cookers, Bicycles, Washing Soaps, Blades, Tea, Salt and Tooth Powder (Ichalkaranje, S.M., & Mane-Patil, 2012).The rural market for Fast Moving Consumer Goods (FMCG) products is growing much faster than its urban counterpart.

According to a study conducted by the McKensey Group (2007) even with increasing urbanisation and migration, 63 per cent of India's population will still live in rural areas by 2025. Thus, the rural market has been, and will remain, vitally important to the Indian economy. By 2025 the Indian consumer market is expected to be the sixth largest market in the world. Premiumisation, shift from commodities to brands and from indulgence to regular purchases will mark the growth of the rural market (Nielsen, 2011).

Rural markets represent the last frontier for global brands looking to expand into newer geographies. The recent slowdown in growth in the broader economy has made rural markets more attractive as marketers try to restore top-line growth. However, the complexity of these markets has to be understood. With the knowledge that marketing strategies that worked for urban markets do not necessarily work for the rural ones (TWT, 2009) manufacturers and service providers are designing strategies that are specific to the rural communities.

Management *Guru* C. K. Prahalad (2006) saw untapped market at the bottom of the economic pyramid. Most of those who live at the bottom of the pyramid in India are in rural areas. Rural markets are important for the marketing companies for their sheer size.

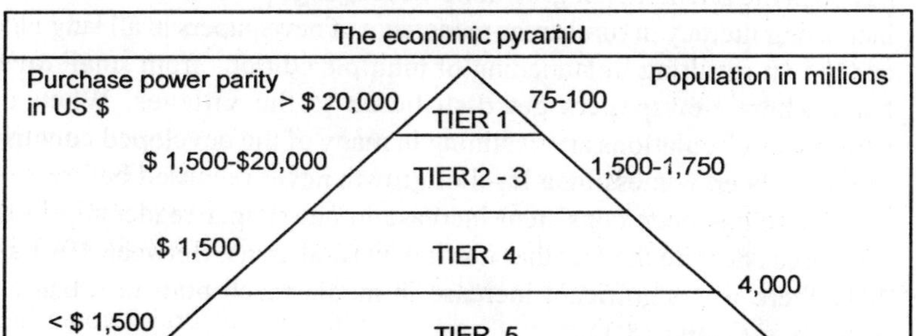

Figure 18.1: World Population and Purchasing Power Parity
Source: Prahalad, C.K. (2006). The fortune at the bottom of the pyramid: Eradicating poverty through profit. *Upper Saddle River*: Prentice Hall.

The multinational and Indian companies have been making inroads into the rural market in the last two decades. Banking, micro-finance, healthcare and FMCG companies have begun tapping the rural market in a big way. As the rural consumer market is growing it is essential that the consumers have adequate information about what are the obligations of the service providers and manufacturers and what are the ways to get their grievance redressed if deficient services or losses or injuries are caused.

This chapter attempts to examine the growth of media and its implications for the rural consumers and analyse media content with regard to consumer affairs. The focus of the chapter is on language newsperson and community radio as tools of creating consumer awareness among the rural communities with special reference to Karnataka.

Media Reach in Rural Areas

Unprecedented growth has taken place in the media market in the last two decades. While there has been rapid growth of media in big cities, media reach in smaller towns and rural areas has shown significant expansion. With the growth of the market for goods and services in the rural areas the media market has also expanded. A higher percentage of people in the rural areas are accessing the media today. Television has emerged as the most accessed medium both in urban and rural areas. However, one of the revolutionary developments in the last two decades has been the phenomenal growth of the language press in India. With the increasing literacy in rural areas readership of newspapers in all languages has grown resulting in launching of multiple editions from small towns from where newspapers get distributed to the villages. When the newspaper circulations are declining in many of the developed countries India has been witnessing a level of growth never recorded before.

There has been consistent increase in newspaper readership in the rural areas despite the fact that it is low in rural areas. Between 1991 and 2011 there was significant increase in media reach both in urban and rural areas (Table 18.1).

A national youth readership survey conducted by the National Council for Applied Economic Research across 207 districts for rural and 199 towns for urban India showed that two-third of the literate youth were in rural areas (*Financial Express*, February 9, 2010, p.10). As many as 15

Table 18.1: Media Reach

Media	*1991*		*2011*	
	Urban	*Rural*	*Urban*	*Rural*
TV	58.0	23.0	82.4	45.4
Press	26.8	8.7	41.0	14.8
Radio	21.1	14.0	23.2	18.2

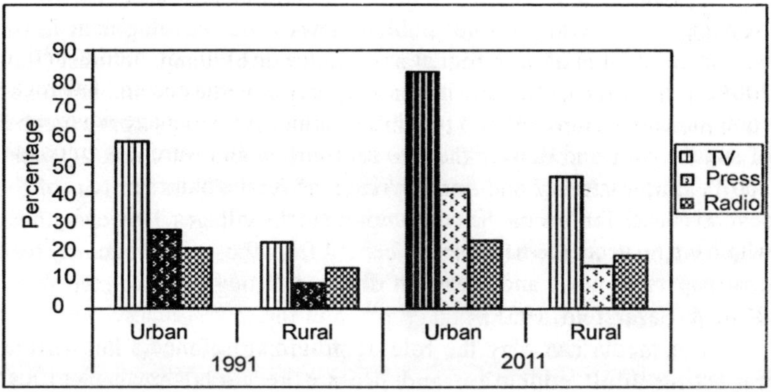

Fig. 18.2: Media Reach

Source: Arthique, A. (2012). *Indian Media*, Cambridge: Polity Press.

per cent of the households in rural areas had subscribed to newspapers as against 39 per cent in urban areas. Among the rural youth the most popular source of information was television (70%) followed by newspapers (45.9%). And nearly 21 per cent of the rural the youth (22.5% urban, 20.6% rural) listen to radio. Internet is accessed by only 1.3 per cent of the youth in rural areas as compared to 7.7 in urban areas.

With over 70 per cent of the Indian population living in the rural regions as compared to about 30 per cent living in the urban regions, media, to a large extent, ought to cater to the needs of the rural masses. When one talks about rural India, the focus has to be on over 700 million people living in nearly 6,40,867 villages spanning over 150 million households.

Print Media and Consumer Affairs

Although many of the language newspapers have considerable circulation in the rural areas the content tends to be biased towards urban India.

Table 18.2: Sources of Information for Urban and Rural Youth

	Urban	*Rural*
Television	91	70
Newspaper	65.3	45.9
Radio	22.5	20.6
Magazine	21.5	12
Internet	7.7	1.3

Source: National Youth Readership Survey 2009.

Newspapers generally do not publish news about development in the village unless it is of exceptional importance or of human interest (Ray, 2009). Expansion of literacy increased purchasing power and improved communications have made it possible to print newspapers from a number of small towns and deliver them to semi-urban and rural areas (Ninan, 2009). Inaccessibility and non-coverage of rural affairs are two of the several causes for low media consumption in the villages. However, those who have no access to newspapers benefit from those who regularly read newspapers as news and ideas get diffused through a "two-step flow" (Katz & Lazarsfeld, 1955).

Print media can play the role of providing scientific knowledge, imparting adult education and promoting social awareness and development. Rural press can disseminate information and knowledge about the rights of the consumers. People in the rural areas often use rural banking facilities, fertilisers, high yielding variety seeds, pesticides and machines without knowing what they should do in the event of loss or injury caused to them. They can be effective when they cover stories about the successful defence of the rights of the consumers.

The rural press can also make public participation in consumer affairs more informed, relevant and meaningful. Apart from broadening the educational base of its readers, the rural press can break down the barriers of isolation and thus, be a catalyst for change and growth. Thus, rural press has a rich potential, an educational and constructive role to play in terms of creating consumer awareness (Ray, 2009).

Readership surveys in India from 1995 to 2010 show that rural readership has been increasing although marginally. Since, rural population is more than double the size of the urban population even an increase of two or three per cent in readership looks significant.

With the gradually increasing percentage of literate rural population

Table 18.3: Newspaper Readership (Per cent of Adults)

Year	*Urban Readers*	*Rural Readers*
1990 NRS	44	—
1995 NRS	46	10
2000 IRS	45	15
2002 IRS	54	24
2007 IRS	58	30
2009 IRS	61	32
2010 IRS	60	32

Source: Indian Readership Survey.

and the level of general awareness going-up and with improvement of income, rural press can definitely fill the awareness gap. With sustained efforts, innovative approach, training opportunities and governmental support and incentives, it is possible to expand the base of the rural press.

A content analysis[1] of newspapers in Karnataka showed that the coverage of consumer news in the daily press is negligible. Of the total number of news stories published between September 2011 and August 2012 consumer affairs accounted for less than one per cent editorial content.

Table 18.4: Coverage of Consumer News in Daily Press of Karnataka

Newspaper Category	*News Stories*	*News Stories about Consumer Affairs*	*Percentage*
Major English dailies	21888	175	0.80
Major Kannada dailies	14592	134	0.92
District newspapers	8928	64	0.72
Town/Taluk newspaper	5184	28	0.54

Source: Indian Readership Survey.

Coverage of consumer affairs is greater in major Kannada dailies than in English dailies. Although the coverage in Kannada newspapers which have huge chunk of readership in rural areas is higher than in English newspapers it is still below one per cent. Consumer news in district level and taluk level newspapers is still lesser. Despite the fact that markets have expanded and that a large number of people are buying branded goods and services, issues related to consumer rights and ways of getting the grievances redressed seldom appear in media.

Although the total quantum of news about consumer affairs is presently negligible there have been cases of newspapers playing advocacy role with regard to consumer rights. One such case is that of Udayavani, a major Kannada newspapers of Karnataka with a large circulations in the villages. The newspaper carried a weekly column on consumer affairs titled "*Bahujana Hitaaya, Bahujana Sukhaaya,*" (for the welfare of the greatest number, for the well-being of the greatest number) for over ten years starting from 1997. Although the primary objective of the column was to discuss consumer affairs, human rights issues were also discussed frequently. The column, authored by a consumer and human rights activist Dr. Ravindranath Shanbhag, a pharmacologist by profession, contributed greatly to the growth of consumer movement in coastal Karnataka. Dr. Shanbhag was associated with Basrur Consumer Forum from its inception in 1980. The column began with the initiative taken by the editor of

Udayavani who sought articles on commoners' plights and possibilities (Hiregange, 2009).

Bureaucratic delays, violations of norms by educational institutions, deficient services in the matters like housing, taxation and banking figured in the column. As many readers started responding to the issues discussed in the column *Udayavani* opened a public grievance cell. The grievances were not directly published. They were sent to the government officials concerned or service providers with a note. If the officials or service provider responded within 30 days and the grievance was addressed satisfactorily it would not publish the grievance. The explanation provided by the service provider would also be published. *Udayavani* received nearly 800 letters in three years out of which it was compelled to publish 62. Rest of the issues were settled on their own. As many as 16 issues, raised in the column during that time, were raised in Karnataka Assembly as well. Four issues were settled in the Court (Shanbhag, 2001).

In certain cases, readers were asked at the end of the article, if they were convinced of the cause, to write a post-card to the authorities urging action[2] (Shanbhag, 2001). In several cases hundreds of letters post-cards were sent to the authorities.

Prajavani, the second largest circulated newspaper in Karnataka, began regularly carrying consumer news in 1998 as part of its business supplement under the heading "*grahaka sukha duhkha*". Court cases, complaints by consumers and activists and opinions of consumer rights experts appeared in the column. But, the column started appearing less frequently because of lack of space[3] in the business supplement as it had to accommodate more news from the world of commerce. Advertising space on the supplement also expanded leaving lesser space for the editorial content. Besides, a commissioned study by the newspaper showed that there was lack of interest on the part of the readers. Now, consumer news appears in the supplement but not regularly.

Vijaya Karnataka, the largest circulated Kannada daily newspaper, publishes a weekly column "*Customer Care*". It was the first newspapers to make inroads into the rural areas in the state. Besides carrying articles and news reports related to consumer affairs it also invites readers to write on consumer issues. Contact details are provided to help consumers seek information and redressal of their grievances.

Smaller newspapers can play a vital role in creating awareness among rural consumers. Frequent interaction between consumer rights organisations and the journalists working for these newspapers is necessary to ensure that important cases of consumer rights violations are reported.

Awareness about consumer rights protection can increase only when the media highlight incidences of consumer being deceived or made to suffer loss or injury. With newspapers now reaching remote villages it is possible to bring key consumer issues to the attention of the readers.

Radio and the Rural Consumers

Radio has been described as the most appealing tool for participatory communication and development (Naronha, 2004). It has also been seen as the ideal medium for change. Radio, particularly community radio stations can serve rural communities with content that is appropriate to the local language, culture and needs. Despite the technological advances in the communication field, radio is still the most pervasive, accessible, affordable, and flexible mass medium available. In rural areas, it is often the only medium that can rapidly disseminate to large and remote audiences, critical information about markets, weather, crops and livestock production, natural resource protection. Rural Radio implies a two-way process, which calls for the active participation of the communities in the planning and production activities of the radio broadcasts. It is the expression of the community rather than a channel for the community. It promotes the exchange of views, brings people closer together, stimulates information, and enhances the value of local knowledge. Community radio could be an effective medium of spreading consumer awareness. With 4,000 community radio stations expected to be set-up in the near future (Thomas, 2012) more and more rural communities will have access need-based information. Some of the community radio stations are airing consumer awareness programmes.

Community radio stations such as Sangham Radio in Pastapur village of Medak district in Andhra Pradesh (Deccan Development Society), Radio Bundelkhand in Orchha village of Tikamgarh district of Madhya Pradesh (Development Alternatives), Namma Dhwani in Bhudikote of Kolar district of Karnataka (Madhyam Communications), Rudi no Radio in Manipur Village of Ahmedabad district of Gujarat (SEWA), Kalanjiam Samuga Vanoli in the Vilunthamavadi Village of Nagapattinam in Tamil Nadu (Dhan Foundation), Mann Deshi Tarang in Mhaswad village of Satara district in Maharashtra (Mann Deshi Foundation), Radio Namaskar at Konark in Odisha (*Young India*), Hevalvaani Samudayik Radio in Udham Singh Nagara of Chamba district in Uttarakhand (J.P. Pant Agricultural University), *Lalit Lokvani* in Alapur village of Lalitpur district of Uttar Pradesh (Sai Jyoti Gramodyog Seva Sansthan) have become tools of empowerment have given broadcasting opportunities to unsung members of the community. Although these stations have been functioning only for the last few years the awareness they have created and the involvement they have generated is unprecedented.

Some of the community radio stations are run and managed by self-help groups (SHG) of women. They have contributed greatly to building of capacities for discursive interaction among women. More and more women are becoming programme producers bringing in locally relevant and gender issues (Jacob, 2007). If these women are given adequate support in planning and producing programmes related to consumer affairs rural consumer awareness can be expanded.

That community radio can be an effective tool of rural communication has been amply demonstrated by Namma Dhwani, the first community radio project in a village. A Bangalore-based NGO, Madhyam Communications, launched this project a decade ago (2001) in Budikote village of Kolar District in Karnataka. As NGOs had not been given licence to operate community radio stations programmes were transmitted to hundreds of homes for two hours through television cables. As Budikote's Namma Dhwani project began giving much needed information to the villagers the network was extended to 60 self-help groups (SHG) in 35 villages around Bhudikote (Sudhindra, 2007). In November 2006 the government announced that NGOs and other reputed voluntary organisations would be allowed to run FM broadcasting stations. The earlier decision to allow only "reputed" educational institutions set-up and run radio stations was amended. Non-profit organisations are allowed to set-up a station to "serve the community" with a range of 10-15 km. Namma Dhwani was issued licence to broadcast under the new regulation in June 2008.

Namma Dhwani broadcasts several programmes related to the obligations of manufacturers and service providers. One of the key features of Namma Dhwani is participation of women in managing the studio and producing the programmes. There are 10 women and 2 two men on the management committee. A study carried out by Singh *et al.* (2010) says that there was a significant gain in knowledge among the listeners of Namma Dhwani about food, health and sanitation. Several such radio stations are needed to create awareness among the rural listeners.

Conclusion

With the expansion of the rural market and increase in media consumption there are greater possibilities of educating rural consumers about their rights and responsibilities. However, an analysis of the media content shows that consumer issues are infrequently covered in the newspapers. While it is expected that newspapers close to the communities would highlight the problems of the consumers an examination of the content indicates that the reality is otherwise. District and local newspapers carry lesser news about consumer affairs compared to state level newspapers. Although newspaper coverage of consumer issues is presently negligible there are examples of some language newspapers launching unique columns to help common readers find ways of getting their problems redressed. There is a need to create awareness among the publishers and journalists of small newspapers about the long term social benefits of covering consumer affairs. Community radio stations run by educational institutions and non-governmental organisations have the capability to enlighten the rural consumers. The expanded media reach in the rural areas should lead to expanded consumer awareness.

Notes

1. Six constructed weeks (Budd *et al.*, 1967) constituted the sample for the period between September 2011 and August 2012. A constructed week procedure is more efficient than pure random or consecutive day sampling because constructed week sampling assumes cyclic variations of content for different days of the week being represented (Riffe *et al.,* 1993). To select the required weeks the sample year was divided into six sub-periods and 48 issues of each newspaper were selected.
2. One example Shanbhag (2001: 37) provides is the case of Vanajamma Achari who filed an application for a loan to construct a small house under Indira Awas Yojana. When she came to know that her name found a place in the list during 1999-2000, she dismantled her old dilapidated hut to lay the foundation for the new one. Later, suddenly her name disappeared from the list of beneficiaries which made her undergo a traumatic phase for a year. She approached the Basrur Consumer Forum and the issue appeared in *Bahujana Hitaaya*. The readers were asked to send mails to the Udupi District Deputy Commissioner if they were convinced of the injustice meted out to her. Finally, the administration responded and Vanajamma's house was constructed. In another case Ms. Poornima Bhandari did not receive her BA final year marks card from Karnataka Univerisity, Dharwad. Despite repeated efforts, the varsity did not respond. Then Basrur Forum took-up the issue and the varsity clarified that her name was mis-spelt in the records and she had to pay a fine to get the mark-sheet. Ms. Poornima did not understand why she should pay fine for an error which an official had

committed. It also became a major issue and nearly 1500 readers wrote to the University pressurising for justice (Shanbhag, 2001: 111).

3. Interview with Mr. Viju Poonacha, associate editor, *Prajavani*, September 05, 2012.

References

Agarwal, S. (2012), "Rural Consumers Aspire for More Urban Products", http://www.livemint.com/Companies/xJzhjobuhZEi4GC87DUM2O/Rural-consumers-aspire-for-more-urban-products.html

Arthique, A. (2012), *Indian Media*. Cambrdige: Polity Press.

Bijapurkar, R., & Shukla, R. (2009), "*The Rural Consumer Myth-II*", Livemint.com.

Bob, D. (2010), "Changing Face of Rural India", *Indian Today*, February 15, p. 37.

Budd, R.W., Thorp, R.K., & Donohew, L. (1967). *Content Analysis of Communications*. New York: MacMillan Co.

Hiregange, V. (2009), "*Bahujana Hitaya*: Medium and the Movement." Paper presented at the National seminar on "*Consumer Protection and Welfare: The Role of Media*". Kuvempu University, March 17-18.

Hoggart, R. (2012), *Mass Media in a Mass Society*. New York: Continuum.

Ichalkaranje, S.M., & Mane-Patil, U. (2012), "Change in Rural Market: Gateway to Modern Business", *Golden Research Thoughts*, 1 (11): 1-5.

Jacob, N. (2007), "Radio Revolution", *The Hindu*, February 4, p. 16.

Jeffrey, R. (2000), *India's Newspaper Revolution*, New Delhi: Oxford University Press.

JWT (2009). *"Why the Rural Market is Different", http://www.wpp.com/wpp/marketing/marketing/why-the-rural-market-is-different.htm*

Kamath, K. P. S. (2007). *Odeyaralla Sevakaru*. Udupi: Rashtrakavi Govind Pai Samshodhana Kendra.

Kanjilal, A., Das, I., & Srivastava, R. (2010). *"Media Effects and its Measurement in rural India"*, www.exchange4media.com/e4m/media_matter/matter_110804.asp

Katz, E., & Lazarsfield, P. (1955). *Personal Influence*. New York: Free Press.

Krishmacharyulu, C.S.G., & Ramakrishnan, L. (2011). *Rural Marketing: Texts and Cases*. New Delhi: Dorling Kindersley.

Malik, K.K. (2009). "Community Radio: Eliminating Voice Poverty", *The Hoot*, February 9, 2012.

Mathew, V. (2003). "Rural India and Media: Emerging Permutions", *The Hindu*, November 28, p.10.

Ninan, S. (2007). *Headlines from the Heartland: Reinventing the Hindi Public Sphere*. New Delhi: Sage Publications.

Noronha, F. (2004). "Community Radio: A 'Most Appealing Tool' for the Common Man", http://www.cityradio.nu/waves.htm (accessed January 29, 2004).

Prahalad, C.K. (2006). *The Fortune at the Bottom of the Pyramid: Eradicating Poverty through Profit.* Upper Saddle River: Prentice Hall.

Ray, G.N. (2009, January). *Print Communication in Rural India.* Keynote address at Centre for Journalism & Mass Communication, Santiniketan, Kolkata.

Riffe, D., Aust, C.F., & Lacy, S. (1993). "The Effectiveness of Random, Consecutive Day and Constructed Week Sampling in Newspaper Content Analysis", *Journalism & Mass Communication Quarterly*, 70 (1): 133-139.

Sapna Agarwal, S. (2012). "*Rural Consumers Aspire for More Urban Products*", http://www.livemint.com/2012/03/06210445/Rural-consumers-aspire-for-mor.html

Schuster, T. (2012). *The Markets and the Media.* Oxford: Lexington Books.

Shanbhag, R. (1997). *Bahujana Hitaaya Bahujana Sukhaaya.* Manipal: Manipal Printers and Publishers.

Shanbhag, R. (1998). *Bekitte Ee Pariya Swatantrya.* Manipal: Manipal Printers and Publishers.

Shanbhag, R. (2001). *Janajagritiya Mahayajna.* Basruru: Basruru Balakedarara Vedike.

Shanbhag, R. (2005). *Janabhiprayada Mahapoora.* Udupi: Human Rights Protection Foundation.

Singh, A.K. & Pandey, S. (2007). *Rural Marketing: Indian Perspective.* New Delhi: New Age International Publishers.

Singh, B.K., Kumar, K.R., Yadav, V.P., Singh, D., & Singh, H.L. (2010). "Social Impact of Community Radio in Karnataka", *Extention Education*, 10(2), 10-14.

Sudhindra, H.R. (2007). "Namma Dhwani in Karnataka", http://www.caluniv.ac.in/Global%20mdia%20journal/Commentaries-june-2010/h%20r%20sudhindra.pdf.

Supraja, C. (2004). "Tune into this Silent Revolution". *Deccan Herald*, March 9, p. 13.

The Bird of Gold: The Rise of India's Consumer Market. McKinsey & Company (2007). San Francisco: McKinsey Global Institute.

Thomas, J. (2012). "Community Radio: on Air with a Heart". http://www.mxmindia.com/2012/08/community-radio-on-air-with-a-heart/ (accessed October 1, 2012).

19
Role of Various Media in Tourism Marketing and Influencing Consumers in Rural Areas of Himachal Pradesh

Arvind Kumar

Introduction

Media is a way of communicating messages collectively to masses in an effective manner. Media is further divided into different forms: press media (newspapers, magazines and journals), broadcast media (radio and television), outdoor or mutual advertising (posters, boards, electric display, vehicular advertising, sandwich board and sky writing etc.), direct mail advertising media (circulars, envelops, price lists, catalogues, leaflets, folders, booklets, gifts, novelties and personal letters etc.), promotional advertising media (window display, interview display, showrooms, exhibitions, trade shows, demonstration, samples and couponed premiums etc.), miscellaneous advertising media (cinema slides, cinema and loud speaker etc.) and internet etc. Media is making improvement in their structures, forms and features with the passage of time. Due to globalisation, and enhancement of technology, there is a rise in the economy and standards of living of people across the country. As a result of economic developments people are availing to different media seek information and knowledge. Due to this different kind of media is penetrating not only the urban areas, but also making their reach to distant and remote corners of the country. This is helping rural consumers to know new trends, lifestyles and experience new things in their life. Different kinds of media are promoting the concept of tourism, even to rural parts of the country. There is also an increase in spending leisure time as a result of which people are various tour packages.

Impact of Globalisation on Tourism

The travel industry is affected by increased competition through globalisation, diversified customer demands and expectations as well as growing of computer-based knowledge. Travel and tourism products are ideal for marketing on the internet, this is because tourism is an information intensive industry and internet is the most effective and efficient means in information exchange worldwide. Tourism is very information intensive and information is often dubbed as the "life-blood" or cement of the industry, which holds together the different producers within the travel industry—airlines, tour operators, travel agencies, attractions, car rentals, cruise lines and other supplies. In few other areas of activity, are the generation, gathering, processing, application and communication of information as important for day-to-day operations, as they are for the travel and tourism industry. Tourism became one of the first industries to widely apply information technology and conduct electronic commerce from the 1960s in the form of Computerised Reservation Systems (CRSs) and then Global Distribution Systems (GDSs). The web can also deliver the information in a greater variety of formats from text to photos, graphs, audio and video clips, whereas in the past, tourists primarily relied on the printed brochures as the limited copies of videos of a limited number of tourism destinations or holidays were only available to the major travel agents. The complex process of choosing among the hundreds of holidays using browser generated selections from back end databases linked to web servers, whereas the printed brochures are usually arranged and indexed by one way, often by destination. Through internet video telephony, tourists can also test drive a prospective holiday by viewing real time scenes through cameras placed in hotels, club restaurants, scenic spots and other sites in the destination and transmitted by the internet. Video clips can also show episodes and scenes of festivals, art performances and service delivery to facilitate tourists in the comparison and evaluation of intangible services, the quality of which is otherwise difficult to assess in advance (Harish Bhatt, 2006). The most commonly used promotional techniques are like preparing printed material such as brochures, posters, maps, travel agent manuals and distributing these to travel agents, tour operators and consumers; preparing audio-visual material, slide, film and video-shows for use in travel seminars and other type of presentations and advertising in newspapers, magazines, radio and television aimed at the tourist consumers and in travel trade publications aimed at tour operations (Ratandeep Singh, 2000).

One to one marketing allows you to take advantage of new technology. It is a concrete way to capitalise on the benefits of new technology. Technology is evolving at an amazing rate and is becoming more and more interactive. A few years ago, the internet was an unknown commodity to most of people but the rate of its adoption into the home has been enormous. The adoption and utilisation of new technology and new commerce should not be ignored or under-estimated. Modern technology can lead to quick and powerful marketing; it ignores country boundaries and effectively contracts the size of the world. Traditional methods of mailing have become expensive and slow, when compared with the inexpensive, fast and effective new technology of e-commerce. All over the world, cyber travel agencies are being developed, whereby the customers do the work and have direct access to tour operators and airlines to book their own holiday (B.S. Badan and Harish Bhatt, 2007). Internet has generated a whole new sub-category of media, from flashy web-based newspapers and magazines to simple electronic newsletters. This means, there are more potential outlets to carry your message (Sanjeev Gulati, 2008). The use of internet has also assisted in spreading information about various tourist destinations in India. Every state has a tourism website showcasing the places to visit in that state and providing information on how to reach those places. They also provide various package tours targeted at different tourists of different economic status. The Himachal Pradesh Tourism Development Corporation has been using print media to promote tourism in the state. These include advertisements in newspapers and publishing books like Unforgettable Himachal. The department has also used TV channels, primarily news channels to advertise tourism. It participates in various national level tourist festivals across the country and also conducts road shows to draw more tourist attention.

Tourism in Himachal Pradesh

Tourism is an important industry in Himachal Pradesh. Of late rural tourism is being promoted in the state on a large scale to uplift the rual population through additional income. The state has a huge potential for rural tourism. Himachal is a highly state where it takes time to travel so use of media can be effective in reducing time and space. There is a need to create market through the use of media particularly the electronic media. In Himachal Pradesh approximately 90 per cent of the population lives in rural areas. Thus, media can play a major role in boosting tourism and allied activities in the state thereby increasing the flow of tourists who avail services offered by various tour operators and service providers. Media can also play a significant role in generating awareness among the people living in rural areas about the need of tourists coming to the state. Media exposes people to innovative, economical and interesting tour packages which are being offered by various tour operators and travel agencies at competitive prices. Tour operators are approaching potential tourists directly through their travel agents, sales persons and indirectly through various modes of communication like T.V., radio, internet, newspapers and other awareness campaigns, seminars and conferences etc. and influencing them to avail tourism products.

Use of Media in Tourism

Media is playing an important role in tourism marketing and influencing consumers in rural areas. Media is an important medium of selling the concept of tourism to the public, irrespective of their geographical locations. Various tourism products (goods and services) like tour packages (adventurous, religious and cultural etc.) and souvenirs etc. are being marketed in the villages with the help of media. Media empowers the consumers by providing information. Marketing is about customers. It is about how to find them, how to satisfy them and how to keep them. Without customers, there will be no money to pay staff, creditors and shareholders. Without customers, there can be no reason for the organisation to exist. For planning effective innovative marketing strategies, two important key points need to be considered. They are: (1) Marketing mix-4P's, i.e. product, price, place and promotion. (2) Positioning of tourist spots. Tourism marketing is the managerial process of anticipating and satisfying existing and potential visitor wants more effectively than competitive supplies. The management of exchange is driven by profit, community gain or both, either way long-term success depends on a satisfying interaction between consumer and supplier. It also means securing environmental and societal needs as well as core consumer satisfaction. They can no longer be regarded as mutually exclusive.

When it comes to selecting the most appropriate techniques to convey the desired message and induce a response from target markets, a variety of choices are at the disposal of tourism marketers. The traditional choices are: Public relations are planned and sustained efforts to establish and maintain goodwill and mutual understanding between an organisation, its products or services and public. Although public relations, when conducted professionally can be highly credible and of low cost, its implementation is often imprecise with considerable difficulty often encountered when trying to target specific markets accurately. Media relations, crisis management, product placement, sponsorship and attendance at exhibitions and travel fairs are public relations activities common to tourism. Advertising: is non-personal, paid form of mass communication by an identified sponsor in a commercially available medium. Advertising is increasingly convincing to public and is highly appropriate for long term image building. Effective advertising often legitimizes the brand and can be very economical in terms of cost per thousand. On the other hand, it is frequently very costly and remains prohibitive for large sections of tourism industry. Sales Promotions are temporary, short term incentives designed to stimulate some kind of action in the target audience. They are very popular, when it comes to inducing brand trial and increasing the frequency of purchase. Direct Marketing and Database Marketing: there are instances, where an organisation promotes and deals directly with the customer. Driven by database technology, direct marketing frequently uses intranets (within an organisation), extranets (networks of suppliers and key customers) and the internet. Growth in direct marketing is attributed to its ability to target precisely and personalise communications and in its ability to induce a behavioural response. Personal Selling: involves verbal communication between one or more prospective purchasers and a salesperson for the purpose of making a sale. Personal selling involves personal interaction, which can be very costly, but on the other hand, personal selling can be highly beneficial, when attempting to build relationships in the trade. Other emerging forms of communication include telemarketing, e-mail and the creation and distribution of CDs, videos and DVDs. These are particularly popular at the destination level. Each of above elements of communication has the capacity to achieve different communication objective. However, prior to selecting the most appropriate vehicle, one needs to consider the wider objectives of the organisation, the nature of the product or service, the characteristics of the market place, the need for either a push or pull approach to communication strategy, the readiness stage of the buyer, the stage of product's life cycle and the evolutionary stage of the market. With regard to actual choice of media, a number of further factors need to be considered, including audience size, audience type, audience mood, cost of production, reach frequency, impact and the availability of media space.

Research Framework

Substantial review of literature suggests that different media are important means of conveying message to different communities living in urban as well as rural areas. They help marketers to focus upon marketing mix as well as positioning of tourist spots. Media help in provision of information to rural consumers regarding different products (goods and services), ordinary as well as tourism products, i.e. tour packages etc. Public relations, advertising, sales promotion, direct marketing and data base marketing and personal selling etc., all these are efforts of marketing different products and are feasible through various media. Information technology is providing information directly to rural people through computers and mobile phones enabled with internet. Information technology is playing an important role in marketing of tourism products across the world. Tourism industry is utilising the services of information technology, as a media for tourism marketing for a long time. Computerised reservation system has urged individuals to experience tourism products in villages also. Cyber travel agencies operational across the globe are helping individuals in remote places, i.e. villages, to access information related to varied tour packages and booking tour packages, airlines tickets etc. One to one marketing, i.e. personal approach to rural consumers by different tour operators and travel agencies through their travel agents is also empowering the efforts of tourism marketing in rural areas of Himachal Pradesh.

Objectives of the Study

1. To study the role of various media in tourism marketing in rural areas of Himachal Pradesh; and
2. To study the role of various media in influencing rural consumers of Himachal Pradesh to utilize tourism services.

Methodology

Total sample of 100 respondents from the villages located in Shimla and

Kullu district of the state (Himachal Pradesh), were selected for the study. Using stratified random sampling, an opinion survey was administered on the sample. The survey consisted of "eight opinion statements" identified by the researcher to study the role of media in tourism marketing and influencing rural consumers. Response to each statement was evaluated on three point scale of Agree, Disagree or Cannot Say and opinions were assessed through statistics using frequency and percentage of respondents on each statement.

Major Findings

Respondents Perceptions: Role of Media in Tourism Marketing and Influencing Rural Consumers

From responses it has emerged that out of 100 respondents for each statement, 90 per cent agree with the view that various media have generated awareness among consumers residing in villages of Himachal Pradesh towards tourism activities through updated information.

Ninty two per cent of the respondents are of the opinion that different media like newspapers, radios, televisions, mobile phones, internet etc. have provided information about various tour packages to consumers in villages. Eighty eight per cent of people responded in affirmation that different media have generated thrust among rural consumers to experience different tour packages available in the market. Eighty three per cent of the respondents have expressed the opinion that various media have provided competitive prices of different tour packages and an opportunity to compare prices offered by different travel agencies to rural consumers in Himachal Pradesh. Eighty six per cent agree with the view that different media have played an important role in promotion of different tour packages and tourism services in rural parts of the state. Seventy five per cent agree with the view that various media have made different tourism trends like eco-tourism, cultural tourism, medical tourism etc. popular among rural consumers. Seventy two per cent have opined that different media have influenced rural consumers to utilise different tour packages and enjoy holidays in innovative manners. Eighty four per cent have agreed with the view that direct or personal contact of rural consumers by different travel agents has influenced them towards the utilisation of sustainable tourism trends and tour operations.

Table 19.1: Perceptions of Rural Respondents of Himachal Pradesh

Sl. No.	*Role of Different Media in Tourism Marketing and Influencing Rural Consumers (Opinion Statements)*	*Responses (100)*		
		Agree	*Disagree*	*Can't Say*
1.	Various media have generated awareness among rural consumers of Himachal Pradesh towards tourism activities through updated information.	90 90%	10 10%	0 0%
2.	Different media like newspapers, radios, televisions, mobile phones, internet etc. have provided information about various tour packages to consumers in villages.	92 92%	8 8%	0 0%
3.	Different media have generated thrust among rural consumers to experience different tour packages available in the market.	88 88%	12 12%	0 0%
4.	Various media have provided competitive prices of different tour packages and an opportunity to compare prices offered by different travel agencies to rural consumers in Himachal Pradesh.	83 83%	17 17%	0 0%
5.	Different media have played an important role in promotion of different tour packages and tourism services in rural parts of the state.	86 86%	15 15%	0 0%
6.	Various media have made different tourism trends like eco-tourism, cultural tourism, medical tourism etc. popular among rural consumers.	75 75%	25 25%	0 0%
7.	Different media have influenced rural consumers to utilise different tour packages and enjoy holidays in innovative manners.	72 72%	28 28%	0 0%
8.	Direct or personal contact of rural consumers by different travel agents has influenced them towards the utilisation of sustainable tourism trends and tour operations.	84 84%	16 16%	0 0%

Source: Primary Data through Questionnaires.

Conclusion

From the study it is evident that by the use of various kinds of media awareness among rural consumers of Himachal Pradesh towards tourism activities has been enhanced. Different kinds of media like newspapers, radios, televisions, mobile phones, internet etc. have provided information to consumers about various tour packages available in the rural areas. various kind of media has generated thrust among rural consumers to experience different tour packages available in the market. Various media have provided competitive prices of different tour packages and an opportunity to compare prices offered by different travel agencies to rural consumers in Himachal Pradesh. Different media have played an important role in promotion of different tour packages and tourism services in rural parts of the state. Various media have made different tourism trends like eco-tourism, cultural tourism, medical tourism etc. popular among rural consumers. Different media have influenced rural consumers to utilise different tour packages and enjoy holidays in innovative manners. Direct or personal contact of rural consumers by different travel agents has also influenced them towards the utilisation of sustainable tourism trends and tour operations. Thus, it can be said that various media have played an important role in marketing of tourism products in rural parts of the state and influenced consumers to a large extent.

References

Badan, B.S. and Bhatt, Harish (2007). *Tourism Marketing,* New Delhi: Commonwealth Publishers, pp. 28-29.

Bhatt, Harish (2006). *Hospitality Marketing,* New Delhi: Crescent Publishing Company, pp. 118, 155, 157-158.

Fyall, Alan and Garrod, Brian (2006). *Aspects Tourism—Tourism Marketing: A Collaborative Approach,* New Delhi: Viva Books Private Limited, pp. 27, 43, 120-121.

Gulati, Sanjeev (2008). *New Dimensions of Public Relation and Press,* New Delhi: Cybertech Publications, p. 151.

Gupta, Deepak Raj and Gupta, Anil (2008). *Travel and Tourism Management: Contemporary Issues and Trends,* Chandigarh: Abhishek Publications, pp. 113, 115.

http://www.kpmg.com/IN/en/IssuesAndInsights/ArticlesPublications/Documents/Tourism-in-himachal-pradesh.pdf

Singh, Ratandeep (2000). *Tourism Marketing: Principles, Policies and Strategies,* New Delhi: Kanishka Publishers and Distributors, p. 155.

20
Role of Communication Media in Rural Marketing

Mahendra Kumar Padhy

Introduction

The rural retail market of India is fascinating and challenging. It offers large scope on account of its size and potential. About 75 per cent of the total population is rural by nature. Rural India has a populations of 83.3 crore spread across six lakh thirty eight thousand villages. A report by National Council of Applied Economic Research (NCAER) shows that rural segment comprise more than 50 per cent of consumers constituting a prime market for consumer goods. Corporate businesses in India are under pressure to capture the untapped rural market to increase their profitability and market share. Companies are adopting rural marketing in a broader context of sustainability in the era of intense competition to grow their businesses and thereby also contributing towards the economic development and the welfare of the rural economy.

The Indian rural market has a huge demand base and offers great opportunities to marketers. Two-third of Indian consumers live in rural areas and almost half of the national income is generated here. The reasons for heading into the rural areas are fairly clear. The rural consumer durable market for products like colour TVs, washing machines, refrigerators and air conditioners is growing annually at between 7 per cent and 10 per cent.

Marketing Defined

Marketing is described as the process of understanding, defining, anticipating and observing consumer demands, and organising all the available resources of the processing units to satisfy their requirements. In fact, satisfaction of customer's needs and wants provides the rationale for the organisations existence. Knowledge of consumer behaviour, therefore, is of vital importance for a firm to achieve its marketing goals. The consumer's behaviour comprises the acts, processes and social relationships exhibited by individuals, groups and organisations in searching, obtaining, and consequent experience with products and services. An understanding and knowledge of the motives underlying consumer behaviour helps a firm in seeking better and more effective ways to satisfy its customers. It helps to select appropriate sales and advertising strategies, and to plan marketing programme in a more efficient manner.

The rural market of India started showing its potential in the 1960s. The 1970s and 1980s witnessed its steady development. And, there are clear indications that the twenty first century is going to see its full blossoming. In our country, where research on consumer behaviour has been nominal, not much systematised information is available about the rural consumers. Only a few enlightened companies, known for their marketing orientation, *viz*., Hindustan Lever, Philips India, Asian Paints, Singer & Larsen and Toubro have made concrete efforts in this direction. But, by and large, we have still to understand the rural buyer through their habits, attitudes and behaviour, particularly from the marketing point of view.

Many assumptions prevail about rural marketing. For instance, one assumption is that the rural buyer is not very discriminating. Once he is persuaded to buy a particular product, he develops a strong affinity for it, and if satisfied, becomes brand loyal. As a result, Indian manufacturers are generally known to prefer selling fewer items at higher prices than selling more items at lower prices. A contrary view is that the rural buyer, being suspicious of the marketer's hard sell techniques, is quite discriminating, and is not easily persuaded. Yet another assumption is that the rural buyer is not particularly keen about quality and packaging. Some other assumptions can be quoted. But, all these need deep probing for arriving at valid and reliable conclusions. Consumer research, thus, is indispensable for entering the rural segment of the market.

Literature Review

Advertising as an important promotion mix element used in rural markets is an upcoming and growing field of marketing, wherein not much research study has been done so far. Discussion and analysis related to the topic have been reviewed as follows:

Tan and Chia (2007), empirically explored the relationship between the general attitude towards advertising and the attitude towards advertising in specific media vehicle that is television and print. The researchers concluded that future research could involve a replication of the current study with new indicators.

J. Jethwanee (2009) distinguished the purchasing behaviour of rural and urban buyers to make out whether the local background of consumers influences their buying decisions or not. The analysis says that, the rural consumers found product packaging more useful than their urban counterparts and they strongly believed that better packages, lightness of weight, simplicity, transparency and consistency of package has relatively less influence on buying decision of rural consumers.

O'Guinn, Thomas (2010), conducted the study to examine the trustworthiness of advertising media *verses* publicity media and to examine the credibility of advertising including a promotional endorser. The study concluded saying that consumers tended to rely on publicity more than advertising.

Objectives of the Chapter

The main objectives of this chapter are as follows:

(a) To examine the marketing communication strategies in rural India and shift of multinational corporations focus towards the Indian rural/retail marketing.
(b) To identify the various communication media used by the marketers for promoting their goods and services in the rural market.
(c) To study and analyse the role of advertising in transforming way of life of rural consumers.

Meaning of Rural Marketing

The words "rural marketing" used to be an umbrella term for the people who dealt with rural people in one way or other. This term got a separate meaning and importance after the economic liberalisation in India after 1990. So, before entering into the other aspects of rural marketing let us discuss the development of this area in different parts which is briefly explained here.

Nature of Rural Market

In the past days, due to the lack of marketing facilities available in the rural areas, the rural consumer went to the nearby urban point to buy branded goods and services. But at present, the marketers have realised the potential in the rural market which has become critical for them, be it for a branded soap or any electronic gadgets. Earlier, vehicle campaigns, cinema commercials and a few wall paintings sufficed the purpose of the marketers to entice the rural folks under their folds. But today, television has made the customers in a rural area quite literate about countless products that are on offer in the market place. Rural marketing is planning and implementation of marketing function for rural areas. It is a two way marketing function process which encompasses the discharge of business activities that direct the flow of goods from urban to rural areas for manufactured goods and *vice versa* for agricultural produce. The rural markets in India have become an area that corporate just cannot afford to ignore. The product offered to rural consumers may or may not be different, but the ways these products are marketed ought to be different. Marketers always look for innovative ways to make their presence felt. Due to regional disparities, customised communication strategy for each region is need of the hour. The researcher is of the view that, an effective communication is one that leads to purchase decision, brand registration in consumers mind, brand recall and right brand associations. Interpersonal communication accounts for about 80 per cent of the rural communication process. The communication package should generate lot of words of mouth publicity, so that the brand acquires top of the mind recall value. Marketers can use a mix of both conventional and unconventional media. The communication should be such so as to make the product category relevant to rural folks.

Rural Marketing Prior to Economic Liberalisation

Rural marketing referred to selling of rural products in rural and urban areas and agricultural inputs in rural markets. It was treated as synonymous to "agricultural marketing". Agricultural produces like food grains and industrial inputs like cotton, oil seeds, sugarcane etc. occupied the central place of discussion during this period. The supply-chain activities of firms supplying agricultural inputs and of artisans in rural areas received secondary attention. The local marketing of products like bamboo baskets, ropes, window and door frames, and small agricultural tools like ploughs by sellers like black smiths, carpenters, cobblers, and pot-makers were emphasised in general. This was totally an unorganised market where all *banias* and *mahajans* (local business people) dominated this market. In this era, green revolution resulted from scientific farming and transferred many of the poor villages into prosperous business centres. As a result, the demand for agricultural inputs went up especially in terms of wheats and paddies. Better irrigation facilities, soil testing, use of high yield variety seeds, fertilisers, pesticides and deployment of machinery like powder tillers, harvesters, threshers etc. changed the rural scenario. In this context, marketing of agricultural inputs took the importance.

Post-Economic Liberalisation Period

The products which were not given attention so far during the two earlier phases were that of marketing of household consumables and durables to the rural markets due to various reasons. Firstly, the economic conditions of the country were as such that the rural people were not in a position to buy these kinds of products. Secondly, our market was in a close shape and we allowed companies (foreign) to operate in Indian market. Thirdly, the small villages/hamlets were widely scattered making reach difficult and expensive consequently. Fourthly, the rural markets were seen an adjunct to urban market and conveniently ignored. However, since 1990s, India's industrial sector has gained in strength and maturity. Its contribution to GNP increased substantially. The economic reforms further accelerated the process by introducing competition in the markets. Steadily, the rural market has grown for household consumables and durables. Rural marketing represented the emergent distinct activity of attracting and serving rural markets to fulfil the needs and wants of persons, households and occupations of rural people.

Characteristic Features of Indian Rural Market

The Indian rural market with its size and market demand offers great opportunities to the marketers. Two-thirds of country's consumers live in rural areas and almost half of the national income is generated here. It is only natural that rural markets form an important part of the total market of India. Our nation is classified in approximately six lakh villages, which can be sorted in different parameters such as literacy levels, income levels, penetration, distances etc.

Table 20.1: Disposable and Per Capita Annual Income

	Disposable Annual Income between Rs. 45000-2,15,000	*Per Capita Annual Income in Rs.*
Rural	27.4 million	9,481
Urban	29.5 million	19,407
Total	56.9 million	28,888

Source: NCAER 2011.

Among the mass media at some point in the late 50s and 60s, radio was considered to be a potential medium for communication to the rural people. Another mass media is television and cinemas. Statistics indicate that the rural areas account for hardly 2500 to 4000 mobile theatres, which is far less when compared to the number of villages. The features of Indian Rural Market are as follows:

1. Agriculture is the backbone of Indian economy.
2. Rural consumers have diverse socio-economic backwardness.
3. The per capita income is seasonal and fluctuating in nature.
4. The rural market of India is geographically large and scattered.
5. It shows linguistic, religious and cultural diversities and economic disparities.
6. The market is undeveloped, as the people who constitute it still lack adequate purchasing power.
7. It is largely agriculture oriented, with poor standard of living, low per capital income, and socio-cultural backwardness.
8. It exhibits sharper and varied regional preferences with distinct predilections, habit patterns and behavioural characteristics.
9. Rural marketing process is both a catalyst as well as an outcome of the general rural development process. Initiation and management of social and economic change in the rural sector is the core of the rural marketing process. It becomes in this process both benefactor and beneficiary.
10. The literacy rate is low in rural areas as compared to urban areas.

Corporate Strategies for Rural Markets

Although the rural market does offer a vast untapped potential, it should also be recognised that it is not that easy to operate in rural market because of several problems. Most MNCs are, therefore, accepting the challenges of the rural markets with the help of the 4 A's, i.e. availability, acceptability, affordability, and awareness. Over the years, India's largest MNC, Hindustan Unilever Ltd., has built a strong distribution network, which helps it to reach the interiors of the rural market for selling products like sunsilk and clinic plus shampoos in small and economic pack. It has also launched a variant of its largest selling soap brand, Lifebuoy at Rs. 2 for 50 gms. The move is mainly targeted at the rural market.

Pepsi, which considers rural India as a future growth driver has evolved a hub and spoke distribution model to reach the villages. Because of the lack of electricity and refrigerators in the rural areas, Pepsi has also provided low cost ice-boxes for its outlets. Pepsi has addressed the affordability issue by introducing the returnable 200 ml. glass bottle at Rs. 5. Samsung electronics in 2000 developed a specially designed TV set for the rural market named small screen which was a big success. For this model, the company introduced a new technology that provided better reception in low locations which is a common problem in rural areas.

The insurance companies that have tailor made products for the rural market have performed well. Lack of awareness is also one of the major challenges of rural marketing being faced by most of the firms. Mass Media is able to reach only to 57 per cent of the rural populations. Fairs and *melas* are used as occasions for brand communication. Cinema vans, shop-fronts, walls and wells are other media vehicles that have been utilised to increase brand and pack visibility. Hindustan Unilever relies heavily on its own company-organised media. These are promotional events organised by stockists. Godrej consumer products which is trying to push its soap brands into the interior areas uses radio to reach the local people using the local language.

Problems in Rural Marketing

There are many problems to be tackled in rural marketing, despite rapid strides in the development of the rural sector. Some of the common problems are discussed below:

Transportation

Transportation is an important aspect in the process of movement of products from urban production centres to remote villages. The transportation infrastructure is extremely poor in rural India. Due to this reason, most of the villages are not accessible to the marketing man. In our country, there are six lakh villages. Nearly 50 per cent of them are not connected by road at all. Many parts in rural India have only *kachcha* roads. During the monsoons, even these roads become unserviceable. Regarding rail transport, though India has the second largest railway system in the world, many parts of rural India, however, remain outside the rail network.

Communication

Marketing communication in rural markets suffers from a variety of constraints. The literacy rate among the rural consumers is very low. Print media, therefore, have limited scope in the rural context. Apart from low levels of literacy, the tradition-bound nature of rural people, their cultural barriers and their overall economic backwardness add to the difficulties of the communication task. Post, telegraph, and telephones are the main components of the communication infrastructure. These facilities are extremely inadequate in the rural parts of our country.

Availability of Appropriate Media

It has been estimated that all organised media in the country put together can reach only 30 per cent of the rural population of India. The print media covers only 18 per cent of the rural population. The radio network, in theory, covers 90 per cent. But, actual listenership is much less. TV is popular, and is an ideal medium for communicating with the rural masses. But, it is not available in all interior parts of the country. It is estimated that TV covers 20 per cent of the rural population. But, the actual viewership is meagre. The cinema, however, is a good medium for rural communication. But, these opportunities are very low in rural areas.

Low Level of Literacy

The literacy rate is low in rural areas as compared to urban areas. This again leads to problem of communication for promotion purposes. Print medium becomes ineffective and to an extent irrelevant for in rural areas since its reach is poor and so is the level of literacy.

Scattered Market

Rural areas are scattered and it is next to impossible to ensure the availability of a brand all over the country. Seven Indian states account for 76 per cent of the country's rural retail outlets, the total number of which is placed at around 3.7 million. Advertising in a highly heterogeneous market, it is very expensive.

Role of Communication Media for Promotion

Advertising is a measure of growth of civilisation and a sign of striving of human race for betterment and perfection. The drive for survival and satisfaction and the limits of human endeavour have been succinctly summed-up by Maslow in his holistic dynamic theory of the subject (Maslow, 1954).

Advertising goes hand in hand with economic growth. With liberal economic environment and increasing rural prosperity, marketers are keen to inform villagers about the benefits of buying and consuming their products and services. Prior to the introduction of economic liberalisation in 1990s, there was little incentive for marketers to advertise their products and services, as rural markets were predominantly a seller's market. The influence of the electronic media particularly television, video, radio and film industry are contributing to the growth of rural aspirations which are being manifested in rural India in the form of increasing consumerism.

The rural environment is different from the urban and therefore, communication to potential customers in a proper and effective manner is a major challenge for corporate marketers. The majority of advertisements designed by corporate marketers are largely urban oriented and extend themselves to rural areas without any consideration to the values and sensitivities of the rural audiences, which are often in striking contrast to those of their urban counterparts. This has led to a negative perception in the minds of villagers about urban media planners and advertisers.

Rural communication is not a peripheral activity. It does not, for instance, involve taking an audio-visual van to a village and assuming that this step is enough to reach out to customers. It requires an entirely different mindset, which demands getting rid of many mental barriers. Companies have to realise that rural is a long-haul market, as gains in the short-term are neither immediate nor large.

Challenges in Rural Communication

The communication pattern in any society is a part of its culture. No

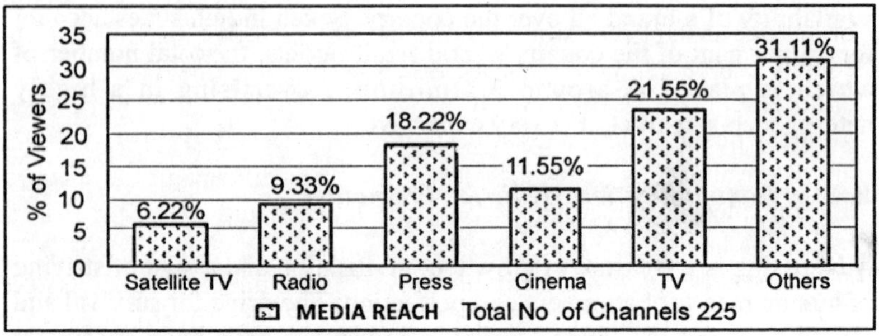

Source: Media Survey Report, 2011.

Fig. 20.1: Media Reach

communication medium can exist in a cultural vacuum. Communicating the message to rural consumers has posed enormous challenges to the rural marketer, because of the large numbers of consumer's scatters across the country. The problem is further compounded by the heterogeneous nature of consumers on there are 16 scheduled languages and 114 local vernaculars.

Limited Media Reach

The limited reach of the mass media imposes limitations on universal communication to rural consumers. These factors lead to poor message comprehension and negligible impact, which fail to translate into consumer awareness and hence fail in generating consumer pull.

Targeted Rural Audience

It is not sufficient to understand rural communication challenges as stated above Rather, what is equally crucial is the need to understand the behavioural and psychographic characteristics of the rural audience, in order to develop an effective rural communication strategy.

Advertisements Meant for Rural Audience

Television is often regarded as the king of advertising media. Majority of people spend more hours watching TV per day in comparison to any other medium. Television uses the combination of sight, colour, sound and motion to create an effect. TV has proved its credibility in influencing human behaviour repeatedly. Advertising on television can give a product or service instant reliability and reputation. Different segments of the society can be captured by scheduling the time for advertisements like children can be reached during cartoon programming. TV offers the greatest possibility for creative advertising by taking the audience anywhere and shows tem almost anything through the magic of a camera. TV audience is divided into very large segments and television enables to reach a larger yet more diverse audience.

To make advertising media successful, Communication experts need to keep the following factors in mind when creating advertisements for rural audiences:

(a) Understanding the mindset of potential customers including their hopes, fears, aspirations and apprehension conducting a qualitative study among the target audience would help in better understanding of the consumer mindset.

(b) Tricky, clever, gimmicky or even suggestive advertising does not work with the rural audiences. Flicks using very expensive computer graphics without any human presence go over the heads of rural audiences.

(c) Pick-up 'gems' in the form of idioms, expressions, words etc. in relation to the product category for later use in the creative.

(d) Combing education with entertainment is a good route to take when targeting rural audiences, using locally popular film stars or even featuring religious events (*Melas*) popular in the region, helps strike a chord with rural audiences. According to a study, it is Mithun, Dharmendra and Shahrukh Khan who are most popular among rural folk in north India.

(e) Quickies do not register well with rural audiences. Advertising agencies need to provide for ample time and space to communicate a message properly and effectively to the intended audience. This is seen for instance, in the popularity of the two-minute theatre commercials screened in rural cinemas.

Rural Media for Marketing

Rural Media can be broadly classified into conventional mass media, non-conventional media and personalised media. The different media vehicles used for rural marketing are as follows:

Table 20.2 : Various Media Vehicles for Rural Marketing

Conventional Mass Media	*Non-Conventional Media*	*Personalised Media*
Television	*Hat* and *Mela*	Direct mailer
Radio	Folk Media (Puppet Show)	Point of sale (Demonstration)
Press	Video Van	Word of Mouth
Cinema	*Mandi*	Int. Personal Communication
Outdoor: Wall Painting, Hoarding	*Nautanki, Yatra, Yakshagana*	Animator

Source: Media Survey Report, 2011.

Innovative Media

Outdoor Media

Wall Painting: This medium is the most widespread form of advertising and is the favourite of the Indian rural masses, as they can view it at their leisure. Wall paintings are important because they constantly remind rural people about name and logos in addition to highlighting the key brand promise. They also reflect the vibrant economic and social life of the area.

Folk Media

Folk media consist of folk songs, folk dances and other theatrical corms, including puppetry, street theatre and magic shows which are an intrinsic part of the culture and heritage of the land. They are capable of communicating message about contemporary issues, topics and concerns as per the needs and demands of a changing society. Folk media may be divided into folk theatre, magic show, puppet show, interactive games and folk theatre.

Concluding Remark

The rural Market of India is lucrative and challenging. It offers large scope on account of its vast size and it is growing steadily. Even a small growth can push-up the sales of a product substantially, in view of the huge base despite the fact that there are enormous amount of problems. It is an attractive market from this angle also that the urban market is highly competitive; the rural market is relatively quiet. In fact, for certain products, it is a totally virgin market. Economic reforms in India brought about major changes in the whole marketing environment. With these changes, rural marketing will become an important playground for our marketers.

Successful rural marketing calls for a review of the rural marketing environment, developing proper understanding of the nature and profile of rural consumers, designing the right products to appeal to them, and adopting suitable media as well as appropriate strategies for communication and distribution. It is generally believed that markets are created, not found. This is especially true in case of the rural market of India. It is a market for the truly creative marketer.

To sum up, it is clear that in any form of rural communication, while we may have a national strategy, we have to think and act locally. The need for focused communication aimed at the rural market, should not be underestimated. This calls for innovation and substantive changes in marketing of what can best be characterised as the 4-R principle such as relevance, reliability, reach, and re-innovation.

If the Indian advertising industry is to reach out to rural India in an effective and efficient manner, it has to be grounded firmly in rural perceptions, value and traditions. It has to immerse itself in local colours, customs, and modes of communication in order to make itself relevant to the needs and desires of rural society. It has to gain the trust of the masses by undercutting its own excessive dependency on western styles of advertising, on the one hand and on its use of deceptive and manipulative claims, on the other. It has to reach out to rural consumers and relate to them at an appropriate level, so that, it can bring about the desired behavioural changes. Finally, it has to find ways to reincarnate innovation.

Annexure

Table A-1 : Rural and Urban Populations (*in crores*)

	2001	2011	Difference	Growth Rate in % 1991-2001	Growth Rate in % 2001-2011	Difference
India	102.9	121.0	18.1	21.5	17.6	–3.9
Rural	74.3	83.3	9.0	18.1	12.2	–5.9
Urban	28.6	37.7	9.1	31.5	31.8	0.3

Source: Census Report, 2011.

Table A-2 : Literacy Rate in Rural and Urban India (%)

	2001	2011	Differences
India	64.8	74.0	9.2
Rural	58.7	68.9	10.2
Urban	79.9	85.0	5.1

Source: Census Report, 2011.

Table A-3: Marketing Opportunities (Low Penetration Rates in Rural India)

Durables/FMCGs	Urban	Rural	% of Rural H.H.
CTV	30.4	4.8	12.1
Refrigerators	33.5	3.5	12.0
Mobile Phones	40.0	12.0	18.0
Shampoo	66.3	35.2	44.2
Tooth Paste	82.2	44.9	55.6

Source: NACER, 2011.

References

Badi, R.V. and Vadi, N.V. (2006). *Rural Marketing Environment,* Mumbai: Himalaya Publishing House.

Bijoor, Harish (1999). "Go Rural", *Economic Times*, June 14.

Dertouzos, James, N. and Garber, S. (2006). *"Effectiveness of Advertising"*, Vol. 35, No.2, pp.111-122.

Dorga, Balaram and Ghuman, Karminder (2008). *Rural Marketing: Concepts and Practices,* New Delhi: Tata McGraw Hill Publishing Company Ltd.

Gopalaswamy, T.P. (1997). *Environment: Problems and Strategies*, New Delhi: Wheeler Publishing.

Gopalswamy, T.P. (2008). *Rural Marketing Environment: Problems and Strategies*, New Delhi: Vikas Publishing House.

Jethwanee, J. (2006). *Advertising Management*, Oxford University Press, New Delhi.

Kotler, Philip (1997). *Marketing Management—Analysis, Planning, Implementation and Control*, Prentice Hall of India, 9th edition.

Krishnamurthy, R. (2008). *Introduction to Rural Marketing*, Mumbai: Himalaya Publishing House.

Maslow, A.H. (1954). *Theory of Human Motivation, Motivation and Personality*, New York: Harper & Row Publishers Inc., pp. 80-101.

O'Guinn, Thomas, (2007). *Advertising and Integrated Brand Promotion*, New Delhi: Thompson.

Serra Inci, Celebi (2007). "The Credibility of Advertising *verses* Publicity for News FMCGs in Turkey", *Corporate Communications,* Volume 12, 2007, pp. 161-176.

Shukla, R.K. (1997). "New Perspective in Marketing", *Rural Marketing: Thrust and Challenges*, New Delhi: National Publishing House.

Tyagi, Lalit Kumar (2000). Rural Communication, *Kurukshetra*, May.

Vaish, T. (2007). Strategies for Rural Markets in India, *"Marketing Mastermind,* ICFAI University Press, pp. 35-41.

21

ICT: Availability, Awareness, Use and Information Seeking Behaviour of Rural Farmers in Southern India

K. Soundararajan

Introduction

In India, Information and Communication Technology (ICT) in agriculture is an emerging field that focuses on development of farming sector and rural economy. This field tends to apply the recent trends in ICT in farming sector. As it provides exact information to the farmers, it is found to enhance the agricultural output by assisting them in decision-making. In India, rural population primarily depends on agriculture for employment. However, the profits to the small farmers are not in line with their efforts and cost inputs. As a result, national food security and productivity has become poorer. So, it becomes necessary to apply recent technologies and scientific knowledge so as to improve the economic status of the farmers. Moreover, there is no problem in terms of R&D efforts and availability of technologies. But the major issue is the distribution of required data and knowledge among the farmers. To overcome this challenge Information and Communication Technology (ICT) can be used to distribute the information in farming sector. In India, twenty four percentage of GDP and fifteen percentages of overall export earnings are contributed by the farming field. Furthermore, it employs around 56.7 per cent of the individuals. Mathur and Ambani (2005) and Sekhar (2012) pointed out that the primary source of resource mobilisation in Indian economy such as industrial goods and services, and rural domestic savings are highly influenced by this sector.

There have been some structural changes in Indian economy with the expected fall in the share of this sector in the GDP. During 1950-51 its share was around 55.1 per cent and it became seventeen percentages during 2008-09. Though there has been a fall in the share of this sector, its importance has not reduced due to the following reasons. At macro-level, the national food production was self-sufficient. However, the high population of malnourished as well as poor children has become a major challenge for the country. As a result, the agriculture sector has become highly responsible to produce food as per this requirement. There has been a fall in the contribution of farming field to GDP. But, still, the rural population mainly depends upon this field for employment. The farming community has been exploited and the agricultural supply chain has become defective due to the asymmetry in the information at all stages of this chain in the developing economies.

Most of the developing economies such as India face many challenges due to this reason. To overcome these challenges, the farming population has to improve its scientific and technical knowledge. So, there is a need for proper production planning, better cultivation practices, useful post-harvest management and marketing approaches. In India, the farming systems are extremely complex and discontinuous. So, the information and knowledge needed at each stage will differ from each other. Empowering the Indian farmers by means of sharing relevant information regarding better agricultural practices and price discovery to assist them in decision-making is the major aim of e-Choupal.

In rural areas, the supply side perspective is involved with technical and organisational aspects to offer access to ICT-based services across the agricultural supply chain. The technical aspects comprise connectivity, computers and peripherals, software and applications, and capacity building of farmers and other application in rural areas. The organisational aspects comprise the formation of an organisational structure to build and maintain the technical infrastructure, provision of services, and capacity building in using ICTs in rural areas. In India, there are two types of organisational structures that have become transparent, i.e. one which is the origin of corporate agribusiness model and the other on basis of public sector or non-government organisation (NGO) service models and each has its own specification.

Farmers make significant decisions all through the year which comprise the ones established through selection of crops, seeds, water, power, fertilisers and pesticides and its market transactions, farm actions, i.e. tillage, sowing, water management, fertiliser management, pest management, harvest, and post-harvest operations and transactions including storage, transport, marketing, processing etc. (Saha *et al.*, 1998). Additionally, there are many non-farm decisions at the level of households in relation to savings, investments, education, health and consumption affecting the farm operations. Usually, the farmers depend on gathered experience and the reinforcement of local organisations. For example, input suppliers, rural credit agencies, extension services, NGOs to collect information perspective to farm and non-farm decisions (Meera *et al.*, 2004). The information is also gathered from radio and television broadcasts by experts and professionals from far distant sources. Frequently, this system proves to be inadequate and most decisions are performed with available information. These decisions are focused to high transaction costs and time delays. The ICTs functionality in these situations is basically to render timely information, increase choice, decrease the cost involved in transaction and contribution to emphasise the efficiency of decision-making to uplift the income level of rural communities and improve their quality of life.

In India, there are many challenges such as expenses, illiteracy and unawareness when it comes to distribution of relevant information in the farming sector. Furthermore, there is a view that capitalistic firms would not get benefits from rural agricultural markets. This is the major challenge to this initiative. This is because, in the present era, besides governmental efforts, the entrepreneurial initiatives of firms are also important to achieve a goal. It is necessary to evaluate the awareness and information sharing attitude of the farmers so as to carry out the process of information dissemination successfully. The innovativeness and economic status of the farmers will be improved only if they get adequate gains and returns. To assess the role of ICT in breaking the challenges in information dissemination and in providing a sustainable and profitable agricultural growth is the focus of this study.

From the previous studies, the role of ICTs as a medium of dissemination of information and knowledge in agricultural development is well documented and discussed. Nevertheless, the above discussions pertain to a very broad perspective. There exist limited empirical evidences on how ICT interventions facilitate farmers in corresponding informed decisions. The current study focuses in comprehending the effect of better availability of information and knowledge on agriculture decision-making processes. With the help of the primary information through structured surveys of farmers, the existing differences in decision-making abilities on activities across the agriculture supply chain between the user and non-user farmer groups have been empirically investigated. The results obtained provide extensive implications for designing and implementing ICTs enabled information dissemination policies for Indian and also globalised agricultural systems. The outcomes also improve the understanding of the complex role played by ICT enabled services in enhancing agrarian communities' decision-making.

Research Framework

Geographic Location and Sample Survey

The data for the research study has been gathered from 100 farmers from the two taluks in India, which are Chunampet and Cheyyur Taluk. A structured questionnaire was used to conduct the survey. The responses were recorded by contacting these farmers personally. Overall, 5 e-Choupals in above two selected taluks were considered and for the each e-Choupal, a minimum range of 10 user farmers and 10 non-user farmers were randomly chosen. These user farmers were selected from the record of farmers provided by the *Sanchalak*, managing a specific village. The other sectors of non-user farmers were selected from village which is located at a distance of 15 km away from the locality of the e-Choupal. The concluding sample of 100 farmers comprised 52 user farmers and 48 non-user farmers. From this sample twenty farmers were chosen for a focus group discussion for identifying perceived advantages and disadvantages of ICT.

Survey Instruments

A pre-tested structured questionnaire was used to conduct the survey and this questionnaire comprised items on many agricultural practices. In consideration to comprehend the language and obtain greater response from the participants, the questionnaire was developed in Tamil language. Also, it was assumed that respondents could answer with increased confidence that provides accurate and unbiased information on the other. Additionally, the questions were associated to agricultural decision-making and they also contained items on socio-demographic profiles of the respondents. The questionnaire was categorised into three different stages pertaining to agriculture sector:

(i) Production planning,
(ii) Cultivation practices, and
(iii) Post-harvest management and marketing.

The questionnaire incorporated items on activities in each of the three stages and the awareness as well as information seeking behaviour were identified.

Major Findings

Table 21.1 provides a summary profile of ICT user and non-user farmers included in this study. All our respondents are male. The majority of the respondents are in the age group of 35-50 years. Interestingly, the maximum number of respondents were found to be in the same age group among both the groups. In terms of education, the ICT uses had more years of schooling, mostly had primary education. The results of the chi-square test reveal a significant difference in education levels between users and non-users of ICT (chi-square = 6.851, ρ = 0.009). As far as social groups are concerned, number of the ICT users belong to general category – the group which represents the higher social groups – whereas non-users were comparatively from the lower social classes (ρ = 0.048). On the economic dimension, about half of the respondents have income less than 2000. Chi-square statistic (ρ = 0.001) indicates a significant difference between income levels of user and non-user groups. On the basis of land holding, the sample can be divided into four categories:

Table 21.1 : Demographics

Age in Years	*Are You Aware of ICT Initiatives in Your Area*				*Total*		*Chi-square Statistics*
	User	*%*	*Non-User*	*%*		*%*	
Less than 25	8	15.4	5	10.4	13	13.0	3.971 (0.46)
25-35 yrs	8	15.4	4	8.3	12	12.0	
35-50 yrs	21	40.4	19	39.6	40	40.0	
50-65 yrs	12	23.1	11	22.9	23	23.0	
>65 yrs	3	5.8	9	18.8	12	12.0	
Total	**52**	**100.0**	**48**	**100.0**	**100**	**100.0**	
Education							
Illiterate	17	32.70	7	14.60	24	24.00	6.851(0.009)
Primary school	16	30.80	13	27.10	29	29.00	
High school	9	17.30	9	18.80	18	18.00	
Graduate and above	10	19.20	19	39.60	29	29.00	
Total	**52**	**100.0**	**48**	**100.0**	**100**	**100.0**	

Source: Based on Field Survey Data.

large (land holding equal to or more than 4 ha), medium (land holding 2–4 ha), small (land holding 1–2 ha) and marginal (land holding less than 1 ha). Chi-square statistic ($\rho = 0.001$) indicates a significant difference between land use of user and non-user groups ($\rho = 0.022$).

All the decision making questions were based on a five point Likert scale system in which 1 meant strong agreement and 5 meant strong disagreements. ANOVA technique was utilised to compare the variances in user and non user farmers, in order to determine whether the usage of information and services being provided by the ICT. ICT initiative has any impact on the quality of decision-making of the farmers at various levels of agricultural supply chain. However, as mentioned before, there are statistical differences among both the non-users as well as users when it comes to areas like education, size of landholdings, incomes and social category. In rural India, the society is still patriarchal in nature with the male members provide most of the information as well as take decisions and therefore, the quality of decision-making in the two groups cannot be ruled out. Thus, ICT users and non-users who had similar profiles with respect to factors such as land holding sizes, education, income etc. were compared using ANOVA techniques in order to control the discrepancies introduced by these differences. The results indicate that the quality of decision-making is much different in most activities across users and non-users if they are either illiterate or less educated. Our results are in line with some previous studies (Agwu, Ekwueme, and Anyanwu, 2008; Taragola and Van Lierde, 2010) which have indicated that educated farmers are more likely to make better-informed decisions on agricultural practices and they are expected to adopt ICTs for their information requirement.

The results of our study indicate that the use of ICT does seem to have a significant impact on socially lower classes since the quality of decision-making is almost equally poor in this category across user and non-user farmers. This is comparable to the views of study Nazarea-Sandoval (1995) which found that decision-making is not homogenous across the social classes and is greatly influenced by the internal social and cultural structure of the society. Results presented in show that there is not much difference in the quality of decision-making of user and non-user farmers whose landholdings are marginal. However, the differences between these two groups – users and non-users of ICT enabled services – become significant when their landholding size increases. The study by Alvarex and Nuthall (2006) supports this statement. From the focus group discussion, it was found that awareness level on ICT among farmers was

Table 21.2: Awareness about ICT Initiatives

Age in Years	*Are You Aware of ICT Initiatives in Your Area*				*Total*		*Chi-square Statistics*
	User		*Non-User*				
Social category							
General	21	40.40%	11	22.90%	32	32.00%	3.910 (0.048)
BC and OBC	14	26.90%	13	27.00%	27	27.00%	
SC/ST	11	21.20%	12	25.00%	23	23.00%	
Unwilling to disclose	6	11.50%	12	25.00%	18	18.00%	
Total	**52**	**100.0%**	**48**	**100.0%**	**100**	**100.0%**	
Agriculture land Holding							
Marginal (<1.00 ha)	16	30.80%	24	50.0%	40	40.0%	5.255 (0.022)
Small (1.01–2.00 ha)	16	30.80%	15	31.30%	31	31.0%	
Medium (2.01–4.00)	11	21.20%	5	10.40%	16	16.0%	
Large (>4 ha)	9	17.30%	4	8.30%	13	13.0%	
Total	**52**	**100.0%**	**48**	**100.0%**	**100**	**100.0%**	
Agriculture land Income							
Less than 2000	51	98.10%	7	14.60%	58	58.0%	71.451 (0.001)
2001-5000	1	1.90%	33	68.80%	34	34.0%	
More than 5000	—	—	8	16.70%	8	8.0%	
Total	**52**	**100.0%**	**48**	**100.0%**	**100**	**100.0%**	

Source: Based on Field Survey Data.

very low and they mostly relied on middlemen, local and official sources for agricultural information. Although mobile phones were widely available to the farmers, its use was mainly for sale enquiry rather production efficiency. The awareness among farmers did not mediate the relationship between the buyer and the seller.

Conclusion

In several developing countries, the publicly funded extension services are mainly involved in delivering information on agriculture technologies and practices. But, the effectiveness of agriculture extension services in developing countries like India is found to be uncertain. The introduction of ICT provides a new dimension on delivering improved agriculture technologies and practices to the farmers. The introduction of ICTs resulted in improving the knowledge regarding the technological advancement in agriculture along with enhancement in the decision-making process among farmers. So, the initiatives in ICTs, which are involved in providing transactional services, must be further expanded and strengthened. In India, the productivity of crop in recent past years seems to be standstill, so that the income of farmers has not increased much which leads to reduction in the overall economic growth of the country. As a result, there is a necessity to enhance the productivity by means of avoiding social unrest due to rural-urban separation followed by improvement in the income of the farmers so as to feed the growing population. One of the ways to increase the productivity and farmers' income is to enhance the decision-making process of farmers by means of improving the knowledge about the advancement of agricultural technology and practices. However, the socio-demographics profile such as education, social category, income and landholding size have been identified from the finding of the study as an important factors that influence the usage of information in decision-making process. Hence, these factors should be considered while launching ICTs enabled information system by both public as well as private sectors. On the basis of the findings, three important recommendations have been made by the researchers.

First, a unique design of information delivery system should not be made for whole village because it could not produce effective results. So, the model should be designed in a way that it covers the demographic profile of the users. Similarly, the content as well as the user interface should be framed in reference with user group. Secondly, the level of education of the user group should be enhanced together with making information and knowledge available to farming communities. The governments in all-around the world though have made more efforts in this direction; our intention of conducting this study is to emphasise the need for speeding-up the implementation regarding the effectiveness of ICT enable information delivery system. Third, the decision-making quality of ICT enabled initiatives for lower social group having low income with marginal landholding have not generated more difference in comparison with the non-users. From this, it is understood that the availability of information as well as knowledge in those sections of the society is not enough to show better behaviour or actions.

The limitation of resources among the farmers community may be a reason for such consequences. So, the ICT enabled initiatives have to pay more attention on providing integrated solutions to the users by using holistic approach. In the midst of all services, the ICT enabled initiatives must give more attention on financial service, so that the farmers can increase their knowledge as well as information regarding information delivery system.

References

Abdullah, M.O., Yung, V.C., Anyi, M., Othman, A.K., Ab. Hamid, K.B. and Tarawe, J. (2010). "Review and Comparison Study of Hybrid Diesel/Solar/Hydro/Fuel Cell Energy Schemes for a Rural ICT Telecenter", *Energy*, 35(2), pp. 639-46.

Adhiguru, P. and Mruthyunjaya (2004). "Institutional Innovations for Using Information and Communication Technology in Agriculture", *Policy Brief* No.18. NCAP, ICAR, New Delhi, India.

Annamalai, K. and Rao, S. (2003). *What Works: ITC's ICT and Profitable Rural Transformation*, University of Michigan, Ann Arbor, MI, USA: World Resources Institute, Digital Dividend Project.

Balakrishnan, P., Golait, R. and Pankaj, K. (2008). "Agricultural Growth in India since 1991", *Development Research Group (DRG),* Study No. 27, Mumbai: Reserve Bank of India.

Bertolini, R. (2006). "Making Information and Communications Technologies Work for Food Security in Africa", *An IFPRI 2020 Vision Conference Brief,* IFPRI, Washington, USA.

Bhalla, G.S. and Singh, G. (2009). "Economic Liberalisation and Indian Agriculture: A State-wise Analysis", *Economic & Political Weekly*.

Birkhaeuser, D., Evenson, R. E. and Feder, G. (1991). "The Economic Impact of Agricultural Extension: A Review", *Economic Development and Cultural Change,* 39, pp. 607-50.

Cash, D.W. (2011). "In Order to Aid in Diffusing Useful and Practical Information: Agricultural Extension and Boundary Organisations", *Science Technology and Human Values,* 26(4), pp. 431-53.

Dancy, R. J. (1993). "The Evolution of Agricultural Extension in England and Wales", *Journal of Agricultural Economics,* 44(3), pp. 375-93.

Dinar, A. (1996) "Extension commercialization: How much to charge for extension services", *Am. J. Agric. Econ.*, 78, pp. 1-12.

Dossani, R., Misra, D.C. and Jhaveri, R. (2005). *Enabling ICT for Rural India*, Asia Pacific Research Centre, Stanford University and National Informatics Centre, Available at: http://iisdb.stanford.edu/pubs/20972/ICT_full_Oct05.pdfôôsearch=%22ict%20governance%20india%20rural%22 (Accessed: 30 September 2006).

Eggleston, K., Jensen, R. and Zeckhauser, R. (2001). "Information and

Communication Technologies, Markets and Economic Development", *The Global Competitiveness Report 2001-2002 (GCR)*. Harvard University and the Institute for Strategy and Competitiveness, Harvard: World Economic Forum (WEF) in collaboration with the Centre for International Development (CID).

Emrouznejad, A., Cabanda, E. and Gholami, R. (2010). "An Alternative Measure of the ICT—Opportunity Index", *Information & Management,* 47(4), pp. 246-54.

Ghosh, A. (2011). "Initiatives in ICT for Rural Development: An Indian Perspective", *Global Media Journal,* 2(2).

Giri Rao, J.S. and Pattnaik, S.N. (2006). "Technology for Rural Development Role of Telecommunication Media in India", *Indian Media Studies Journal,* 1(1).

Gollakota, K. (2008). "ICT Use by Businesses in Rural India: The Case of EID Parry's Indiagriline", *International Journal of Information Management,* 28(4), pp. 336-41.

Jhunjhunwala, A., Ramachandran, A. and Bandyopadhyay, A. (2004). "n-Logue: the Story of a Rural Service Provider in India", *Journal of Community Informatics,* 1(1), pp. 30-38.

Kalusopa, T. (2005). "The Challenges of Utilising Information Communication Technologies (ICTs) for Small-scale Farmers in Zambia", *Library Hi Tech.,* 23(3), pp. 196-204.

Kannan, E. and Sundaram, S. (2011). Analysis of Trends in India's Agricultural Growth, *Working Paper 276.*

Kizilaslan, N. (2006). "Agricultural Information System: National case study", *Library Review,* 55(8), pp. 497-507.

Lio, M. and Liu, M. (2006) "ICT and Agricultural Productivity: Evidence from Cross-Country Data", *Agricultural Economics,* 34, pp. 221-228.

Mathur, A. and Ambani, D. (2005). "ICT and Rural Societies: Opportunities for Growth", *The International Information & Library Review,* 37(4), pp. 345-51.

Meera, S., Jhamtani, A. and Rao, D. (2004). "Agricultural Research and Extension Network", *Network Paper No.135*, National Institute for Smart Government 3rd Annual Report.

Palaskas, T.B., Harriss–White, B. and Crowe, T. (1997). "The Evolution of Local Market Commodity Price Behaviour in South India, 1972–92", *Journal of International Development,* 9(1), pp. 101-15.

Planning Commission (2002). "Report of the Steering Group on Agriculture and Allied Sectors", *For The Tenth Five Year Plan 2002-2007,* Government of India, New Delhi.

Poole, N.D. and Kenny, L. (2003). "Agricultural Market Knowledge: System for Delivery of a Private and Public Good", *Journal of Agricultural Education and Extension,* 9, pp. 117-26.

Puri, S.K. (2007). "Integrating Scientific with Indigenous Knowledge:

Constructing Knowledge Alliances for Land Management in India", *MIS Quarterly,* 31(2), pp. 355-79.

Rajalakshmi, K.G. (2007). "E-governance Services through Telecentres: The Role of Human Intermediary and Issues of Trust", *Information Technologies and International Development,* 4(1), pp. 19-35.

Rao, C. H. (2006). "Growing Regional Disparities in Development in India—Post-Reform Experience and Challenges Ahead", *The Indian Economic Journal,* 54(1).

Rao, N. (2008). *Good Women do not Inherit Land: Politics of Land and Gender in India*, New Delhi, India: Social Science Press and Orient Blackswan.

Rao, S.S. (2007). "Social Development in Indian Rural Communities: Adoption of Telecentres", *International Journal of Information Management,* 28(6), pp. 474-82.

Rao, S.S. (2008). "Social Development in Indian Rural Communities: Adoption of Telecentres", *International Journal of Information Management,* 28, pp. 474-82.

Ravallion, M. (1986). "Testing Market Integration", *American Journal of Agricultural Economics,* 688, pp. 102-109.

Saha, B., Dien, B., Bothast, R. (1998). "Fuel Ethanol Production from Corn Fiber: Current Status and Technical Prospects", *Appl. Biochem. Biotechnol.,* 70-72, pp. 115-25.

Sekhar, C.S.C. (2012). "Agricultural Market Integration in India: An Analysis of Select Commodities", *Food Policy,* 37(3), pp. 309-22.

Streeter, D.H., Sonka, S. T. and Hudson, M. A. (1991). "Information Technology, Coordination and Competitiveness in the Food and Agribusiness Sector", *American Journal of Agricultural Economics.*

Swaminathan (2005). *How can ICTs play a Role?,* Available at: *http://www.14donline.net/feb05/introduction.asp* (Accessed: 14 December, 2005).

Thompson, S. and Sonka, S.T. (1997). "Potential Effects of Information Technologies on the Economic Performance of Agricultural and Food Markets", *American Journal of Agricultural Economics, Agricultural and Applied Economics Association,* 79(2), pp. 657-62.

Tilman, D., Cassman, K.G., Matson, P. A., Naylor, R. and Polasky, S. A. (2002). "Agricultural Sustainability and Intensive Production Practices", *Nature,* 418, pp. 671-77.

Umali, D.L. and Schwartz, L. (1994). *Public and Private Agricultural Extension: Beyond Traditional Frontiers,* World Bank Discussion Papers No. 236, Washington, DC: World Bank.

Upton, D.M. and Fuller, V. A. (2004). "The ITC ICT Initiative", *Harvard Business School Case*, pp. 1-20.

Vaidyanathan, A. (2010). *Agricultural Growth in India, Role of Technology, Incentives, and Institutions*, New Delhi: Oxford University Press.

22
Role of ICT in Empowering Rural Consumers

Sheetal Kapoor

Introduction

"*The spirit of India lives in its villages*" has been rightly said by Mahatma Gandhi. Two-third of India's consumers live in rural areas and almost half of the national income is generated here. Our country is classified around 450 districts and approximately 6,40,867 villages, which can be classified on the basis of different parameters such as, literacy levels, accessibility, income levels, penetration, distances from nearest towns etc. Villagers who used to crack open peanuts are now demanding chocolates, charcoal teeth are a rare sight, so is the case with twigs of *neem* and *babul* tree. Today, the ultra bright shine of Colgate or some international brand holds more appeal than the traditional methods of cleaning teeth (like tooth powder or '*Dant Manjan*') in rural areas. Consumerism and Globalisation is invading parts of rural India and the villages which were once inconsequential dots on maps, are now are connected with telephone and internet getting the attention of global marketing and media planners.

Information is the key to democracy. With the advent of Information Technology (IT), it has become possible for common man to access global information. Information in a broader sense includes oral communication, voice in telephony, text in fax and newspapers, images in video and television broadcasting, and data in computers. All information can be digitised, transported, stored, retrieved, modified and then distributed. Emerging digital techniques, new network alternatives including intelligent networks, high bandwidth communication technology and state-of-the-art software for network functions and services, are the new technology trends evident in the development of electronic communication systems. The swift emergence of a global "information society" is changing the way people live, learn, work and relate. Rural marketers have to successfully communicate with a much larger, but scattered audience characterised by variations in language, culture and lifestyles. The requirement, therefore, is to develop region specific and right communication strategies to induce target audience to buy the product.

The chapter discusses the need to focus on Indian rural consumers to empower them to access information, knowledge by deploying the Information and Communication Technologies (ICTs) and to explore the available media at the different locations. Analyse the factors preventing rural communities from reaping the benefits of ICTs, government initiatives to overcome the factors, and to identify the bottlenecks and solutions, and lessons learned.

What Constitutes Rural?

There is no specific definition which defines what a rural area is. The Census of India defines urban areas having the following features:[1]

I. a minimum population of 5,000;
II. at least 75 per cent of male working population engaged in non-agricultural pursuits; and
III. a density of population of at least 400 per sq. km. (1,000 per sq. mile).

Definitions for rural India abound while the most convenient one is, "anything that is not urban", is considered as rural.[2] The rural market in India is not a separate entity in itself and it is highly influenced by the sociological and behavioural factors operating in the country. The concept of rural marketing in India is often been found to form ambiguity in the minds of people who think rural marketing is all about agricultural marketing. However, rural marketing determines the carrying out of business activities bringing in the flow of goods from urban sectors to the rural regions of the country as well as the marketing of various products manufactured by the non-agricultural workers from rural to urban areas. The rural markets dominate Indian marketing scene and need special attention for the expansion of marketing activities and also for providing better life and welfare to the rural people.

What makes Rural Markets Attractive?

- Rural India constitutes 70 per cent of India's population.
- Villagers now account for the majority of consumers spending in the country, more than $100 billion a year.
- There are more mobile phones than Radio in Rural India (100 million subscriber base).
- Seventy per cent of India's population lives in 6,40,867 villages in rural areas. According to the NCAER study, there are twice as many "lower middle income" households in rural areas as in the urban areas.
- There are 1.6 million households in rural areas at the highest income level as against 2.3 million urban households. Middle and high-income households in rural India are expected to grow from 80 million to 111 million by 2007.
- While in urban India, the middle and high-income households are expected to grow from 46 million to 59 million by 2007.

Thus, the absolute size of rural India is expected to be double that of urban India.

Opportunity

The Indian rural market with its vast size and demand base offers a huge opportunity for the marketers. With 128 million households, the rural population is nearly three times the urban. Because of certain socio-economic changes the rural consumer has become aware about his needs and upgradation of his standard of living. Information technology, government policies, corporate strategies and satellite communications are the factors responsible for development of the rural markets. The increase in procurement prices has contributed to a rise in rural demand. A series of good harvests on the back of several good monsoons boosted rural employment in agricultural and allied activities. Government schemes like NREGS [National Rural Employment Guarantee Scheme, which guarantees 100 days of employment to one member of every rural household] reduced rural underemployment and raised wages. Also, farmers benefited from loan waivers. The increase in rural purchasing power is reflected in rural growth across a number of categories.

According to Ernst and Young in 2012 rural Indians would account for over 60 per cent of the total telecom subscriber base. As per TRAI the subscriber additions in rural areas exceeded additions in the metros. The unprecedented growth in rural retail market has attracted domestic retail firms including Godrej, Dabur, and many others who have already set-up farm linkages. ITCs e-chaupal, Tata's Kisan Sansars, Hindustan Unilevers Ltd's. Project Shakti, DCM's Kisan Bazaars are established rural retail hubs.[3] The State Bank of India (SBI) has started a zero-balance bank account programme for villagers. Called the SBI Tiny account, there are no physical branches or officials, just a paid volunteer who is equipped with a small box and a cellphone. The box enables biometric measurements (fingerprints), at the time of opening the account to confirm the account holder's identity. The cellphone enables communication with the zonal office to check on available balance. Payments under programmes such as the NREGS and pensions are made directly to these accounts. The advantage for the villagers is that they can withdraw money from their accounts at any time of the day or night (Withdrawals are never more than a few dollars). SBI hopes to cover 1,00,000 villages by 2012. The bank has tied-up with India Post for some services.[4]

Features of Indian Rural Market[5]

- *Large and Scattered Market*: The rural market of India is large and nearly 50 per cent of the villages in the country do not have proper roads. Moreover, the number of families residing in a particular village is not always large.
- *Major Income from Agriculture*: Nearly 60 per cent of the rural income is from agriculture. Hence, rural prosperity is tied with agriculture and adequate monsoons in non-irrigated rural areas.
- *Traditional Outlook*: The vast majority of rural consumers value old customs and traditions. However, education and economic change is also bringing a slow change in outlook.
- *Diverse Socio-economic Backwardness*: Rural consumers have diverse socio-economic backwardness, which is different in different parts of the country. This is related to linguistic and regional development factors.
- *Many Languages and Dialects*: The number of languages and dialects vary widely from state-to-state, region to region, and from district to district. Even though the number of recognised languages in India are only 16, the dialects are estimated to be around 850.

Problems Faced by Rural Consumers Regarding Unethical Marketing Practices[6]

Many rural consumers are illiterate and are easily vulnerable to the unscrupulous and unethical marketing practices of 'greedy' marketers.

1. *Prevalence of Spurious Brands and Seasonal Demand*: For any branded product there are a multitude of 'local variants' which are cheaper and, therefore, more desirable in rural markets or even small towns. Sub-standard and spurious products are being passed on to the rural consumers under counterfeit brand names which are deceptively similar to the popular brand names. For example, 'Calgote' for Colgate. The rural consumer is gullible to quacks, fake ayurvedic drugs and cosmetics due to lack of awareness and knowledge.
2. *Misleading and Deceptive Pricing*: Since the rural consumers lack product and price information and possess less bargaining power and buying insight they are prone to being deceived by the traders. On the pack of the products the 'MRP' the maximum retail price is printed, but many rural consumers do not check that. As provided by the law no dealer can charge more than the MRP of an item although they can reduce the price to any extent.
3. *Misleading Advertisements*: The prohibition of drugs and magic remedies is often openly flouted in the rural areas where the quacks and self-styled medical practitioners play with the lives of people with impunity.
4. *Distribution of Goods*: Certain products which are advertised in the rural areas or through the local media are not available with the vendors and sometimes the re-order time may even be more than 15 days, so that, the villagers have to wait or to go for some other substandard brand.
5. *Counterfeits:* There may be products that use fake standard marks. Gullible consumers may be duped by fake standard marks like ISI, Agmark etc. which have been put without conformity assessment procedures being followed. In other cases some manufacturers copy the brand name of popular companies and sell them to consumers who are unable to notice that they are counterfeits and have not been produced by the brand owner.
6. *Sale of Unpacked Goods*: When products are sold loose they become prone to adulteration. The adulteration may take place

deliberately to make more profit or it may be accidental due to exposure to heat, dust, storage conditions etc.

Single Media Campaign Misfit for Rural Markets

As mentioned earlier the rural market poses several problems with regard to various methods available for communicating effectively with them. Further, the rate of literacy among the rural consumers is low and this limits the use of printed words. Any communication can simply serve little or no purpose unless it uses local language or idioms. According to Hindustan Unilever Ltd., mass media reaches only 57 per cent of the rural population. On the one hand, traditional media, such as, puppetry, folk theatre, demonstrations, *haats* and *melas*, wall paintings, post cards and posters are popular in communicating messages to the rural folk as rural audience are heterogeneous and languages and dialects change from region to region.[7] Gradually, the reach of TV is expanding in the rural areas and now has become a prime medium. Recent introduction of Direct to Home (DTH) facility has further increased the TV penetration in the rural areas. Irrespective of the literacy levels of the people, topography and geographical locations of the areas of residence, the Radio reaches rural people easily. Cinema is the next important medium of communication. Television viewership is increasing in the rural areas. Ownership is being increased by the marketers of TV sets as well as the satellite television influx in regional languages. The Southern States account for as many as 20 channels in regional languages.[8]

Role of Consumer Education

Educated and well informed consumers are an asset to any society. An aware consumer lays foundation for building-up a superior society. The main aim of consumer education is to enhance the skills of rational thinking based on logic and adopt a realistic attitude towards optimum utilisation of resources. It educates the purchaser of what to buy, where to buy, how to buy and how to make the best use of what he buys in order to get the best value for his money. In reality consumers are often exploited due to ignorance and lack of unity amongst them. Consumer awareness at the time of purchase and knowledge of the law which gives consumers power in the market place, helps in reducing the losses caused by ignorance.

Rural Consumer Education

The success of any consumer movement depends on the consciousness and awareness of rural consumers. A number of awareness programmes should be taken-up in local language to teach the consumers to avoid being duped by the traders. Some of the initiatives are:

- Rural consumers should be made aware of their rights as a consumer. They should be taught to check quality marks on the products they purchase, so that they do not fall prey to greedy traders.
- They should be taught to take a receipt after purchase and check the expiry dates of an item.
- It is required that the individuals, government and non-governmental organisations should work hand-in-hand for educating the rural consumers, so that, their hard earned money is not wasted.
- Marketers also need to look long term because if they supply substandard products they would loose the trust of the people. So, short term profiteering should be avoided.
- The rural youth are more open to fresh concepts as against their elderly family members so, it is better to build awareness about consumer education at a very young age. For example, consumer education should be taken-up as a subject in school's curriculum.
- The Central Government although is building awareness among consumers through radio and television. Further focusing on the opinion leaders which play an important role in communicating a message to the rural consumers.

"Jago Grahak Jago" – an Initiative towards Consumer Education and Awareness

The slogan "*Jago Grahak Jago*" has now become a household name as a result of publicity campaign undertaken by the Department of Consumer Affairs. Through the increased thrust on consumer awareness in the Five Year Plan, the Government has endeavoured to inform the common man of his rights as a consumer. As part of the consumer awareness scheme, the rural and remote areas have been given top priority. In a big country like India, given the scenario of economic disparity and level of education and ignorance, educating the consumers remains a gigantic task.

Government has taken-up number of activities and schemes in creating consumer awareness in the country as part of this Consumer Awareness Scheme.

Sayani Rani which comes as the spokes girl in the Department of Consumer Affairs advertisements is a smart rural consumer who exercises her rights and is not ready to be cheated by the market. She always thinks rationally while making purchases, is conscious of her rights and responsibilities and is not swayed by the false and deceptive claim of the traders. She is aware of her consumer rights, such as right to safety, right to information, right to choose, right to be heard, right to seek redressal and right to consumer education.

Use of ICT Techniques by Government

As part of the Multi-Media publicity campaign various activities undertaken by the government are:

1. Publicity through Print Media Using Newspaper Advertisements

To educate the consumers about their rights and responsibilities, the Department has been releasing small advertisements through Department of Audio-Visual Publicity (DAVP) in National dailies as well as regional newspapers in local languages in accordance with the Advertisement Policy of the DAVP.

2. Publicity through Electronic Medium by Telecast of Video Spots

The Department has got produced video spots of 30 seconds duration on various consumer related issues such as Grievance Redressal System, MRP, ISI, Hall-Mark, Alternate Dispute Redressal System, Weights and Measures, Rights of Consumers etc. which are being telecast through Doordarshan, Cable and Satellite channels such as Sony, Star Plus, Zee News, Star News, Doordarshan National Network, Kalyani Programme of DD-I, Krishi Darshan, Regional Channels, Sun Network, ETV Network, ZEE TV Network, Discovery and other private popular satellite channels. Special programmes have been telecast on DD News and Lok Sabha TV also to highlight the issues relating to consumer awareness. Issues pertaining to rural and remote areas have been given prominence in the various advertisement spots.

3. Telecast of Video Spots in North-Eastern States

The Department has produced 6 video spots in regional languages of North-Eastern States of 20 seconds and 30 seconds duration on various consumer related issues such as M.R.P. (Maximum Retail Price), short measurement, expiry date on medicine, adulteration, damaged product, redressal system and telecast them through Doordarshan Kendras of North-Eastern States.

4. Meghdoot Postcards

The Department in consultation with Department of Posts has disseminated consumer awareness messages through Meghdoot Posts cards to reach far-flung rural areas including North-East States. A bigger plan of partnership with the Department of Posts to use the vast network of postal department for spreading the message of consumer awareness has been chalked out Calendars containing the message of consumer awareness are being displayed through the vast network of 1.55 lakh Post-Offices.

5. Printed Literature

The Department has re-printed a folder entitled "Consumer Awareness Mission" containing the salient features of Consumer Protection Act, 1986, Consumer Resource kit as well pocket calendars and posters for distribution during various events such as IITF, *Nukkad Nataks* and also through the State Governments at grassroots level. The publicity material relating to consumer awareness has also been translated in regional languages and is being disseminated to various State Governments.

6. Nukkad Nataks

The Department in consultation with Song & Drama Division of Ministry of Information and Broadcasting has organised more than 1 000 programmes in all the States/UTs to create awareness at grassroots level.

7. National Consumer Helpline and State Helplines

The Department has initiated a pilot project National Consumer Helpline, this can be accessed through a Toll Free Number 1800-11-4000 which is being operated by Delhi University for counselling the consumers to redress their grievances. The Toll Free number facility is available to consumers from 9.30 a.m. to 5.30 p.m. on all the working days (Monday–Saturday). Through the various advertisements pertaining to Department of Consumer Affaris adequate publicity has been given to National Helpline so that the affected consumers can seek guidelines/counselling through the national helpline.

8. Core Centre

Another, technology-based site CORE scheme has been taken-up to counsel the aggrieved consumers. The Consumer Online Resource Empowerment Centre provides online counselling and a complaint redressal mechanism to consumers from across India. Consumers can access its website www.core.nic.in for a comprehensive database on consumer issues.

9. Use of Sports Events

In order to reach maximum number of consumers, the Department has telecast video spots containing consumer related information during the popular sports events such as Tri-series cricket tournament, Indo-Pak Series, Indo-Australia Series, Indo-England Cricket Series etc.

10. Use of Internet to Generate Consumer Awareness

We are a young country with more than 70 per cent population being under 35 years. The youngsters are using the internet in a big way for various purposes and also happen to be major consumers. Realising this, a major initiative is being taken to spread consumer awareness through the online medium. The advertisements being brought out by the Department are also being displayed on the website of the Ministry www.fcamin.nic.in.

11. Advertisements in journals of Publication Division

The Department has entered into a tie-up with Publication Division under the Ministry of Information and Broadcasting. As part of the tie-up advertisements are being published to educate consumers in all the journals brought out by Publication Division such as *Yojana*, *Kurukshetra*, *Bal Bharati*, *Aajkal* and their regional editions. Focussed articles on consumer awareness are being published in these magazines keeping in view their target readership. Employment News, the flagship publication of Publication Division, which is the largest selling career weekly of its kind occasionally publishes articles that are of interest to youngsters in keeping them informed about their rights. The advertisements of Department are also published regularly in *Employment News/Rojgar Samachar*, so that the youth of the country are made aware of their consumer rights.

12. Participation in India International Trade Fair

Keeping in view the large number of visitors to India International Trade Fair, the Department displayed its activities through a stall in IITF. Publicity material regarding main provisions of Consumer Protection Act, Standardisation, Weights & Measures, ISI, Hall-marking and other issues of consumer interest was distributed free of cost. On the spot guidance was also given to consumers during the Trade Fair.

Need for Collborative Action

Seven hundred and twenty million consumers in India which comprises the bottom of the pyramid have a huge potential. According to CAGR the total income of rural India in 2010-11 has been $425 billion, i.e. an increase in 12 per cent as compared to 2004-05.[9] Therefore, the need of the hour is to have a joint initiative from industry, consumer organisations, media and the government.

1. *Business Response*: As many big business houses are increasingly generating profits more than the GDP of some smaller nations, it is now being felt that profit-maximisation should not be the sole objective of corporates. Many transnational corporations are richer and more powerful than the state that seeks to regulate them. It is increasingly being felt that corporations have a responsibility towards the society as a whole and there has been an increased focus on corporate social responsibility and ethical practices. There have been many initiatives taken by Federation of Indian Chambers of Commerce and Industry (FICCI). FICCI has constituted a Consumer Business Forum which discusses issues relating to the consumer. Similarly, the Indian Council of Advertisers have established Advertising Standard Council of India to deal with consumer complaints. According to ASCI it is

trying to inculcate self-regulation in its members. ASCI is a voluntary body of advertisers and has drawn up a comprehensive code for self-regulation. Now-a-days, all big companies have a customer care centre for easy and speedy redressal of complaints.

2. Businessmen should act as trustees of society's wealth. Fraudulent, unethical and monopolistic trade practices on the part of traders should be avoided by following the law diligently. Businessmen should take all measures to provide safe goods and services, disclose full information about products and services, disclose full and fair information in advertisements.
3. *Role of Consumer Organisations*: Consumer organisations are voluntary associations established for the purpose of safeguarding the interests of the consumers. These organisations create awareness in consumers about their rights, help individual consumers to fight with malpractices of traders, do research on comparative testing and take-up the issues of wrong business practices. Some of the NGOs which are actively working in the area of consumer protection are, VOICE (Voluntary Organisation in the Interest of Consumer Education), CERC (Consumer Education and Research Centre), Common Cause, Upabhokta Seva Samiti etc.
4. *Mass Media*: The media is increasingly sensitive to consumer needs. Both radio and television offer information and helpline-based programmes. In the print media almost every daily newspaper as well as journals and magazines run regular columns in support of consumers.
5. *Government Response*: The government till now has enacted 24 pro-consumer Acts to control buyer-seller relations at the market place. The major consumer protection legislations in India are:
   - The Indian Penal Code, 1860
   - The Indian Contract Act, 1872
   - The Sale of Goods Act, 1930
   - The Agricultural Produce (Grading and Marking) Act, 1937
   - The Drugs and Cosmetics Act, 1940
   - The Drug (Control) Act, 1950
   - The Industries (Development and Regulation) Act, 1954
   - The Prevention of Food Adulteration Act, 1954
   - The Essential Commodities Act, 1955

- The Monopolies and Restrictive Trade Practices Act, 1969 (to be repealed and replaced by The Competition Act, 2002)
- The Standards of Weights and Measures Act, 1976
- The Trade Marks Act, 1999
- The Cigarettes (Regulation of Production, Distribution and Supply) Act, 1975
- The Standards of Weights and Measures Act, 1976
- The Prevention of Black Marketing and Maintenance of Supplies of Essential Commodities Act, 1980
- The Standards of Weights and Measures (Enforcement) Act, 1985
- The Bureau of Indian Standards Act, 1986
- The Consumer Protection Act, 1986
- The Competition Act, 2002

Certain government departments such as, telecommunications and electricity organise Lok Adalats from time-to-time, so that, the grievances of consumers relating to their departments can be addressed. This is a practical method to handle consumer grievances and seek a solution. Some departments such as, railways have made their services efficient and guide the consumers through information. In the banking sector Ombudsman are there for speedy redressal of consumer grievances relating to deposit accounts, dishonour of cheques, credit cards, debit cards, ATMs etc.

Children are the backbone of any society. A scheme has been taken up to set-up Consumer Clubs in schools and colleges. It would try to educate students about their rights as a consumer and to mobilise youngsters to strengthen the consumer movement in the country. Thus, many new schemes have been started by the government to empower the rural consumers. The cost and time involved in litigation is so much that Alternative Dispute Resolution Mechanisms are required and ICT measures can play an important rile in empowering the rural consumers.

Notes

1. Information from Census of India, 2001.
2. Kotler Philip and Prafulla Agnihotri *et al.*, *Principles of Marketing: A South Asian Perspective* (Pearson 2011), Appendix 3.
3. Michael Etzel, Walker *et al.*, (2010). *Marketing*, (14th Ed.) Tata McGraw Hill Education Pvt. Ltd., pp. 700-706.

4. "Why Companies See Bright Prospects in Rural India", 2009 Published: June 18, 2009 in India Knowledge@Wharton
5. Kapoor, Sheetal, (2005). "Growing Consumerism in Rural India", *Consumer Voice*, July-August.
6. Kapoor, Sheetal (2005). *Consumer and the Market*, IIPA, New Delhi.
7. Kumar, Rajendra (2009). *Rural Marketing*, A.P.H. Publishing Corporation, New Delhi.
8. Kazmi, S.H.H. and J.P. Mahajan (2012). *Principles of Marketing*, Excel Books.
9. Sinha, Dheeraj (2011). Consumer India: Inside the Indian Mind and Wallet (*Time Business Series*).

Index